Looking at Philosophy

Looking at Philosophy

The Unbearable Heaviness of Philosophy Made Lighter

SIXTH EDITION

Donald Palmer

*Professor Emeritus at College of Marin
(Formerly Visiting Assistant Professor,
North Carolina State University)*

Mc Graw Hill

Connect
Learn
Succeed™

The McGraw-Hill Companies

Connect
Learn
Succeed™

For Katarina & Christian

LOOKING AT PHILOSOPHY: THE UNBEARABLE HEAVINESS OF PHILOSOPHY MADE LIGHTER, SIXTH EDITION

3 4 5 6 7 8 9 0 DOC/DOC 1 0 9 8 7 6 5

ISBN 978-0-07-803826-6
ISBN 0-07-803826-X

Vice President and Editor-in-Chief: Michael Ryan
Vice President & Director Specialized Publishing: Janice M. Roerig-Blong
Sponsoring Editor: Amy Mittelman
Marketing Coordinator: Angela R. FitzPatrick
Project Manager: Mary Jane Lampe
Design Coordinator: Margarite Reynolds
Buyer: Laura Fuller
Media Project Manager: Sridevi Palani
Compositor: Cenveo Publisher Services
Typeface: 12/17 Tekton
Printer: R. R. Donnelley

Library of Congress Cataloging-in-Publication Data

Palmer, Donald.
    Looking at philosophy : the unbearable heaviness of philosophy made lighter / Donald Palmer, Professor Emeritus at College of Marin (Formerly Visiting Assistant Professor, North Carolina State University). — Sixth edition.
        pages cm
    Includes bibliographical references and index.
    ISBN 978-0-07-803826-6 (pbk.)
    1. Philosophy—History.   2. Philosophy—History—Caricatures and cartoons.   3. American wit and humor, Pictorial.   I. Title.

    B74.P26   2012
    190—dc23   2012010384

www.mhhe.com

Preface

Wittgenstein once said that a whole philosophy book could be written consisting of nothing but jokes. *This is not that book*, nor does this book treat the history of philosophy as a joke. This book takes philosophy seriously, but not gravely. As the subtitle indicates, the goal of the book is to lighten the load a bit. How to do this without simply throwing the cargo overboard? First, by presenting an overview of Western philosophy from the sixth century B.C.E. into the early twenty-first century in a way that introduces the central philosophical ideas of the West and their evolution in a concise, readable format without trivializing them, but at the same time, without pretending to have exhausted them or to have plumbed their depths. Second, following a time-honored medieval tradition, by illuminating the margins of the text. Some of these illuminations, namely those that attempt to schematize difficult ideas, I hope will be literally illuminating. Most of them, however, are simply attempts in a lighter vein to interrupt the natural propensity of the philosophers to succumb to the pull of gravity. (Nietzsche said that only the grave lay in that direction.) But even these philosophical jokes, I hope, have a pedagogical function. They should serve to help the reader retain the ideas that are thereby gently mocked. Thirty years of teaching the subject, which I love—and which has provoked more than a few laughs on the part of my students—convinces me that this technique should work. I do not claim to have achieved Nietzsche's "joyful wisdom," but I agree with him that there is such a thing and that we should strive for it.

Before turning you over to Thales and his metaphysical water (the first truly heavy water), I want to say a word about the women and their absence. Why are there so few women in a book of this nature? There are a number of possible explanations, including these:

1. Women really are deficient in the capacity for sublimation and hence are incapable of participating in higher culture (as Schopenhauer and Freud suggested).
2. Women have in fact contributed greatly to the history of philosophy, but their contributions have been denied or suppressed by the chauvinistic male writers of the histories of philosophy.
3. Women have been (intentionally or unintentionally) systematically eliminated from the history of philosophy by political, social, religious, and psychological manipulations of power by a deeply entrenched, jealous, and fearful patriarchy.

I am certain that the first thesis does not merit our serious attention. I think there is some truth to the second thesis, and I may be partially guilty of suppressing that truth. For example, the names of at least seventy women philosophers in the late classical period alone have been recorded, foremost of which are Aspasia, Diotima, Aretê, and Hypatia. (Hypatia has been belatedly honored by having a journal of feminist philosophy named after her.) Jumping over centuries to our own age, we find a number of well-known women contributing to the history of philosophy in the first half of the twentieth century, including Simone de Beauvoir, Susanne Langer, and L. Susan Stebbing.

However, no matter how original, deep, and thought-provoking were the ideas of these philosophers, I believe that, for a number of reasons (those reasons given in the second and third theses are probably most pertinent here), few of them have been treated by historians of thought with as much attention as have their male counterparts. Fortunately, things have begun to change in the past few years. An adequate account of contemporary philosophy could not in good faith ignore the major contributions to the analytic tradition of philosophers Iris Murdoch, Philippa Foot, G. E. M. Anscombe, and Judith Jarvis Thompson, nor those contributions to the Continental tradition made by Gayatri Chakravorty Spivak, Monique Wittig, Luce Irigaray, and Julia Kristeva. Furthermore, a new wave of women philosophers is already beginning to have considerable impact on the content of contemporary philosophy and not merely on its style.

So, despite the risks, I defend the third thesis. I truly believe that if women had not been systematically excluded from major participation in the history of philosophy,[1] that history would be even richer, deeper, more compassionate, and more interesting (not to mention more joyful) than it already is. It is not for nothing that the book ends with a discussion of the work of a contemporary woman philosopher and with a question posed to philosophy herself, "Quo vadis?"—Whither goest thou?

The sixth edition proceeds with the refinement of presentation begun as early as the second edition and with the addition of new material initiated in the third edition. I have added a short section on Skepticism to Chapter 3, deleted some outdated material throughout, removed some less successful illustrations and added some new ones, and rewritten a number of passages for the purposes of clarity and precision. I have also tried to make the book more student-friendly by adding to the end of each chapter outlines of the most important philosophical ideas in each section. The other large change is the division of old Chapter 7 into two chapters, now 7 and 8. I have called the new Chapter 7 "The Phenomenological Tradition and Its Aftermath," and the new chapter 8 "Pragmatism and the Analytic Tradition." I don't really like the names we give those two rather divergent directions that philosophy has taken in the twentieth century, but I feel stuck with them. Philosopher Stanley Cavell, who in his own work somehow manages to straddle the divide, thinks that these are superficial and misleading names, but goes on to say, "there is no nonirritating pair of titles for this . . . intellectual divide."[2] I have had some help with all six editions of this book. I'd like to thank the reviewers who made suggestions for the sixth edition. They include Marcia Andrejevich, Ivy Tech Community College; Allison DeBoer, Grays Harbor College; Susanna Goodin, University of Wyoming; Matthew Laurents, Austin Community College; John Harding, Troy University; and Mark Rauls, College of Southern Nevada. For suggestions with the earlier editions, I am grateful to the Rev. Robert Mode, Trocaire College; Jeff Delbel, Cayuga CC; Pamela Pumpton, Warner Pacific College; Amber Katherine, Santa Monica CC; Timothy R. Allan and Robert Caputi, Trocaire College; Dasiea Cavers-Huff, Riverside Community College; Job Clement, Daytona Beach Community College; Julianna Scott Fein, Mayfield Publishing Company; Will Griffis, Maui Community College; Hans Hansen, Wayne State University; Fred E. Heifner Jr., Cumberland University; Joseph Huster, University of Utah; Janine Jones, University of North Carolina, Greensboro; Ken King, Mayfield Publishing Company; James Lemke, Coker College; Robin Mouat, Mayfield Publishing Company; Kirby Olson, SUNY Delhi; Don Porter, College of San Mateo; Brian Schroeder, Siena College; Matt Schulte, Montgomery College; Yukio Shirahama, San Antonio College; Samuel Thorpe, Oral Roberts University; William Tinsley, Foothill College; James Tuttle, John Carroll University; Kerry Walk, Otis College of Art and Design; Stevens F. Wandmacher, University of Michigan, Flint; Andrew Ward, San Jose State University; Robert White, Montgomery College; and David Auerbach, North Carolina State University. Jim Bull, my editor at Mayfield Publishing Company for the first two editions, had faith in this project from its inception. For the new edition, my editor at McGraw-Hill, Mark Georgiev, and the development editor, Craig Leonard, have been exceptionally helpful. Also at McGraw-Hill, I am indebted to Mary Jane Lampe, the project manager. My wife, Leila May, has been my most acute critic and my greatest source of inspiration. She kept me laughing during the dreariest stages of the production of the manuscript, often finding on its pages jokes that weren't meant to be there. I hope she managed to catch most of them. There probably are still a few pages that are funnier than I intended them to be.

Notes

1. See Mary Warnock, ed., *Women Philosophers* (London: J. M. Dent, 1996).
2. Stanley Cavell, *Little Did I Know: Excerpts from Memory* (Stanford: Stanford University Press, 2010), 350, 456–57.

Contents

Introduction

The story of Western philosophy begins in Greece—or, more specifically, in the Greek settlements on the coast of the Persian Empire, in present-day Turkey.

The Greek word "Logos" is the source of the English word "logic" as well as all the "logies" in terms like "biology," "sociology," and "psychology," where "logos" means the theory, or study, or rationalization of something. "Logos" also means "word" in Greek, so it involves the act of speaking, or setting forth an idea in a clear manner. "Logos," therefore, designates a certain kind of thinking about the world, a kind of logical analysis that places things in the context of reason and explains them with the pure force of thought. Such an intellectual exercise was supposed to lead to wisdom (Sophia), and those who dedicated themselves to Logos were thought of as lovers of wisdom (love = philo), hence as philosophers.

What was there before philosophy, before Logos? There was *Mythos*—a certain way of thinking that placed the world in the context of its supernatural origins. Mythos explained worldly things by tracing them to exceptional, sometimes sacred, events that caused the world to be as it is now. In the case of the Greeks, Mythos meant tracing worldly things to the dramatic acts of the gods of Mount Olympus. The narratives describing these origins—myths—are not only explanatory but also morally exemplary and ritualistically instructive; that is, they provide the rules that, if followed by all, would create the foundation of a genuine community of togetherness—a "we" and an "us" instead of a mere conglomeration of individuals who could only say "I" and "me." Hence, myths are

You will wear your baseball cap backward because the gods wore theirs backward!

What's baseball?

Explaining Ancient Greek Customs

often conservative in nature. They seek to maintain the status quo by replicating origins: "So behaved the sacred ancestors, so must we behave." Myths had the advantage of creating a whole social world in which all acts had meaning. They had the disadvantage of creating static societies, of resisting innovation, and, many would say, of being false. Then, suddenly, philosophy happened—Logos broke upon the scene, at least according to the traditional account. (There *are* other accounts, however, accounts that suggest that Western Logos—philosophy and science—is just *our* version of myth.) But let us suppose that something different *did* take place in Greece about 700 B.C.E.[1] Let's suppose that the "first" philosopher's explanation of the flooding of the Nile River during the summer (most rivers tend to dry up in the summer) as being caused by desert winds (*desert winds*, not battles or love affairs among gods) really does constitute novelty. Natural phenomena are explained by other natural phenomena, not by supernatural events in "dream time"—the time of the ancient gods. In that case, Greece truly is the cradle of Western philosophy.

A Modern Myth?

Why Greece, and not, for example, Egypt or Judea? Well, let's be honest here. Nobody knows. Still, a number of historical facts are relevant to the explanation we seek. For one, there was a very productive contact between ancient Greece and the cultures of the eastern Mediterranean region—Persia, Mesopotamia, Phoenicia,

Cyprus, southern Italy, and Egypt, among others. The Greeks were a well-traveled group and were extremely adept at borrowing ideas, conventions, and artistic forms from the cultures they encountered and applying these elements creatively to their own needs. There is also a controversial theory that Greek culture derives greatly from African sources.[2] It is at least certain, as one historian of Greek ideas has recently said, that "the cultural achievements of archaic and classical Greece are unthinkable without Near Eastern resources to draw upon,"[3] and eastern North Africa fits into this map.

Also, unlike the case in some of the surrounding societies, there was no priestly class of censors in Greece. This observation does not mean that Greek thinkers had no restrictions on what they could say—we will see that several charges of impiety were brought against some of them in the period under study—but that they were able nevertheless to get away with quite a bit that went against prevailing religious opinion.

Dreaming in Detail

Another historical fact is that the Greek imagination had always been fertile in its concern with intimate detail. For example, Homer's description of Achilles' shield takes up four pages of the *Iliad*. In addition, the many generations of Greek children who grew up on the poems of Homer and Hesiod[4]—two of the main vehicles that transmitted Greek religion—recognized in them their argumentative, intellectually combative, and questioning nature. The polemical nature of Greek drama and poetry would find a new home in Greek philosophy.

A final component of the world into which philosophy was born is the socioeconomic structure that produced a whole leisured class of people—mostly *male* people—with time on their hands that they could spend meditating on philosophical issues. It is always jolting to remember that during much of Greece's history, a major part of the economic foundation of its society was slave labor and booty from military conquests. This fact takes some of the luster from "the Glory that was Greece."

Still, for whatever reasons, the poetry and drama of the Greeks demonstrate an intense awareness of change, of the war of the opposites—summer to winter, hot to cold, light to dark, and that most dramatic change of all, life to death.

Indeed, this sensitivity to the transitory nature of all things sometimes led the Greeks to pessimism. The poets Homer, Mimnermus, and Simonides all expressed the idea, "Generations of men fall like the leaves of the forest."[5]

Generations of Men Fall like the Leaves of the Forest

But this sensitivity also led the Greeks to demand an explanation—one that would be obtained and justified not by the authority of religious tradition but by the sheer power of human reason. Here we find an optimism behind the pessimism—the human mind operating on its own devices is able to discover ultimate truths about reality.

But let us not overemphasize the radicalness of the break made by the Greek philosophers with the earlier, mythical ways of thinking. It's not as if suddenly a bold new **atheism** emerged, rejecting all religious explanations or constraints. In fact, atheism as we understand it today was virtually unknown in the ancient world.[6] Rather, these early Greek philosophers reframed the perennial puzzles about reality in such a way as to emphasize the workings of nature rather than the work of the gods. For instance, they tended to demote **cosmogony** (theories about the *origins* of the world) and promote **cosmology** (theories about the *nature* of the world).

This new direction represents the beginnings of a way of thinking that the Greeks would soon call "philosophy"—the love of wisdom. We can discern in these early efforts what we now take to be the main fields of the discipline that we too call philosophy: **ontology** (theory of being); **epistemology** (theory of knowledge); **axiology** (theory of value), which includes **ethics,** or **moral philosophy** (theory of right behavior), and **aesthetics** (theory of beauty, or theory of art); and **logic** (theory of correct inference).

In fact, the theories put forth in ancient Greece could be called the origins of Western science with as much justification as they can be called the origins of Western philosophy, even though at that early period no such distinctions could be made. Roughly, I would say that *science* deals with problems that can be addressed experimentally by subsuming the observable events that puzzle us under the dominion of natural laws and by showing how these laws are related causally to those events. *Philosophy,* on the other hand, deals with problems that require a speculative rather than an experimental approach. Such problems often require **conceptual analysis** (the logical scrutiny of general ideas) rather than observation or data gathering. Consider these questions, paying special attention to the underlined words:

> Can we <u>know</u> why on rare occasions the sun darkens at midday?
> Is it <u>true</u> that the moon's passing between the earth and the sun <u>causes</u> such events?
> Can there be <u>successful</u> experiments that <u>explain</u> this phenomenon?

These questions are scientific questions. Now compare these questions to the following ones, paying attention again to the underlined words:

> What is <u>knowledge</u>?
> What is <u>truth</u>?
> What is <u>causality</u>?
> What is <u>value</u>?
> What is <u>explanation</u>?

These questions invite conceptual analysis, which is part of philosophy.

But we are moving too fast and looking too far ahead. As I said, such distinctions had not yet been clearly drawn in the ancient world. The thinkers there were satisfied to have asked the kinds of questions that were foundational both to philosophy and to science.

Notice that I stress the *asking* of the questions that the pre-Socratics posed rather than the *answers* given. *Logos* strives for truth and completeness, but is not always able to provide them. However, this is not simply a problem for the ancient Greek philosophers; even twenty-first-century scientists are loath to claim that their theories lead to absolute certainty, rather they assert only the hope that their theories prove to be superior to earlier theories and more approximate to the truth. (As we will see later, conceptual analysis of the idea of "truth" finds even it to be philosophically problematical.) I would venture to say that philosophers should be even more wary of claims to truth and absolute certainty than are scientists. Science is at least somewhat constrained by observable facts (though, of course, the concept of "fact" also needs philosophical analysis), while philosophy, often looking for "the bigger picture," appeals to some happy combination of reason and imagination. Reader, beware of the results (but be *philosophically* aware).

Topics for Consideration

1   Pick some observable phenomenon, such as what we now call the eclipse of the sun, and explain it from the perspective of science, and then again from some system of myth. (You may have to visit the library for this exercise.) Then use these two "stories" to demonstrate the difference between Logos and Mythos.

2. Think about your own patterns of belief. Are there any of them that you would acknowledge as Mythos rather than Logos? Here are two examples: (A) If you have religious beliefs, how would you characterize them in terms of this distinction? (B) What do skeptics about science mean when they assert that science itself is simply an instance of Western Mythos?

Notes

1. I have chosen to use the new dating coordinates B.C.E. (Before the Common Era) and C.E. (Common Era) rather than the older B.C. (Before Christ) and A.D. (Anno Domini, or The Year of Our Lord) because the attempt to gauge the whole of human history from the perspective of a particular religious tradition no longer seems tenable. But let's face it: This new system is a bit artificial. Probably there is something arbitrary about all attempts to date historical events. At least I am not following the lead of the nineteenth-century philosopher Friedrich Nietzsche, who proclaimed, "History begins with my birth." (We'll study Nietzsche later.)

2. Martin Bernal, *Black Athena: The Afroasiatic Roots of Classical Civilization*, vol. 1, *The Fabrication of Ancient Greece 1785–1985* (New Brunswick, N.J.: Rutgers University Press, 1987).

3. Robin Osborne, "The Polis and Its Culture," in *Routledge History of Philosophy*, vol. 1, *From the Beginning to Plato*, ed. C. C. W. Taylor (London and New York: Routledge, 1997), 14.

4. Homer, *The Iliad*, trans. Michael Reck (New York: IconEditions, 1994); Homer, *The Odyssey*, trans. Robert Fitzgerald (New York: Farrar, Straus & Giroux, 1998); Hesiod, *Theogony: Works and Days*, trans. Dorothea Wender (Harmondsworth, England: Penguin, 1976).

5. This sentiment can be found in the poems published in *Greek Lyric: An Anthology in Translation*, ed. and trans. Andrew M. Miller (Indianapolis and Cambridge: Hackett Publishing, 1996), 27, 117, 118.

6. See Catherine Osborne, "Heraclitus," in *From the Beginning to Plato*, 90.

1

The Pre-Socratic Philosophers

Sixth and Fifth Centuries B.C.E.

The thinkers who were active in Greece between the end of the seventh century B.C.E. and the middle of the fourth century B.C.E. are known today as the pre-Socratic philosophers, even though the last of the group so designated were actually contemporaries of Socrates. (Socrates was born in 469 and died in 399 B.C.E. We look at his thought in the next chapter.) What all the pre-Socratic philosophers have in common is their attempt to create general theories of the cosmos (kosmos is the Greek term for "world") not simply by repeating the tales of how the gods had created everything, but by using observation and reason to construct general theories that would explain to the unprejudiced and curious mind the secrets behind the appearances in the world. Another commonality was that all the pre-Socratic philosophers stemmed from the outlying borders of the Greek world: islands in the Ionian Sea or Greek colonies in Italy or along the coast of Persia (in today's Turkey). Knowledge of these thinkers is tremendously important not only for understanding the Greek world of their time, but—as I have suggested in the Introduction—for grasping the origins of Western philosophy and science.

The problem is that in fact very little is known about the pre-Socratic philosophers. Most of the books that they wrote had already disappeared by the time that the philosopher Aristotle (384–322 B.C.E.) tried to catalog and criticize their views. Today's understanding of the pre-Socratics is based mostly on summaries of their ideas by Aristotle and by later Greek writers who had heard of their views only by word of mouth. Many of these accounts are surely inaccurate because of distortions caused by repetition over several generations by numerous individuals. (Have you ever played the game called Telephone, in which a complicated message is whispered to a player, who then whispers it to the next player, and so on, until the message—or what's left of it—is announced to the whole group by the last player in the circle?) Also, these summaries often contained anachronistic ideas, that is, ideas from the later time projected back into the earlier views. Only fragments of the original works remain in most cases today, and even those few existing passages do not always agree with one another. Remember, these "books" were all written by hand on papyrus (a fragile early paper made from the crushed and dried pulp of an Egyptian water plant), and all editions of these books were copied manually by professional scribes. Furthermore, the meaning of many of the fragments is debatable, both because of the "fragmentary" nature of the scraps—key words are missing or illegible—and because of the obscure style and vocabulary in which many of these works were written. Nevertheless, a tradition concerning the meaning of the pre-Socratics had already developed by Aristotle's time, and it is that version of their story that influenced later philosophers and scientists. Aristotle is not the only source of our information about the pre-Socratics, but unfortunately most of the additional information comes from post-Aristotelian commentators giving interpretations of Aristotle's remarks. We do not know to what extent the material provided by these other sources is informed by extraneous sources. So Aristotle appears to be our real source, and we have no clear idea of his accuracy because he paraphrases the various pre-Socratics.[1] Therefore, the tradition that I report here is flawed and distorted in many ways.

Thales

Philosophy makes its first self-presentation in three consecutive generations of thinkers from the little colony of Miletus on the coast of Asia Minor—today's Turkey—in the sixth century B.C.E. The first recorded philosopher is Thales of Miletus (ca. 580 B.C.E.). Apparently, he did not write a book, or if he did, it is long lost.

If we can trust Aristotle and his commentators, Thales's argument was something like this:

If there is change, there must be some *thing* that changes, yet does not change. There must be a unity behind the apparent plurality of things, a Oneness disguised by the superficial plurality of the world. Otherwise the world would not be a *world*; rather, it would be a disjointed grouping of unrelated fragments.

So what is the nature of this unifying, ultimately unchanging substance that is disguised from us by the *appearance* of constant change?

Like the myth makers before him, Thales was familiar with the four elements: air, fire, water, and earth. He assumed that all things must ultimately be reducible to one of these—but which one?

Of all the elements, water is the most obvious in its transformations: Rivers turn into deltas, water turns into ice and then back into water, which in turn can be changed into steam, which becomes air, and air, in the form of wind, fans fire.

Thales's actual words were: "The first principle and basic nature of all things is water."[2]

This obviously false conclusion is valued today not for its content but for its form (it is not a great leap between the claim "All things are composed of water" and the claim "All things are composed of atoms") and for the presupposition behind it (that there is an ultimate stuff behind appearances that explains change while remaining itself unchanged). Viewed this way, Thales can be seen as the first philosopher to introduce the project of **reductionism.** Reductionism is a method of explanation that takes an object that confronts us on the surface as being one kind of thing and shows that the

**Then water it is!
All things are composed of water.**

object can be reduced to a more basic kind of thing at a deeper but less obvious level of analysis. This project is usually seen as a major function of modern science.

I regret to say that I must add three other ideas that Aristotle also attributes to Thales. My regret is due to the capacity of these ideas to undercut what has seemed so far to be a pretty neat foundation for future science. Aristotle says that, according to Thales,

(A) The earth floats on water the way a log floats on a pond.
(B) All things are full of gods.

(C) A magnet (loadstone) must have a soul, because it is able to produce motion.

The first of these ideas, (A), is puzzling because it seems gratuitous. If everything is water, then it is odd to say that some water floats on water. (B) shows us that the cut between Mythos and Logos is not as neat in Thales' case as I have appeared to indicate. (C) seems somehow related to (B), but in conflicting ways. If according to (B) all things are full of gods, then why are the magnets mentioned in (C) any different from everything else in nature? No surprise that over the years scholars have spilled a lot of ink—and, because the debate still goes on, punched a lot of computer keys—trying to make sense of these ideas that Aristotle attributes to Thales.

Anaximander

Several generations of Thales's followers agreed with his primary insight—that the plurality of kinds of things in the world must be reducible to one category—but none of them seems to have accepted his formula that everything is water. His student Anaximander (ca. 610–ca. 546 B.C.E.), also from the city of Miletus, said that if all things were water, then long ago everything would have returned to water. Anaximander asked how water could become its deadly enemy, fire—how a quality could give rise to its opposite. That is, if observable objects were really just water in various states of agitation—as are ice and steam—then eventually all things would have settled back into their primordial liquid state. Aristotle paraphrases him this way: If ultimate reality "were something specific like water, the other elements would be annihilated by it. For the different elements have contrariety with one another. . . . If one of them were unlimited the others would have ceased to exist by now."[3] (Notice that if this view can be accurately attributed to Anaximander, then he subscribed to an early view of the principle of **entropy,** according to which all things have a tendency to seek a state of equilibrium.)

For Anaximander, the ultimate stuff behind the four elements could not itself be one of the elements. It would have to be an unobservable, unspecific, indeterminate something-or-other, which he called the Boundless, or the Unlimited (*apeiron* in Greek). It would *have* to be boundless, unlimited, and unspecific because anything specific is opposed to all the other specific things in existence. (Water is not fire, which in turn is not air, and air is not earth [not dirt and rock].) Yet the Boundless is opposed to nothing, because everything is *it*.

Anaximander seems to have imagined the Boundless as originally moving effortlessly in a great cosmic vortex that was interrupted by some disaster (a Big Bang?), and that disaster caused opposites—dry and wet, cold and hot—to separate off from the vortex and to appear to us not only as qualities but as the four basic elements: earth, water, air, and fire.

Anaximander wrote a book in prose, one of the first such books ever written. But papyrus does not last forever, and only one passage remains that we can be fairly certain comes from his book. However, that passage is a zinger.

> And from what source things arise, to that they return of necessity when they are destroyed, for they suffer punishment and make reparation to one another for their injustice according to the order of time.[4]

There are many possible interpretations of this amazing statement. According to the most dramatic interpretation, the whole world as you and I know it is the result of a cosmic error. Creation is an act of injustice. But justice will be done; the world will eventually be destroyed, and "things" will return to their boundless source and revolve eternally in a vortex. *This* interpretation, which contains at least as much Mythos as Logos, exhibits a bizarre kind of optimism about the triumph of justice.

I've got some good news and some bad news. The good news is that the world is going to end . . .

A less radical, less mythical, and more likely interpretation would be this: Once the four elements were created, they became related to one another in antagonistic ways, but their opposition to one another balances out in an ecological harmony. If one element dominates at one period (say, water in a time of flood), it will later be compensated by the domination of another element at another period (say, fire in a drought). So the original unity of the Boundless is preserved in the apparent war of the opposites.

A very important part of this passage is the claim that the events described occur "of necessity ... according to the order of time." This process, then, is not due to the whims of the gods, and the "punishment" and "reparation" for the "injustice" is not reprisal against individual humans by angry divinities. Natural laws are governing these processes with inevitability. If the working out of these laws is described by Anaximander in the moral and legal language of the old myths, his description simply shows, as the eminent pre-Socratic scholar Malcolm Schofield says, "that Anaximander is a revolutionary who carries some old-fashion baggage with him. That is the general way with revolutions."[5] In any case, the cause of these processes—the apeiron—is immortal and indestructible, qualities usually associated with gods, as Aristotle points out.[6] Again, we see that pre-Socratic philosophy has not completely divorced itself from its religious origins.

Other striking ideas have been attributed to Anaximander: (1) Because the same processes that are at work here are at work everywhere, there is a plurality of universes. (2) The earth needs no support (remember Thales' "floating like a log in water"). Because the earth is right smack in the middle of the universe (well, *our* universe), it is "equidistant from all things." (3) The four elements concentrate in certain regions—in concentric circles—of the cosmos, with earth (the heaviest) in the center, surrounded by a circle of water, then another of air, then one of fire. A wheel of fire circles our slower earth. What we see as the stars are really holes in the outer ring, or "tube-like vents," with fire showing through.

This last cosmological picture painted by Anaximander had an amazingly long life. Merrill Ring quotes the sixteenth-century British poet Edmund Spenser as writing:

> The earth the air the water and the fire
> Then gan to range themselves in huge array,
> and with contrary forces to conspire
> Each against other by all means they may.[7]

And in the early seventeenth century, Miguel de Cervantes relates a heroic adventure of Don Quixote and Sancho in which a group of bored aristocrats trick the knight and his squire into blindfolding themselves and mounting a wooden horse, Clavileño, which they are told is magic and will fly them to the outer reaches of the world. The underlings of the Duke and Duchess blow winds upon our heroes with great billows as they reach the "realm of the air." Turning the wooden peg in the horse's head that he believes controls the horse's speed, Don Quixote says, "If we go on climbing at this rate

Don Quixote and Sancho Pass through the Realm of Fire

we shall soon strike the region of fire, and I do not know how to manage this peg so as not to mount so high that we shall scorch."[8] Their tormentors then brush their faces with torches to convince them that they have indeed reached the realm of fire at the edge of the cosmos.

This magical episode "takes place" some two thousand years after the death of Anaximander and sixty years after the death of Copernicus, so people should have come to realize by then that Anaximander was wrong.

Anaximenes

Some of Anaximander's followers asked, "How much better is an 'unspecific, indeterminate something-or-other' than nothing at all?" They decided that it was no better, that in fact, it was the same as nothing at all, and they also knew that *ex nihilo nihil* (from nothing comes nothing), so they went on searching for the mysterious ultimate stuff.

The air that we experience ("commonsense air") is a halfway house between all the other forms

The next philosopher, Anaximenes (ca. 545 B.C.E.), thought this *apeiron* was air.

into which "primordial air" can be transformed through condensation and rarefaction. The commentator, Theophrastus, says:

> Anaximenes ... like Anaximander, declares that the underlying nature is one and boundless, but not indeterminate as Anaximander held, but definite, saying that it is air. It differs in rarity and density according to the substances [it becomes]. Becoming finer it comes to be fire; being condensed it comes to be wind, then cloud, and when still further condensed it becomes water, then earth, then stones, and the rest come to be out of these.[9]

With the idea of condensation and rarefaction, Anaximenes continued the project of reductionism. He introduced the important claim that all differences in quality are really differences in quantity (just more or less stuff packed into a specific space), an idea with which many scientists would agree today.

These first three philosophers, Thales, Anaximander, and
Anaximenes, are known as the
Milesians because they all came
from the Greek colony of Miletus
on the Persian coast and because
they constitute the first school of
philosophy. Despite the differences
among them, they shared a number
of characteristics, some of which
would eventually become part of the
Western scientific tradition: a desire
for simple explanations, a reliance on
observation to support their theo-
ries, a commitment to **naturalism** (the view that natural phenomena should be explained in terms of other natural phenomena), and
monism (the view that ultimately there is only one kind of "stuff").

Rarefaction

fire
smoke
steam
AIR
mist
water
mud
dirt
stone

Condensation

The School of Miletus ended when the tenuous peace between
the Greek outpost and Persia collapsed and the Persians overran the
city, leaving behind much destruction and death. According to the
historian Herodotus, the Athenians were so distressed at the fall of
Miletus that they burst into tears in the theater when the playwright
Phrynichus produced his drama "The Capture of Miletus." The government banned his play and fined the author one thousand drachmas
for damage to public morals.

Pythagoras

The Milesians' successor, Pythagoras (ca. 572–ca. 500 B.C.E.), from
the island of Samos, near Miletus, did not seek ultimacy in some
material element, as his predecessors had done. Rather, he held the
curious view that all things are numbers. Literally understood, this
view seems absurd, but Pythagoras meant, among other things,
that a correct description of reality must be expressed in terms of

mathematical formulas. From our science classes we are familiar with a great number of laws of nature, all of which can be written out in mathematical formulas (for example, the law of gravitation, the three laws of motion, the three laws of thermodynamics, the law of reflection, Bernoulli's law, Mendel's three laws). Pythagoras is the great-great-grandfather of the view that the totality of reality can be expressed in terms of mathematical laws.

Very little is known about Pythagoras himself. Nothing he wrote has survived. It is almost impossible to sort out Pythagoras's own views from those of his followers, who created various Pythagorean monastic colonies throughout the Greek world during the next several hundred years. He seems to have been not primarily a mathematician but a **numerologist;** that is, he was interested in the mystical significance of numbers. For instance, because the Pythagoreans thought that the number 10 was divine, they concluded that what we would today call the solar system had ten members. This theory turns out to be roughly correct—the sun and nine planets—but not for Pythagoras's reasons. Well, maybe eight and a half planets; in August of 2006, the International Astronomical Union demoted Pluto, declaring it to be a "dwarf planet."

Nevertheless, he anticipated the bulk of Euclid's writings on geometry and discovered the ratios of concord between musical sound and number. From this discovery he deduced a mathematical harmony throughout the universe, a view that led to the doctrine of "the music of the spheres." The ten celestial bodies move, and all motion produces sound. Therefore, the motion of the ten celestial bodies—being divine—produces divine sounds. Their music is the eternal background sound against which all sound in the world is contrasted. Normally, we hear only the "sound in the world" and are unable to hear the background harmony. But a certain mystical stance allows us to ignore the sound of the world and to hear only the divine music of the spheres.

The influence of Pythagoras was so great that the School of Pythagoreans lasted almost 400 years. The spell he cast on Plato alone would be enough to guarantee Pythagoras a permanent place in the history of philosophy. (We shall see that Plato turns out to be the most important philosopher of the Greek period and that he was a fine mathematician as well.) With hindsight, we can now look at Pythagoras's work and see those features of it that mark him and his followers as true philosophers. Nevertheless, it is only artificially that we distinguish that portion of Pythagorean thought that we declare to be philosophical. We should not ignore the less scientific aspect of Pythagoras's teachings, which to him were all part of a seamless whole. He was the leader of a religious cult whose members had to obey a strict number of esoteric rules based on **asceticism,** numerology, and vegetarianism.

Despite their vegetarianism, Pythagoreans had to forswear eating beans because eating beans is a form of cannibalism. A close look at the inside of a bean reveals that each one contains a small, embryonic human being (or human bean, as the case may be).

Xenophanes

Xenophanes was born in Colophon on today's Turkish coast, about fifty miles north of Miletus, in about 570 B.C.E. He left his home in his early twenties when it was violently overrun by a Persian army. Apparently, he spent the rest of his long life wandering in western Greece. We do not know the date of his death, but he tells us in one of his poems that he is ninety-two years old as he writes. Tradition has it that he lived for more than a hundred years. Xenophanes's philosophical credentials were questioned by Aristotle, who is our closest thing to an intellectual historian of the period. Aristotle thought of him as a confused poet, and Xenophanes has been treated as such by a number of historians of philosophy in the modern period, but he had a number of ideas that are worth remarking. Unfortunately, they often appear contradictory—as Aristotle delighted in pointing out—but fortunately, there are relatively numerous fragments extant from his writings (about 120 lines), enough to provoke interpretive attempts to fathom Xenophanes's thought. Indeed, there have been many vicious battles fought by scholars against each other's interpretation of Xenophanes's poems.[10]

after John Tenniel

Alice Prepares Scholars to Fight over the Correct Interpretation of Xenophanes

We will look at only a few of the welter of ideas put forth by Xenophanes in the fragments of his work that still exist. I will start with one of his clearer claims on whose meaning there is something of a consensus. First, it is fairly obvious that he sees his main purpose as that of attacking the religious and moral views presented to the Greek people by their greatest poets, Homer and Hesiod. Concerning the moral problem, he writes: "Homer and Hesiod attributed to the gods all things which are disreputable and worthy of blame when done by men; and they told of them many lawless deeds, stealing, adultery, and deception of each other."[11] (You will soon discover that Plato—perhaps the most prominent philosopher of ancient Greece—picked up Xenophanes's moral criticism of Homer and Hesiod and intensified it.) Concerning the theological problem, Xenophanes says:

> But mortals suppose that the gods are born (as they themselves are), and that they wear man's clothing and have a human voice and body. (frag. 5)
> But if cattle or lions had hands, so as to paint with their hands and produce works of art as men do, they would paint their gods and give them bodies in form like their own—horses like horses, cattle like cattle. (frag. 6).

Xenophanes seems angry at the human propensity to **anthropomorphize** divinity. God, or the gods, are not simply bigger people with more power than we, hence with the ability to get away with more than we manage to get away with. If gods do not die, then they are not born either, because that would imply that there was a time when they did not exist. They do not wear clothes, nor sit on thrones, nor have emotional tantrums.

This is an interesting and advanced theological critique, so what does Xenophanes himself think about divinity? Well, this is one of those topics that has provoked conflict among the scholars: "God is one, supreme among gods and men, and not like mortals in body or in mind" (frag. 1). Yet this passage contains some of the complexity that puzzles serious readers of Xenophanes. He speaks both of "God" and of "the gods." Is Xenophanes a **monotheist** or a **polytheist?** Most historians of Greek philosophy ignore the plural reference to "gods" and attribute it to the stylistic poetic requirements of the day. According to them, Xenophanes is the first true monotheist. But those in the monotheist camp are divided over whether he is a **pantheist,** believing that the cosmos itself

Zeus throws a tantrum

is god, or whether he sees god as an embodied divinity located somewhere in the universe. The pantheist camp is aided by fragment 8: "For all things come from earth, and all things end up by becoming earth." This passage can be read as claiming that earth itself is god. Or, this passage can be read in such a way as to deny that any god of any sort is needed to explain apparent change in the cosmos. Some scholars have read it as placing Xenophanes's project among the one initiated by the Milesians. If Thales says that all things are water, and Anaximenes that all things are air, and Heraclitus that all things are fire, then Xenophanes fills the final possibility: all things are earth. Others say this is a misreading, pointing to the next fragments, 8 and 9: "For we are all sprung from earth and water." "All things that come into being and grow are earth and water."

Whatever else he was, this old man was not above having a good time. In fragment 17, he says:

"The following are fit conversations for men reclining on a soft couch by the fire in the winter season, when after a meal they are drinking sweet wine and [crunching hazelnuts]: Who are you, and what is your family? What is your age, my friend?"

Then, one last swipe at Homer and Hesiod: "… but there is nothing praiseworthy in discussing battles of Titans or of Giants or Centaurs, fictions of former ages, nor in plotting violent revolutions" (frag. 21).

Heraclitus

The next philosopher to demand our attention is Heraclitus (ca. 470 B.C.E.) of Ephesus, only a few miles from Miletus. Almost 100 trust-worthy passages from Heraclitus's book remain for our perusal. We know more about what Heraclitus actually said than we know about any other pre-Socratic philosopher. Unfortunately, we don't neces-sarily know more about what he *meant*. Like Anaximander, Heraclitus wrote in prose, but he chose to express himself in aphorisms—short, pithy outbursts with puzzling messages that seem to dare the reader to make sense of them. Rather than review the great vari-eties of scholarly effort in recent years trying to convey the many

possible meanings of Heraclitus's fragments, here I
concentrate on the meaning
attributed to Heraclitus's
views by the generations
that followed him in the
Greek and Roman world in
the years after his death.
The picture that emerges
from the commentators of
that early period is fairly
uniform, if perhaps mis-
guided, but after all, that
picture has guaranteed Heraclitus's fame for
centuries and has been influential in the history
of ideas.

One of Heraclitus's most famous aphorisms concerns fire. He wrote: "There is an
exchange of all things for fire and of fire for
all things."[12] Many commentators understood
Heraclitus to be naming fire as the basic stuff
of reality and therefore to be in the line of Milesian cosmologists who tried to reduce all things
to one element. Others realized that Heraclitus
was using the image of fire in a more subtle,
figurative sense. There is something about the
nature of fire that gives insight into both the appearance of stability (the flame's form is stable) and the fact of change (in the flame,
everything changes).

Heraclitus drew some striking conclusions from this vision:

> Reality is composed not of a number of things but of
> a process of continual creation and destruction.

But these passages too should be understood symbolically and not
literally.

"War is father and king of all."
"Conflict is justice."[13]

Another one of Heraclitus's aphorisms evokes the image of flowing water:

"You cannot step into the same river twice."[14]

Heraclitus explained this idea by saying "Everything flows and nothing abides; everything gives way and nothing stays fixed."[15] Commentators interpreted Heraclitus to be saying that the only thing that does not change is change itself; on this account, not fire but change would be the ultimate truth about reality, and fire would be change's best example, as well as a metaphor standing for change.

Heraclitus was called the Dark One and the Obscure One because of the difficulty of his aphorisms. Justifiably or not, his ideas were interpreted pessimistically by later Greeks, and this understanding was handed down to posterity. According to this interpretation, his ideas create more than merely a philosophy—they constitute a mood, almost a worldview of nostalgia and loss:

> You can't go home again. Your childhood is lost.
> The friends of your youth are gone.
> Your present is slipping away from you.
> Nothing is ever the same.

Nevertheless, there was something positive in the Heraclitean philosophy. An unobservable Logos—a logic—governed change that made change a rational phenomenon rather than the chaotic, arbitrary one it appeared to be. Heraclitus wrote: "Logos is always so."[16] This Logos doctrine deeply impressed Plato and eventually became the basis of the notion of the laws of nature. It is also directly related to a doctrine claimed by Christianity. Both God and Christ are equated with Logos in the Gospel of John: "In the beginning was the Word [Logos], and the Word [Logos] was with God and the Word [Logos] was God" (John 1:1); "And the Word [Logos] was made flesh, and dwelt among us" (John 1:14).

Parmenides

Heraclitus's successor Parmenides (ca. 515–ca. 440 B.C.E.) went a step further than his predecessor.

In effect, he said that you can't step in the same river once.

Parmenides begins with what he takes to be a self-evident truth: "It is." This claim is not **empirical**—not one derived from observation; rather, it is a truth of Reason. It cannot even be denied without self-contradiction. If you say, "It is not" (i.e., nothing exists), then you've proved that "It is," for if nothing exists, it's not nothing; rather, it is something that exists.

You Cannot Step in the Same River Once

Parmenides believed that Being is rational, that only what can be thought can exist. Since "nothing" cannot be thought (without

thinking of it as *something*), there is no nothing, there is only Being. From the mere idea
of Being it follows that Being is uncreated (if it were created, it would have
been created from nothing, but there
is no nothing), indestructible (if it
were destructible, it could turn into
non-Being, but there is no non-
Being), eternal (if it were not eternal, then it would eventually become
non-Being, which is impossible), and
indivisible (if it could be divided, there
would be spaces of non-Being between
its parts, but there is no non-Being).
Furthermore, Being is spherical, because
only a sphere is equally real in all directions.
(Maybe this notion is related to the idea of
the twentieth-century physicist Albert Einstein, who claimed that
space is curved?) Being has no holes (no vacuum) because, if Being *is*,
there can't be any place where Being is *not*.

From this argument it follows that motion is impossible because
motion would involve Being going from where Being is to where Being
isn't (but there can't *be* any such place as the place where Being isn't).

In fact, for Parmenides the very idea of empty space was an
impossible idea. Either space is a thing, in which case it is *something*
and not nothing, or it is *nothing*, in which case it does not exist. Because all thought must have an object and because nothing is not an
object, the idea of nothing is a self-contradictory idea.

It must be obvious to you that Parmenides has strayed a long
way from common sense and from the facts that are revealed to us
by the senses of sight, touch, hearing, smell, and taste—and primary
among those facts is that motion exists and that things change.
But if people laughed at Parmenides, they didn't laugh for long, because he soon had a powerful ally.

Zeno

The sly old fox Zeno of Elea (ca. 490 B.C.E.–?) wrote a now-famous series of paradoxes in which he defended Parmenides's outrageous views by "proving" the impossibility of motion using a method known as **reductio ad absurdum** ("reduction to absurdity").

In this form of argument, you begin by accepting your opponent's conclusions, and you demonstrate that they lead logically to an absurdity or a contradiction.

Zeno argued that, even granting motion, you could never arrive anywhere, not even to such a simple goal as a door. Before you can get to the door, you must go halfway, but before you can go halfway, you must

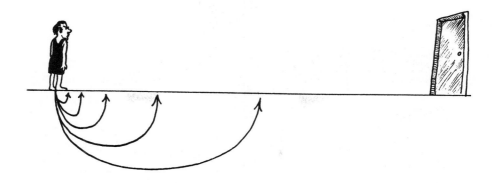

go halfway of the remaining halfway, but before you can do that, you must go halfway of halfway, but before you can go halfway, you must go halfway. When does this argument end? Never! It goes on to infinity. Therefore, motion would be impossible even if it were possible.

In yet another of his paradoxes, Zeno demonstrated that in a race between Achilles and a tortoise, if Achilles gave the tortoise a head start (as would only be fair), the swift runner could never overtake the lumbering reptile. Before Achilles could pass the tortoise, he must arrive at the point at which the tortoise used to be; but given the hypothesis of motion, the tortoise will never still be there. He will have moved on. This paradox will forever be the case. When Achilles arrives at a point at which the tortoise was, the tortoise will have progressed. Achilles can never catch him.

Is Reality One Thing?

Or Many?

The conclusions of these paradoxical arguments of Zeno defending the views of his master, Parmenides, may seem absurd to you, but they are actually derived from the mathematical notion of the infinite divisibility of all numbers and, indeed, of all matter. Zeno's arguments are still studied in postgraduate courses on the foundations of mathematics. Zeno is forcing us to choose between mathematics and sensory information. It is well known that the senses often deceive us, so we should choose the certainty of mathematics. With that suggestion Parmenides and Zeno caused a crisis in Greek philosophy. They radicalized the distinction between information based on the five senses and that based on pure reason (a distinction that would later develop into two schools of philosophy: **empiricism** and **rationalism**). Furthermore, they forced a reevaluation of the monistic presupposition accepted by all Greeks heretofore (namely, the view that reality is composed of one thing), because thinkers came to realize that such a view led directly to Parmenides's conclusions. It appeared that philosophers either would have to accept Parmenides's shocking arguments or they would have to give up monism. In fact, they gave up monism.

Empedocles

The next group of philosophers are known as **pluralists,** precisely because they were unable to accept the monolithic stillness of Parmenides's Being. Therefore, they were forced to believe that ultimate reality is composed of a plurality of things rather than of only one kind of thing.

The first of this group was Emped-ocles (?–ca. 440 B.C.E.), a citizen of the Greek colony of Acragas on the island of Sicily—now part of Italy—who believed that everything was composed of the simplest parts of the four elements: fire, air, earth, and water. He called these ele-ments the "four roots."

But in the face of Zeno's critique of motion, Empedocles be-lieved he needed to posit two forces to explain change and move-ment. These forces he called Love and Strife. Love is the force of unity, bringing together unrelated items to produce new creations, and Strife is the force of destruction, breaking down old unities into fragments.

(A curious version of Empedocles's theory was later accepted by the twentieth-century psychoanalyst Sigmund Freud, who named the two forces Eros and Thanatos [the life instinct and the death instinct]. Freud agreed with Empedocles that these forces formed the bases of all organic matter.)

The first theory of **evolution** developed out of Empedocles's system. Love brings together certain kinds of monsters. "Many heads grew up without necks, and arms were wandering about naked, bereft of shoulders, and eyes roamed about alone with no foreheads. Many creatures arose with double faces and double breasts, offspring of oxen with human faces, and again there sprang up children of men with oxen's heads."[17]

And those that could survive, did survive.

(Aristotle later criticized this view as "leaving too much to chance.")

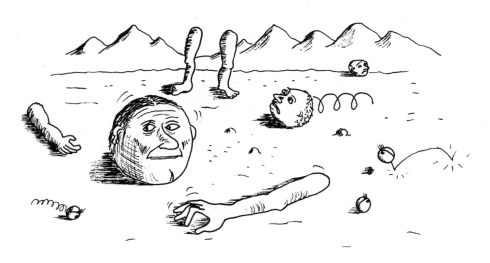

Anaxagoras

The next pluralist, Anaxagoras (ca. 500–ca. 428 B.C.E.) of Clazom- enae, near Miletus, found Empedocles's theory too simplistic. He re- placed the "four roots" with "infinite seeds." Each of these seeds is something like an element in today's chemistry; so in some ways, this theory sounds very modern. Every object in the world contains seeds of all ele- ments, and in each object, the seeds of one element predominate.

"In all things, there is a portion of everything. . . . For how could hair come from what is not hair? Or flesh from what is not flesh?"[18]

Anaxagoras agreed with Empedocles that some force explain- ing motion and change was required, but he replaced Empedocles's all too mythical figures of Love and Strife with one force, a mental one, which he called Nous, or Mind. This assumption means that the universe is organized according to an intelligent, rational order. Anaxagoras's Nous is almost like a god who creates objects out of the seeds, or elements.

Furthermore, there is a distinction between the animate and the inanimate world in that the organic world contains Nous within it as a self-ordering principle, whereas the inorganic world is ordered externally by Nous. Nous itself is qualitatively identical everywhere, but its abilities are determined by the nature of the body that con- tains it. Humans aren't any smarter than carrots, but they can do more than carrots because they have tongues, opposable thumbs, and legs. (You wouldn't act very smart either if you were shaped like a pointy root.)

Notice that Anaxagoras's theory is the first time that a philosopher distinguished clearly between living substance and "dead" matter. The anthropomorphic concept Nous looked promising to two of the most important later Greek philosophers, Socrates and Aristotle, but eventually it disappointed them. Socrates said that at first he found it an exciting idea, but it ended up meaning nothing at all, and Aristotle said that Anaxagoras stood out "like a sober man in the midst of loose talkers."[19] Later Aristotle was disillusioned by Anaxagoras, who used "reason as a **deus ex machina** for the making of the world, and when he is at a loss to tell from what cause something necessarily is, then he drags reason in, but in all other cases ascribes events to anything rather than reason."[20]

Leucippus and Democritus

Precisely because Anaxagoras's view was anthropomorphic, it was still too mythical for Anaxagoras's successors, a group of philosophers, led by Leucippus (ca. 460 B.C.E.–?) and Democritus (ca. 460–ca. 370 B.C.E.), known as the **atomists.**

They saw the world as composed of material bodies, which themselves are composed of groups of "atoms." The Greek word ατομον (atomon) means "indivisible," that which cannot be split.

Democritus made each atom a little piece of Parmenidean Being (uncreated, in-destructible, eternal, indivisible, containing no "holes") and set them moving through empty space travers-ing absolutely neces-

sary paths that are determined by rigid natural laws.

So, contrary to Parmenides's view, both empty space and motion are real. Moreover, like atoms themselves, mo-tion and space are natural and basic, admitting of no further analysis. It is the appearance of *inertia* and not that of motion that needs explaining, and Democritus's explanation, like that of Heraclitus, is that inertia is an illusion. That is to say, it is explained away. Thus, by the year 370 B.C.E., Greek philosophy had been led to a thoroughgoing **materialism** and a rigorous **determinism.** There was nothing in the world but material bodies in motion and there was no freedom, only necessity.

What had the pre-Socratic philosophers achieved? Through them, a special kind of thinking had broken free from its mythical and religious ancestors, developing its own methods and content—a kind of thinking that would soon evolve into what today we know as science and philosophy. Looking back at the pre-Socratics, *we see a direct lineage between them and the great thinkers of our own time:* The dichotomy between reason and the senses that the German philosopher Immanuel Kant was to resolve in the eighteenth century was first made clear by the pre-Socratics; the first attempt to formulate a theory of evolution was made by them; and the first effort to solve the riddle of

THALES

KANT

DARWIN

EINSTEIN

how mathematical numbers hold sway over the flux of reality—all this we see as a more or less unbroken genealogy from their time to ours.

But to the Greeks of the fifth century, the pre-Socratic philosophers had left a legacy of confusion.

The only thing the philosophers had succeeded in doing was to undermine the traditional religious and moral values, leaving nothing substantial in their place. (As the Greek dramatist Aristophanes said, "When Zeus is toppled, chaos succeeds him, and whirlwind rules.")

Besides, "the times they were a-changin'," socially and politically as well as intellectually. The old aristocracy, dedicated to the noble values of the Homeric legends, was losing ground to a new mercantile class, which was no longer interested in the virtues of Honor, Courage, and Fidelity but in Power and Success. How was the new class to achieve these virtues in an incipient democracy? Through politics. And the access to political power was then, as it is today, through the study of rhetoric (read "law")— the art of swaying the masses with eloquent, though not necessarily truthful, argumentation.

Key Philosophical Ideas in Chapter 1

- Overview: New kinds of thinkers appear in the Greek Adriatic colonies in the sixth century B.C.E.

- <u>Explanations</u> of reality and its origins <u>no longer merely mythical</u>.

- <u>Natural phenomena explained in terms of natural processes</u>.

- These first thinkers, the pre-Socratic philosophers ("lovers of wisdom"), were <u>familiar with the four basic elements</u>—water, earth, fire, and air—and used them as their foundations.

<u>Thales</u>:

- The first of the <u>monists</u>: <u>reality is composed of one thing</u>.

- Thales's assumption: <u>If there is change</u> in the world, <u>there must be something that does not change</u>.

- Thales chooses water as the primary element from which all others are derived.

<u>Anaximander</u>:

- There must be <u>a hidden abstract element</u>—the "boundless," the "unlimited"—<u>from which all other elements are derived</u>.

Anaxamines:

- <u>Air is the fundamental element</u> from which all others are derived.
- The world as it appears to us is composed of air in more or less <u>condensed</u> or <u>rarified</u> forms. (Quality is determined by quantity: more or less air in a given space.)

Pythagoras:

- <u>Number</u> is the fundamental <u>building block of reality</u>.
- All <u>explanations must be mathematical</u>.

Xenophanes:

- <u>A criticism of the religious views in Greek mythology</u>: On Olympus, the gods are like very strong, badly behaved, immoral humans.
- If there are gods, they don't look and dress like humans, any more than they look and dress like cows or lions (<u>attack on anthropomorphism in religious thought</u>).

Heraclitus:

- <u>Fire is the basic element</u> from which all other elements derive (<u>or</u>, more likely, <u>fire is a metaphor for</u> the nature of <u>reality</u>).
- <u>Change is</u> the key feature of <u>reality</u>. ("You can't step in the same river twice.")
- Heraclitus is the Dark: his philosophy was interpreted as pessimism.

Parmenides:

- The opposite of Heraclitus: <u>Nothing ever changes; motion is an illusion</u>.
- Only Being is real, because "nothingness" and "change" are self-contradictory concepts.
- <u>Being is uncreated, unchanging, eternal, immovable, indivisible, solid, and spherical (equally real in all directions)</u>.

Zeno:

- Defender of Parmenides's philosophy using <u>reductio ad absurdum argumentation against Parmenides's detractors</u>.

- Zeno's paradoxes are proofs that motion and change are impossible.
- Overview: In the face of the powerful Parmenides's revelation of the implications of monism, <u>either Parmenides's conclusions will have to be accepted or monism will have to be abandoned</u>. In the face of the powerful logical arguments of Zeno, future philosophers who believe in change and motion will have to explain how these phenomena are possible.

Empedocles:

- The first of the <u>pluralists</u>: reality is composed of <u>an irreducible plurality of elements</u>.
- The <u>"four roots"</u>—fire, air, earth, and water—cannot be reduced to something more basic.
- <u>Motion and change are real</u>, produced by <u>two forces</u>: a positive force (<u>Love</u>) and a negative force (<u>Strife</u>).
- First recorded <u>theory of evolution</u>.

Anaxagoras:

- <u>Pluralism</u> continued: everything produced from <u>"infinite seeds"</u> (replacing Empedocles's "four roots").
- <u>Motion and change</u> are <u>caused by</u> <u>Nous</u> (Mind or Reason).

Leucippus and Democritus:

- <u>Pluralism</u> and <u>materialism</u>.
- <u>Atomism</u>: The world is composed of "atoms": invisible, indivisible particles of matter in constant motion travelling in <u>pre-determined paths</u>, colliding, grouping, and scattering <u>according to rigid natural laws</u>.

Conclusion:

- Even though the atomists seem closest to the modern scientific understanding of physical reality, the <u>pre-Socratic period ended without reaching a unified philosophical understanding of the world</u>. What in fact unifies these otherwise desperate philosophical efforts was the belief that <u>the natural world could be explained in terms of natural causes, and that there must be a unifying principle or element from which all natural phenomena emerged</u>.

Topics for Consideration

1. What is the problem of "the One and the Many" that presented itself to the early Greek philosophers? Pick three pre-Socratics with very different solutions to this problem and contrast their views.

2. Apply the distinction you learned in the Introduction between Mythos and Logos to the Milesian philosophers Thales, Anaximander, and Anaximenes. Which camp are they in?

3. If you lived in the Greek world during the sixth century B.C.E. and knew only what could be known at that period, which of the basic substances or entities would you choose as the foundation of reality, based on your own observations? Why? (Before you start, read topic four.)

    (a) Water (Thales)

    (b) Air (Anaximenes)

    (c) Fire (roughly, Heraclitus)

    (d) Earth (Xenophanes, or, very roughly, Democritus)

    (e) An indeterminate "stuff" (Anaximander)

    (f) Numbers (roughly, Pythagoras)

4. Same question as the previous topic, with this qualification: Based on what you *now* know at the beginning of the twenty-first century, but still limited to the categories a through f, which letter or combination of letters would you choose?

5. Contrast as dramatically as you can the theses of Heraclitus and Parmenides. What do you think would be the practical consequences, if any, of seriously accepting the philosophical claim of Heraclitus? of Parmenides?

6. Explain why Zeno's paradoxes provoked such a deep crisis in the intellectual environment of ancient Greece. Show how philosophical progress after Zeno required some compromise between the views of the Parmenidean camp and those of the pre-Parmenidean camp.

Notes

1. These post-Aristotelian sources are primarily Theophrastus (ca. 371–ca. 286 B.C.E.), a pupil of Aristotle; Simplicius, a sixth-century B.C.E. commentator on Aristotle; Eudemus of Rhodes, who wrote around 300 B.C.E.; Hippolytus, Bishop of Rome in the third century C.E.; and Diogenes Laertius, whose books were written about 300 C.E. A readable account of recent scholarship on this topic can be

found in *Routledge History of Philosophy*, vol. 1, *From the Beginning to Plato* (ed. C. C. W. Taylor [London and New York: Routledge, 1997]), Chapter 2, "The Ionians," by Malcolm Schofield; Chapter 3, "Heraclitus," by Catherine Osborne; Chapter 4, "Pythagoreans and Eleatics," by Edward Hussey; Chapter 5, "Empedocles," by M. R. Wright; and Chapter 6, "Anaxagoras and the Atomists," by C. C. W. Taylor. These investigations support large parts of the traditional views of the pre-Socratics as they are reported here, but also give good reasons for skepticism concerning the accuracy of other aspects of those views.

2. Philip Wheelwright, ed., *The Presocratics* (New York: Odyssey Press, 1966), 44. This sentence is one of the four sentences that are attributed to Thales by Aristotle.

3. Ibid., 55.

4. Milton C. Nahm, ed., *Selections from Early Greek Philosophy* (New York: Appleton-Century-Crofts, 1962), 62.

5. Schofield, 47–87, 55.

6. "The unlimited is equivalent to the Divine, since it is deathless and indestructible" (Aristotle, quoted by Wheelwright, 55).

7. Merrill Ring, *Beginning with the Pre-Socratics*, 2d ed. (Mountain View, Calif.: Mayfield Publishing, 2000), 24.

8. Miguel de Cervantes Saavedra, *The Adventures of Don Quixote*, trans. J. M. Cohen (Harmondsworth, England, and New York: Penguin Books, 1983), 731.

9. Simplicius quoting Theophrastus in *A Presocratics Reader*, ed. Patricia Curd, trans. Richard D. McKirahan Jr. (Indianapolis and Cambridge: Hackett Publishing, 1996), 14.

10. For an overview of some of these intellectual squabbles, see W. K. C. Guthrie, *A History of Greek Philosophy*, vol. 1, *The Earlier Presocratics and the Pythagoreans* (Cambridge: Cambridge University Press, 1962), 361–362.

11. Nahm, fragment 7, 109. In subsequent quotations, the fragments will be numbered in parentheses in the text.

12. Wheelwright, 71.

13. Ring, 70.

14. Ibid., 66.

15. Wheelwright, 70.

16. Ring, 62.

17. Nahm, 136.

18. Ibid., 150, 152.

19. Wheelwright, 168.

20. Aristotle, *Metaphysics*, trans. W. D. Ross, in *The Basic Works of Aristotle*, ed. Richard McKeon (New York: Random House, 1941), 697.

2
The Athenian Period
Fifth and Fourth Centuries B.C.E.

The Sophists

Because of the social shift toward political power and the study of rhetoric, it was no surprise, then, that the next group of philosophers were not really philosophers as such but rhetoricians who became known as Sophists ("wise guys"). They traveled from city to city, charging admission to their lectures—lectures not on the nature of reality or truth but on the nature of power and persuasion. Plato and Aristotle wrote a lot about the Sophists, and according to the picture that they handed down to us, not just skepticism but cynicism became the rule of the day.

Protagoras

Perhaps the most famous (and least cynical) of the Sophists was Protagoras (ca. 490–ca. 422 B.C.E.). He taught that the way to achieve success is through a careful and prudent acceptance of traditional customs—not because they are *true*, but because an understanding and manipulation of them is expedient. For Protagoras all customs were relative, not absolute. In fact, *everything* is relative to human subjectivity. Protagoras's famous claim is *homo mensura*—man is the measure.

Man is the measure of all things, of things that are, that they are, and of things that are not, that they are not.[1]

Protagoras's emphasis on **subjectivism, relativism,** and expediency is the backbone of all **sophism.** According to some stories, Protagoras was indicted for blasphemy, and his book on the gods was

burned publicly in Athens—
yet one of the few remaining
fragments of his writ-
ings concerning religion
states, "As for the gods,
I have no way of knowing
either that they exist or
that they do not exist."[2]

Gorgias

Another famous Sophist was
Gorgias (ca. 483–375 B.C.E.).
He seems to have wanted to de-
throne philosophy and replace it with
rhetoric. In his lectures and in a book he
wrote, he "proved" the following theses:

1. There is nothing.
2. If there were anything, no one could know it.
3. If anyone did know it, no one could communicate it.

The point, of course, is that if you can "prove" these absurdities, you can "prove" anything. Gorgias is not teaching us some astounding truth about reality; he is teaching us how to win arguments, no matter how ridiculous our thesis may be.

Thrasymachus

Yet another Sophist was Thrasymachus, who is known for the claim "Justice is in the interest of the stronger." That is to say, *might makes right*. According to him, all disputation about morality is empty, except insofar as it is reducible to a struggle for power.

Callicles and Critias

According to the accounts handed down to us, two of the most cynical Sophists were Callicles and Critias.

Callicles claimed that traditional morality is just a clever way for the weak masses to shackle the strong individual. He taught that the strong should throw off these shackles and that doing so would be somehow "naturally right." What matters is *power*, not justice. But why is power good? Because it is conducive to survival. And why is survival good? Because it allows us to seek *pleasure*—pleasure in food, drink, and sex. Pleasure is what the enlightened person aims for, qualitatively and quantitatively. The traditional Greek virtue of *moderation* is for the simple and the feeble.

Critias (who was to become the cruelest of the Thirty Tyrants, the men who overturned the democracy and temporarily established an oligarchical dictatorship) taught that the clever ruler controls subjects by encouraging their fear of non-existent gods.

So we see that the essence of sophism comprises subjectivism, **skepticism,** and **nihilism.** Everything the pre-Socratics stood for is devalued. There is no objective reality, and if there were, the human mind could not fathom it. What matters is not truth but manipulation and expediency. No wonder Socrates was so offended by sophism.

Yet we must say a few kind words about sophism despite its negativism. First, we might credit the Sophists of fifth-century Greece B.C.E. with anticipating in many ways the **epistemological** relativism of Friedrich Nietzsche—whom you'll study in chapter 6—and the cultural movement called **postmodernism** in the last half of the twentieth century. In this book, the philosophical expression of that movement is called **poststructuralism** and is treated from page 321 forward. There, too, we find strong criticisms of traditional claims about knowledge and attempts to show how the structures of power claim proprietorship of knowledge. Second, many of the Sophists were skilled politicians who actually contributed to the history of democracy. Third, history's animosity toward them is based mostly on reports we have of them from Socrates and Plato, who were enemies of the Sophists. Finally, and most important, sophism had the positive effect of making human beings aware not of the cosmos but of themselves as objects of interest. In pre-Socratic philosophy, there was no special consideration of the human. Suddenly, with Protagoras's "man is the measure," humans became philosophically interested in themselves.

Socrates

The Sophists, who were professional teachers, met their match in a man who was possibly the greatest teacher of all time, Socrates (469–399 B.C.E.). Despite his overall disagreement with them, Socrates followed the Sophists' lead in turning away from the study of the cosmos and concentrating on the case of the human. But unlike the way the Sophists discoursed about the human being,

Socrates wanted to base all argumentation on objectively valid definitions. To say "man is the measure" is saying very little if one does not know what "man" is. In the *Theatetus*, Socrates says:

Socrates's discourse moved in two directions— outward, to objective definitions, and inward, to discover the inner person, the soul, which, for Socrates, was the source of all truth. Such a search is not to be conducted at a weekend lecture but is the quest of a lifetime.

Socrates was hardly ever able to answer the questions he asked. Nevertheless, the query had to continue, for, as we know from his famous dictum,

The unexamined life is not worth living.[3]

Socrates spent much of his time in the streets and marketplace of Athens, querying every man he met about whether that man knew anything. Socrates said that, if there was an afterlife, he would pose the same question to the shades in Hades.

Ironically, Socrates himself professed to know nothing. The oracle at Delphi said that *therefore* Socrates was the wisest of all men. Socrates at least *knew* that he knew nothing, whereas the others falsely believed themselves to know something.

Socrates himself wrote no books, but his conversations were remembered by his disciple Plato and later published by him as dialogues. Very often these Socratic dialogues will emphasize a specific philosophical question, such as "What is piety?" (in the dialogue titled *Euthyphro*), "What is justice?" (in *Republic*), "What is virtue?" (in *Meno*), "What is meaning?" (in *Sophist*), "What is love?" (in *Symposium*). The typical Socratic dialogue has three divisions:

1. A question is posed (e.g., the question of what virtue is, or justice, or truth, or beauty); Socrates becomes excited and enthusiastic to find someone who claims to know something.

2. Socrates finds "minor flaws" in his companion's definition and slowly begins to unravel it, forcing his partner to admit ignorance. (In one dialogue, Socrates's target actually ends up in tears.)

3. An agreement is reached by the two admittedly ignorant companions to pursue the truth seriously. Almost all the dialogues end inconclusively. Of course, they must do so. Socrates cannot give his disciples the truth. Each of us must find it out for ourselves.

In his quest for truth, Socrates managed to offend many of the powerful and pompous figures of Athens. (In fairness to his accusers, it should be mentioned that some citizens suspected Socrates of preferring the values of Sparta to those of his native Athens. Sparta was Athens's enemy in the Peloponnesian War.) Socrates's enemies conspired against him, getting him indicted for teaching false doctrines, for impiety, and for corrupting the youth. They brought him to trial hoping to humiliate him by forcing him to grovel and beg for mercy.

Far from groveling, at his trial Socrates maligned his prosecutors and angered the unruly jury of 500 by lecturing them about their ignorance. Furthermore, when asked to suggest his own punishment, Socrates recommended that the Athenians give him free board and lodging in the town hall. The enraged jury condemned him to death by a vote of 280 to 220.

Ashamed of their act and embarrassed that they were about to put to death their most eminent citizen, the Athenians were prepared to look the other way when Socrates's prison guard was bribed to allow Socrates to escape.

Despite the pleas of his friends, Socrates refused to do so, saying that if he broke the law by escaping, he would be declaring himself an enemy of all laws. So he drank the hemlock and philosophized with his friends to the last moment. In death, he became the universal symbol of martyrdom for the Truth.

The Death o Socrates
(after Jacques-Louis David, 1787)

Plato

The most important of Socrates's young disciples was Plato (427–347 B.C.E.), who was one of the most powerful thinkers in history.

He is also the founder of the first university, the Academy, where students read as exercises the Socratic dialogues that Plato had written.

Because of his authorship, it is often difficult to distinguish between the thought of Socrates and that of Plato. In general, we can say that Plato's philosophy was more metaphysical, more systematic, and more other-worldly than Socrates' philosophy was.

The essence of Plato's philosophy is depicted allegorically in the Myth of the Cave, which

Plato

appears in his most important work, the *Republic*. In this myth Plato has Socrates conceive the following vision: Imagine prisoners chained in such a way that they face the back wall of a cave. There they have been for life and can see nothing of themselves or of each other. They see only shadows on the wall of the cave.

These shadows are cast by a fire that burns on a ledge above and behind them. Between the fire and the prisoners is a wall-lined path along which people walk carrying vases, statues, and other artifacts on their heads. The prisoners hear the echoes of voices and see the shadows of the artifacts, and they mistake these echoes and shadows for reality.

Plato has Socrates imagine that one prisoner is unchained, turned around, and forced to look at the true source of the shadows. But the fire pains his eyes. He prefers the pleasant deception of the shadows.

Behind and above the fire is the mouth of the cave, and outside in the bright sunlight (only a little of which trickles into the cave) are trees, rivers, mountains, and sky.

Now the former prisoner is forced up the "steep and rugged ascent"[4] (Plato's allegory of education) and brought to the sunlit exterior world. But the light blinds him. He must first look at the shadows of the trees (he is used to shadows), then at the trees and mountains. Finally he is able to see the sun itself (the allegory of enlightenment).

Plato suggests that if this enlightened man were to return to the cave, he would appear ridiculous because, dazzled by the sun, on his return to the cave he would see sunspots everywhere and not be able to penetrate the darkness.

And if he tried to liberate his fellow prisoners, they would be so angry at him for disturbing their illusions that they would set upon him and kill him—a clear allusion to the death of Socrates.

The allegory of the liberation of the slave from darkness, deceit, and untruth and the slave's hard journey into the light and warmth of the Truth has inspired many philosophers and social leaders. But Plato meant it as more than just a poetic vision. He also gave it a precise technical application, seen in his Simile of the Line, also found in the *Republic*.[5] It is called "the Line" because it is explained to us in Book VI of the *Republic* when Socrates uses a stick to draw a line on the ground and builds a diagram around it. On the left side of the Line we have an *epistemology* (theory of knowledge); on the right

side, an *ontology* (theory of being). In addition, we have an implicit *ethics* (moral theory) and *aesthetics* (theory of beauty). The totality constitutes Plato's **metaphysics** (general worldview).

The Line reveals the hierarchical nature of the objects of all these disciplines. Reality is a hierarchy of being, of knowledge, and of value, with objects that are most real, most certain, and most valuable at the top. A descending ontological, epistemological, moral, and aesthetic scale cascades down from the highest level in the guise of a mathematically organized series of originals and copies. The whole of the visible world is a copy of the whole of the intelligible world, yet each of these worlds is also divided into originals and copies.

For each state of being (right side of the Line—consult the diagram below), there is a corresponding state of awareness (left side). The lowest state of awareness is that of Conjecture, which has as its object Images, such as shadows and reflections (or images on the TV screen and video games in our day).

The person in a state of conjecture mistakes an image for reality. This level on the Line corresponds to the situation of the cave-bound prisoners watching the shadows.

The next level, that of Belief, has as its object a particular thing—say, a particular horse or a particular act of justice. Like Conjecture, Belief still does not comprise knowledge but remains in the sphere of Opinion, still grounded in the uncertainties of sense perception. It is not yet "conceptual." It is not yet directed by theory (*hypothemenoi*) or by a definition in terms of **necessary conditions** (necessary conditions are features of a concept that *must* be

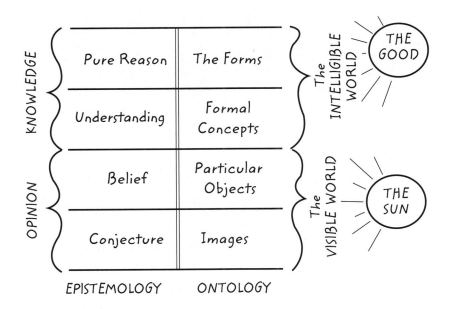

present if the concept is to be deemed correctly defined—e.g., being a member of the biological kingdom of animals is a necessary condition of being defined as a mammal) and **sufficient conditions** (sufficient conditions are features which, when present, guarantee that the concept in question has been correctly defined—e.g.,

possessing mammary glands is a sufficient condition for being identified as a mammal). The person in a state of belief is like a prisoner who sees the artifact held above the wall inside the cave.

Opinion and the objects of which it is aware are all sustained by the sun. Without the sun, there could be no horse and no image of a horse, nor could we be aware of them in the absence of light. (It's easy to get confused here, so be careful. Notice that the sun in the Myth of the Cave is a symbol, standing for the Good in the Simile of the Line, while the sun that appears in the Simile of the Line is literally the sun in the sky. However, in addition to being the real source of light and heat for the world, the sun on the "Line" is *also* symbolic of the Good because the sun plays the same role in the physical world that the Good plays in the intelligible world; namely, it is the source and sustainer of everything in the world that it commands.)

For Opinion to become Knowledge, the particular object must be raised to the level of *theory*. (This stage, Understanding, corresponds to the status of the released prisoner looking at the shadows of the trees in the world above the cave.)

But according to Plato, theories and definitions are not empirical generalizations dependent on particular cases and abstracted from them. To the contrary, rather than coming from below on the Line, theories are themselves images of something higher— what Plato calls the **Forms.** (In the same way that shadows and reflections are merely images of particular things, so theories or concepts are the shadows of the Forms.) When one beholds the Forms, one exercises Pure Reason, and one is like the liberated prisoner who gazed upon the trees and mountains in the sunlit upper world.

Plato's conception of the Forms is very complicated, but I can simplify it by saying that Forms are the eternal truths that are the source of all Reality. Consider, for example, the concept of beauty.

BEAUTY — The Form of Beauty

BEAUTY — The Concept of Beauty

Individual Beautiful Entities

Imitations of Beautiful Entities (paintings, photos, reflections, shadows)

Things in the sensible world are beautiful to the extent that they imitate or participate in Beauty. However, these beautiful things will break, grow old, or die. But Beauty itself (the Form) is eternal. It will always be. The same can be said of Truth and Justice. (Also, more embarrassingly, of Horseness or of Toothpickness.)

Furthermore, just as the sensible world and awareness of it are dependent on the sun, so are the Forms and knowledge of them dependent on the Good, which is a Superform, or the Form of all Forms.

The state of beholding the Good is represented in the Myth of the Cave by the released prisoner beholding the sun itself. Plato's theory is such that the whole of Reality is founded upon the Good, which is Reality's source of being. And all Knowledge is ultimately knowledge of the Good.

If you are puzzled by Plato's conception of the Good, you are in "good" company. Philosophers have debated its meaning for centuries. Clearly it plays a role very much like that of God in certain theological systems. For example, referring to the Simile of the Line, Plato calls the sun a "god" and claims that it is "the offspring of the Good."[6] The Good is the source of being, knowledge, and truth but is something even "more beautiful"[7] than these. It is not surprising that many religiously oriented philosophers in the Middle Ages and the Renaissance—two periods in which Plato's influence was powerful—treated the Good as a **mystical** category. Something that is beyond being and knowledge is something that might be grasped only by a state of mind that transcends rationality. More orthodox religious thinkers treated the Good as identical to God. It was along these lines that Plato deeply influenced the development of Christianity, Judaism, and Islam. It would be a bad pun (and an anachronistic one, since the English language did not yet exist in Plato's time), but an illuminating one, to say that early Christianity dropped one "o" from "Good" and changed the "u" to an "o" in "sun" to create an icon of the relation between God and Christ.

Whatever Plato means by "the Good," he optimistically holds that if one ever comes to know the Good, one becomes good. Ignorance is the only error. No one would willingly do wrong.

How can we learn the Truth? Where can we find the Forms, and especially the Form of the Good? Who can teach us? Plato had curious answers to these questions. In the dialogue called *Meno,* Plato had an unschooled slave boy solve a difficult mathematical problem by answering affirmatively or negatively a series of simple questions posed by Socrates. Plato concluded from this episode that the slave boy always knew the answer but didn't know that he knew. All Truth comes from within—from the soul. One's immortal soul is born with the Truth, having beheld the Forms in their purity before its embodiment. Birth, or the embodiment of the soul, is so traumatic that one forgets what one knows and must spend the rest of life plumbing the depths of the soul to recover what one already knows—hence, Plato's strange doctrine that *all Knowledge is recollection.* Now we see Socrates's role as that of helping his student to remember, just as the psychoanalyst does with his or her patient today. (A modern version of Plato's doctrine of recollection is Freud's theory of unconscious memories.)

The *Republic* is well known not only for its epistemology but also for its social philosophy. The latter for Plato is a combination of psychology and political science. He said that the City (the "Republic") is the individual writ large. Just as the individual's psyche has three aspects—the appetitive, animal side; the spirited source of action; and the rational aspect—so does the ideal City have three classes—the workers and the artisans; the soldiers; and the rulers. In the psyche, the rational part must convince the spirited part to help it control the appetitive. Otherwise, there will be an unbalanced soul, and neurosis will ensue.

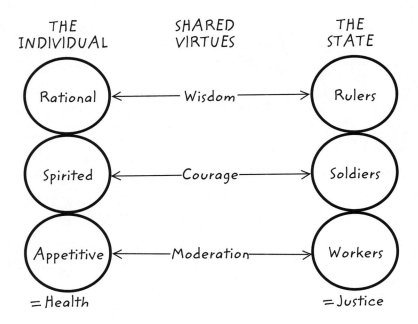

Similarly, in the City, the rulers must be philosophers who have beheld the Forms and therefore know what is good. They must train the military caste to help control the naturally unruly peasants. The latter will be allowed to use money, own property, and wear decorations in moderation, but the members of the top two classes, who understand the corrupting effect of greed, will live in an austere, absolute communism, sleeping and eating together, owning no property, receiving no salary, and having sexual relations on a prearranged schedule with partners shared by all. These rules will guarantee that the City will not be frenzied and anarchic—a strange beginning for the discipline of political science (one from which it has still not recovered)!

The members of the ideal City will be allowed to play simple lyres and pipes and sing patriotic, uplifting songs, but most artists will be drummed out of the Republic. This maltreatment has four reasons: (1) ontological—Because art deals with images (the lowest rung in the Simile of the Line), art is an imitation of an imitation. (Art is "three removes from the throne.");[8] (2) epistemological—The artist, at the conjectural stage, knows nothing but *claims* to know something; (3) aesthetic—

THE GOOD

Art expresses itself in sensual images; hence, it distracts us from Beauty itself, which is purely intellectual; (4) moral—Art is created by and appeals to the appetite side of the soul (Freud's id). Art is either erotic or violent or both; hence, it is an incitement to anarchy. Even Homer must be censored, for he too is guilty of the artist's crimes: fraudulence, ignorance, and immorality.

(The whole enterprise of the *Republic* can be viewed as a plea that philosophy take over the role that art had hitherto played in Greek culture.)

Plato did not live to see the inauguration of his ideal state nor to see the installation of a Philosopher King who would know the Good, but the legacy that Plato left is still very much with us, for better or for worse. The eminent British-American philosopher Alfred North Whitehead once said that the history of philosophy is merely a series of footnotes to the *Republic*.

Plato's Simile of the Line would, to a great extent, lay out the framework of Western metaphysical thought from his time to ours. Many of the philosophers mentioned in this book were influenced deeply by Plato (Aristotle, the Stoics, the Neoplatonists, Saint Augustine, Saint Anselm, Saint Thomas Aquinas, Descartes, Spinoza, Kant, Hegel, Schopenhauer, Kierkegaard, Marx, Russell, and Whitehead, among others). Even those philosophers who hated Plato's philosophy, such as Nietzsche, often admired his intellectual power—a power that even Nietzsche could not escape.

Aristotle

Plato's influence is clearly seen in the thought of one of his best students, Aristotle (384–322 B.C.E.). Aristotle, born in Stagira,

Aristotle

spent twenty years at Plato's academy. Soon after the death of the master, Aristotle left the school because of disagreements with its new chiefs, and he founded an academy of his own, the Lyceum. In Aristotle's school, Platonic philosophy was taught, but it was also criticized.

The main thrust of Aristotle's dispute with his mentor concerned the latter's other-worldliness. For Plato, there were two worlds: the unspeakably lofty world of Forms, and the world of mere "things," which is but a poor imitation of the former. Aristotle contradicted this view, asserting that there is only *one* world and that we are right smack in the middle of it. In criticizing Plato, Aristotle asked: If Forms are **essences** of things, how can they exist separated from things? If they are the *cause* of things, how can they exist in a

Mere Dog Copies

different world? And a most telling criticism has to do with the problem of *change* and *motion*, which the early Greeks had tried to solve.

They thought either that stability was an illusion (the view of
Heraclitus, for example) or that motion was an illusion (the view of
Parmenides). Plato had tried to resolve the dilemma by acknowledging
the insights of both Heraclitus and Parmenides. The former's world
is the unstable and transient realm of the visible. The latter's world
is the immutable realm of the intelligible composed of the eternally
unchanging Forms, which themselves are poorly reflected in the transitory world of the visible. But did Plato's compromise really solve the
problem of motion and change? Is it really comprehensible to explain
"changing things" by saying that they are bad imitations of unchanging things?

Parmenidean Permanence

Heraclitean Hustle

Aristotle thought not. In offering his own solution to the problem, Aristotle employed some of the same terminology as Plato. He said that a distinction must be drawn between *form* and *matter*, but that these two features of reality can be distinguished only in thought, not in fact. Forms are not separate entities. They are embedded in particular things. They are *in the world*. To think otherwise is an intellectual confusion. A particular object, to count as an object at all, must have both form and matter. Form, as Plato had said, is universal, in the sense that many particulars can have the same form. Aristotle called an object's form its "whatness." That is, when you say *what something is* (it's a tree, it's a book), you are naming its form. The form is a thing's *essence*, or nature. It is related to the thing's function (a wheel, a knife, a brick, etc.).

An object's matter is what is unique to that object. Aristotle called it the object's "thisness." All wheels or trees have the same form (or function), but no two have the same matter. Matter is

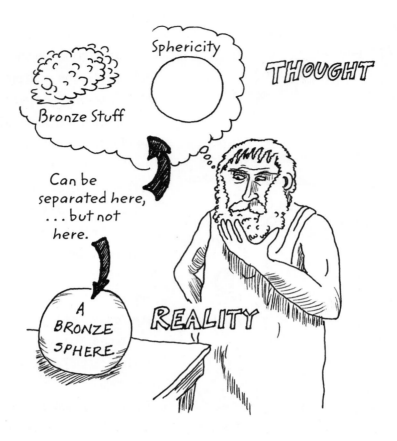

"the principle of individuation." An object with both form and matter is what Aristotle called a **substance.**

Each substance contains an essence, which is roughly equivalent to its form, as in Plato's writings; but unlike in Plato's account, in Aristotle's theory the essence cannot be separated from the substance in question. However, it is possible to perform the purely intellectual act of *abstracting* the essence from the substance. Indeed, part of the philosopher's job is to discover and catalog the different substances in terms of their *essences* and their **accidents,** that is, in terms of those features of the substance that are essential to it, and those that are not essential. (To be human, one must be rational, so rationality is part of the human essence; but although every human either has hair or is bald, neither hairiness nor baldness is essential to human nature. It is neither a necessary nor a sufficient condition.) With this kind of analysis Aristotle initiated a philosophical method that would be pursued well into the modern period.

THIS dog.

Who, me?

Aristotle's anti-Platonic metaphysics holds that reality is composed of a plurality of substances. It is not composed of an upper tier of eternal Forms and a lower tier of matter that unsuccessfully attempts to imitate those Forms. This theory represents Aristotle's pluralism as opposed to Plato's **dualism** (a dualism that verges on **idealism** because, for Plato, the most "real" tier of reality is the nonmaterial). How does Aristotle's pluralism solve the problem of motion and change, a problem that was unsuccessfully addressed by his predecessors? It does so by reinterpreting matter and form as *potentiality* and *actuality* and by turning these concepts into a theory of change. Any object in the world can be analyzed in terms of these categories. Aristotle's famous example is that of an acorn. The acorn's matter contains the potentiality of becoming an oak tree. That is, the acorn's physical structure contains within it the possibility of its developing over time into an oak tree, and that goal, that "form," "oak tree-ness," is the acorn's *actuality* (in other words, when the acorn "actualizes itself," it becomes an oak tree). Therefore, if the oak tree is the actuality of the acorn, the acorn is the potentiality of the oak tree. So, for Aristotle, form is an operating cause. Each individual sub-stance is a self-contained **teleological** (i.e., goal-oriented) system. Notice that a sub-stance's essence does not change, but its accidents do. (From the perspective of twenty-first century science, it may seem that Aristotle makes two errors here—an error of omission and one of commission: he omits all the tough stuff—the biology and chemistry that explain how the material components of an acorn can develop into an oak tree; and he commits what today appears to be the anthropomorphic error of attributing to acorns—and to all other natural objects—internal goals and intentions.)

In fact, Aristotle analyzed all substances in terms of four causes. The *material cause* is the stuff out of which something is made (e.g., a chunk of marble that is to become a statue). The *formal cause* is the form, or essence, of the statue, that which it strives to be. (This form exists both in the mind of the artist and potentially in the marble itself.) The *efficient cause* is the actual force that brings about the change (the sculptor's chipping the block of stone). The *final cause* is the ultimate purpose of the object (e.g., to beautify the Parthenon).

Nature, then, is a teleological system in which each substance is striving for self-actualization and for whatever perfection is possible within the limitations allowed it by its particular essence. In Aristotle's theory, as in Plato's theory, everything is striving unconsciously toward the Good. Aristotle believed that for such a system to work, some concrete perfection must actually exist as the *telos* (or goal) toward which all things are striving.

This entity Aristotle called the Prime Mover. It serves as a kind of god in Aristotle's metaphysics, but unlike the traditional gods of Greece and unlike the God of Western religion, the Prime Mover is almost completely nonanthropomorphic. It is the cause of the universe, not in the Judeo-Christian sense of creating it out of nothing, but in the sense of a

Final Cause; everything moves toward it in the way a runner moves toward a goal. The Prime Mover is the only thing in the universe with no potentiality because, being perfect, it cannot change. It is pure actuality, which is to say, pure activity. What activity?

The activity of pure thought. And what does it think about? Perfection! That is to say, about itself. The Prime Mover's knowl-

edge is immediate, complete self-consciousness.

What we seem to have here is an absolutely divine case of narcissism. (In Greek mythology, Narcissus was an extraordinarily handsome youth who became transfixed by the reflection of his own beauty and remained staring at it until he died.)

Aristotle's moral philosophy, as it appears in his manuscript now called *The Nicomachean Ethics,* reflects his teleological metaphysics. The notion of *goal,* or *purpose,* is the overriding one in his moral theory. Aristotle noted that every act is performed for some *purpose,* which he defined as the "good" of that act. (We perform an act because we find its purpose to be worthwhile.) *Either* the totality of our acts is an infinitely circular series (we get up in order to eat breakfast, we eat breakfast in order to go to work, we go to work in order to get money, we get money so we can buy food in order to be able to eat breakfast, etc., etc., etc.)—in which case life would be a pretty meaningless endeavor—*or* there is some ultimate good toward which the purposes of all acts are directed. If there is such a good, we should try to come to know it so that we can adjust all our acts toward it in order to avoid that saddest of all tragedies—the wasted life.

According to Aristotle, there is general verbal agreement that the end toward which all human acts are directed is *happiness;*[9]

therefore, happiness is the human good because we seek happiness
for its own sake, not for the sake of something else. But unless we
philosophize about happiness and get to know exactly what it is and
how to achieve it, it will be platitudinous simply to say that happiness
is the ultimate good. To determine the nature of happiness, Aristotle
turned to his metaphysical schema and asked, "What is the function
of the human?" (in the same way he would ask about the function of a
knife or an acorn). He came to the conclusion that a human's function is to engage in "an activity of the soul which is in accordance
with virtue" and which "is in conformity with reason."[10] Before grasping this complicated definition, we must determine what "virtue" is
and what kinds of virtues there are. But first, as an aside, I must
mention that Aristotle believed that certain material conditions
must hold before happiness can be achieved.

This list of material conditions reveals Aristotle's elitism: We need good friends, riches, and political power. We need a good birth, good children, and good looks. ("A man is not likely to be happy if he is very ugly.")[11] We must not be very short. Furthermore, we must be free from the need of performing manual labor. ("No man can practice virtue who is living the life of a mechanic or laborer.")[12] I should note that Aristotle's moral theory would be left substantially intact if his elitist bias were deleted.

Let us now inspect Aristotle's idea of virtue. The Greek word is *areté*. It could equally well be translated as "excellence." *Areté* is that quality of any act, endeavor, or object that makes them successful acts, endeavors, or objects. It is, therefore, a *functional* excellence.

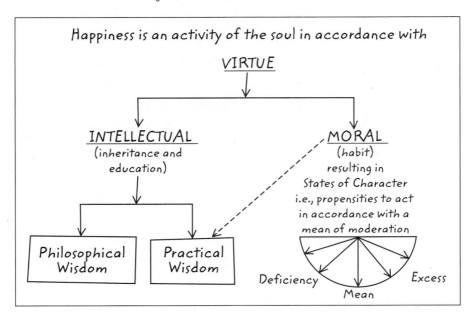

For Aristotle, there are two kinds of virtue: intellectual and moral. Intellectual virtues are acquired through a combination of inheritance and education, and moral virtues through imitation, practice, and habit. The habits that we develop result in states of character, that is, in dispositions to act certain ways, and these states of character are virtuous for Aristotle if they result in acts that are in accordance with a golden mean of moderation. For example, when it comes to facing danger, one can act with excess, that is, show too much fear (cowardice). Or one can act deficiently by showing

too little fear (foolhardiness). Or one can act with moderation, and hence virtuously, by showing the right amount of fear (courage). Aristotle realized that the choices we must make if we are to learn moral virtue cannot be made mathematically; rather, they are always context-bound and must be approached through trial and error.

Returning to the intellectual virtues of practical and philosophical wisdom, the former is the wisdom necessary to make judgments consistent with one's understanding of the good life. It is therefore related to moral virtue (as in the diagram). Philosophical wisdom is scientific, disinterested, and contemplative. It is associated with pure reason, and for Aristotle, the capacity for reason is that which is most human; therefore, philosophical wisdom is the highest virtue. So, when Aristotle defined happiness as "an activity of the soul in accordance with virtue," the activity referred to is philosophical activity. The human being can be happy only by leading a contemplative life, but not a monastic one. We are not only philosophical animals but also social ones. We are engaged in a world where decisions concerning practical matters are forced upon us constantly. Happiness (hence the good life) requires excellence in both spheres.

Aristotle's political views follow from his moral views. Just as happiness (*eudaimonia*) is the function or goal of the human individual, so is it the function of the state. Aristotle agrees with Plato that humans are endowed with social instincts. The state (*polis*) is a natural human organization whose goal is to maximize happiness for its citizens. In fact, the state is more natural than the family because only in the social climate produced by community can human nature be fully self-actualized. We see that in political theory, as everywhere in Aristotle's philosophy, teleology reigns supreme.

According to Aristotle, the distinction between nature and convention so touted by the Sophists is somewhat artificial. Law is natural to humans. Just as humans are naturally social, so is their desire to participate in the political body an innate disposition. But Aristotle recognizes that different constitutional bases produce different kinds of states. As long as the constitution is designed for the common well-being (*eudaimonia*) of all its citizens, it is a just state. There are three possible legitimate forms of the state: governance by one person (a monarchy), governance by an elite group (plutocracy), and governance by the body of citizens itself (a polity—a limited form of democracy). In certain circumstances, Aristotle preferred a monarchy—where a strong individual with excellent political skills steps forward to impose conditions that will be conducive to the well-being of all citizens. But in practice, Aristotle favored a polity, even if many of the citizens are not excellent individuals. "For

A Few Good Men

the many, of whom each individual is but an ordinary person, when they meet together may very likely be better than the few good, if regarded not individually but collectively."[13]

For each of the three sound forms of government, there is a possible perversion. A perverse government is one that has at heart not the interest of the whole of the citizenry, but only the interest of the rulers at the expense of the citizens. The perversion of monarchy is tyranny; the perversion of plutocracy is oligarchy; and the perversion of polity is democracy. Aristotle understood democracy as a government by the majority in a *polis* in which the bulk of its citizens are poor, and the poor look out exclusively for their own interests by taking the wealth of the rich for their own advantage. "If the poor, for example, because they are more in number, divide among themselves the prosperity of the rich—is this not unjust? . . . If this is not unjust, pray, what is?"[14] For Aristotle, this form of mob rule is as unjust as its opposite, the rich robbing and plundering the poor.

Despite Aristotle's predilection for what we would today call a modified democracy, his division of labor within the state was as harsh as Plato's. A great number of the inhabitants of the state—perhaps the majority—would be slaves. Aristotle provided a tortured argument trying to prove that some individuals are natural slaves and hence to be treated as mere property and as animate tools. Even those individuals who are citizens but are artisans or laborers are debarred from full participation in the advantages of citizenship. Furthermore, freedom is severely restricted for all members of the *polis*. At least this restriction is not as oppressive as Plato's was; Aristotle admonished Plato for outlawing private property and marriage in the ruling class. Aristotle believed that the desire to accumulate wealth is based on a natural instinct and should be allowed expression, though the state should control the excesses produced by giving free rein to that instinct.

Aristotle's support for a modified form of democracy makes his political views more attractive to the modern mentality than is Plato's propensity toward totalitarianism, but this advantage is diminished by Aristotle's assumption that the wealth of the state will be based on slave labor, by his disfranchisement of female citizens, by his debasing the class of blue-collar (blue-toga?) workers in his republic.

Just as Aristotle's political philosophy was written in response to Plato's, so was his philosophy of art. Let us recall Plato's objections to most art:

I am not just IGNORANT; I am DANGEROUSLY ignorant

1. Ontological objection: Art is in the realm of images; hence, it has the lowest ontological status in the Simile of the Line. Artistic images are copies of copies of copies.

2. Epistemological objection: The artist is

Homer

ignorant, but he purports to know Truth and to instruct it; therefore the artist is a *dangerous* ignoramus.

3. Aesthetic objection: Beauty (the Form) transcends the physical world, but art always reduces beauty to images, hence, to its lowest common denominator.

4. Moral objection: Art appeals not to the intellect—as does philosophy—but to the passions, which it stirs up, justifies, and loosens on an already chaotic (i.e., unphilosophical) public. Here too the artist is dangerous.

Aristotle agreed with Plato that the function of art is *mimesis*, "imitation" (or, as we would probably say today, "representation"). But he disagreed with Plato concerning the status of the *objects* represented in art. Rather than imitating mere things or individuals, art represents higher truths; hence, art, when successful, is a form of philosophy. Aristotle wrote:

> the poet's function is to describe, not the thing that has happened, but a kind of thing that might happen, i.e., what is possible as being probable or necessary. . . . Hence poetry is something more philosophical and of graver import than history, since its statements are of the nature rather of universals, whereas those of history are singulars.[15]

This philosophy, if correct, eliminates the first three of Plato's objections to representative art. As for the fourth objection, Aristotle argued that, far from provoking the passions, great art can *purge* from the viewers the passions that have built up in them. Aristotle says of the art of tragedy (and remember, it is generally agreed that some of the greatest tragedy ever written was from the Golden Age of Greece) that it achieves its effect "in a dramatic, not in a narrative form; with incidents arousing pity and fear, wherewith to accomplish its **catharsis** of such emotions."[16]

Not only did Aristotle make major contributions to metaphysics, ethics, aesthetics, and politics, but in addition, he singlehandedly created the first system of logic, one that remained pretty much intact until the development of symbolic logic 2000 years later. Even then, the new logic did not reject Aristotle's logic, but absorbed it after making a few corrections. Aristotle did not actually list logic as one of the sciences; rather, he saw it as the precondition of any science, which is why his main book on logic is called *Organon*, meaning "tool" or "instrument" in Greek.

In that book, Aristotle is primarily interested in discussing the idea of **logical entailment,** as is seen in his treatment of the form of argument known as the **syllogism** in which a conclusion follows necessarily from two premises. Look, for example, at this argument, suggested by Aristotle:

> All men are mortal.
> Socrates is a man.
> Therefore Socrates is mortal.

This is a *valid* argument. This means that the first two statements (the argument's *premises*) logically entail the third statement (the argument's *conclusion*). If the premises are both true, then the conclusion is also true. However, the argument would still be valid even if it turned out that the first or second premise was false. Even if it turned out that some men are immortal and that Socrates was actually a fish, the argument would be valid purely in terms of its *form*, which is the following:

> All As are Bs.
> S is an A.
> Therefore S is a B.

In his treatment of logic in his book *Metaphysics*, Aristotle defends what he takes to be the three primary laws of logic: the **principle of identity** (A equals A), the **principle of non-contradiction** (if A, then not not-A), and the **principle of the excluded middle** (either A or not-A). Unlike logicians of today, Aristotle treated these laws as metaphysical; that is, as descriptive truths about being rather than as mathematical-type truths. He did not think that these truths are self-evident. For example, he offered seven proofs of the truth of the principle of non-contradiction.

Aristotle also initiated what today is called "modal logic"; that is, the study of possibility and necessity. Aristotle argued that a proposition is *necessary* if its negation leads to a self-contradiction (e.g., "All mammals are animals"). A proposition is *possible* if its negation does not lead to a self-contradiction (e.g., "All animals are mammals." Notice that this proposition is in fact false and its negation is true, but we could conceive of a logically consistent world in which the original proposition would be true).

Although since the end of the nineteenth century the field of logic has developed into a powerful analytical tool that far surpasses Aristotle's insights, nobody doubts that it was he who was the true pioneer in this field.

Some of Aristotle's empirical claims about the world leave something to be desired (for instance, his claim that falling rocks accelerate because they are happy to be getting home, or his claim that snakes have no testicles because they have no legs). Nevertheless, Aristotle's metaphysics, his ethics, his logic, and his aesthetics remain permanent monuments to the greatness of human thought.

Key Philosophical Ideas in Chapter 2

<u>The Sophists</u>:

- <u>Goal</u>: To <u>replace philosophy with rhetoric</u>, and the pursuit of truth with the pursuit of rhetorical victory for the power it might bring; to <u>replace objectivity with subjectivism</u>, <u>objective truth with relativity</u>, <u>knowledge with skepticism</u>

<u>Protagoras</u>:

- <u>Relativity</u>: "Man is the measure of all things."

<u>Georgias</u>:

- <u>Nihilism</u>: "There is nothing"; <u>skepticism</u>: if there were anything, it couldn't be known; <u>subjectivism</u>: if it could be known it couldn't be communicated.

Thrasymachus:

- Power, not law or morality, should be everyone's goal. *Might makes right*.

Callicles:

- Power, not justice, *is good*. Power is good for survival. Survival allows pleasure. *Food, drink, and sex are the meaning of life*.
- Morality is the *weapon of the weak masses to shackle powerful individuals*.

Critias:

- Clever rulers control their subjects by encouraging the fear of non-existent gods.
- Conclusion: Despite the defense of subjectivism, relativism, and nihilism, the sophists did force philosophical attention away from cosmology and physics toward the human condition, and they participated in the political life of the newly democratic Athens.

Socrates:

- The greatest opponent of the Sophists, challenging them at every level.
- Socrates's motto: "The unexamined life is not worth living."
- Socrates queried everybody on every philosophical topic: knowledge, being, truth, meaning, justice, love, beauty, death, etc.
- He professed to know nothing, being on a permanent quest for knowledge.
- Irony as a tool of analysis.
- Socrates managed to offend powerful figures in Athens, was arrested and tried on bogus charges, and was condemned to death. He became the first recorded martyr for philosophy.

Plato:

- Plato's goal in *Republic*: to establish a complete account of ontology, epistemology, ethics, social and political philosophy, psychology, and philosophy of art through a series of dialogues with Socrates as the spokesman.
- Plato's Main Philosophical Ideas:
  - The Simile of the Line (consult illustration, page 64)
  - Ontology: two main divisions: the "intelligible world" at the top and the "visible world" below, the latter being a mere copy of the former

- Intelligible world divided into the "Forms" at the top, and "Formal Concepts" below, the latter being a mere copy of the former
- Result: a hierarchy of reality: four levels of Being in descending order
- Epistemology: two main divisions, "knowledge" at the top and "opinion" below, the latter being a mere copy of the former
- Knowledge divided into "Pure Reason" at the top and "Understanding" below, the latter being a mere copy of the former
- Opinion divided into "Belief" at the top and "Conjecture" below, the latter being a mere copy of the former
- "The Good" as the god of the intelligible world and the "the Sun" as the god of the visible world
- The Myth of the Cave (consult illustration, page 62), a mythical rendition of the Simile of the Line, with each feature represented symbolically as an account of education: the journey from ignorance to wisdom
- Ethics: the Good as the motive for all human endeavor
- Social philosophy and psychology: the parallel between the make-up of the individual (rational, spirited, and appetitive) and the make-up of the society (rulers, soldiers, and workers)
- Philosophy of art: the condemnation of representative art as ignorant and degenerate, based on imagery and emotion rather than on the Forms and knowledge

Aristotle:

- Aristotle's goal: to preserve the best of Platonism and reject those elements that are too otherworldly, replacing them with more practical elements

- Key Aristotelian Ideas:
  - Critique of Plato:
    - How can essences of objects be separated from those objects?
  - If Forms are unchangeable, how is change possible?
  - Aristotle's analytical division of objects—but not a real division—in terms of form (the "whatness" of the object) and matter (the "thisness" of an object); a substance is an object with form and matter.
  - Change:
    - Each substance (e.g., acorns or humans) strives to actualize its potentiality (a teleological explanation of change—a movement toward a goal).
    - The four causes: (a) material, (b) formal, (c) efficient, and (d) final ([b] and [d] are teleological)

- The <u>Prime Mover</u>: The <u>perfection toward which everything</u> and everyone <u>strives to move</u>, consciously or unconsciously
- <u>Ethics</u>: (See illustration, page 82.)
  - The <u>goal</u> of ethics (and politics) <u>is happiness</u>.
- <u>Happiness</u> is "<u>an activity of the soul . . . in conformity with virtue</u>."
- <u>Virtue: two kinds</u>
  - <u>moral virtue</u> (habitual propensities to act in accordance with <u>moderation</u>—the "<u>golden mean</u>")
  - <u>intellectual virtue</u>: two kinds
    - <u>practical wisdom</u>: the ability to deliberate well in the quest for a golden mean in all action
    - <u>intellectual wisdom</u>: development of philosophical contemplation about those things over which one has no power (the <u>activity of the soul</u> referred to above)
- <u>Politics</u>: <u>Three legitimate forms of government</u>: <u>monarchy, plutocracy, polity</u> (i.e., moderate democracy); <u>monarchy</u> is <u>preferable</u>.
- <u>Aesthetics</u>: Two defenses of art opposing Plato's rejection of art
  - <u>Art is philosophical</u> (it represents a higher truth).
  - <u>Art is cathartic</u> (it purges powerful and destructive emotions).
- <u>Logic</u>: Aristotle as the <u>Father of</u> the science of <u>logic (the rules of entailment</u>)
  - <u>syllogism</u>
  - the <u>principles of logic</u>: <u>identity, non-contradiction, excluded middle</u>

Topics for Consideration

1. It is claimed in this chapter that subjectivism, skepticism, relativism, and nihilism are at the heart of the project of sophism. Contrast these ideas with those seen in the philosophies of the pre-Socratics, and again with those in the philosophy of Plato.

2. Based on the few pages about Socrates that you have read here, write an essay speculating on what Socrates might have meant when he said, "The unexamined life is not worth living."

3. Make an alignment between Plato's Simile of the Line and his Myth of the Cave. Show that for each category or entity in the Simile, there is a corresponding category or entity in the myth.

4. In the Simile of the Line, the sun—the ultimate source of light—is designated by Plato as "the lord of the visible world." That is, everything in the physical world is dependent on the sun, and all visual awareness of the

physical world is because of the presence of light. The sun, in turn, is a copy of the Good, which is the "lord of the intelligible world." What does this analogy between the sun and the Good tell us about the objects and the relationships in the intelligible world and about our knowledge of this world?

5. William Wordsworth's poem "Ode: Intimations of Immortality from Recollections of Early Childhood" and John Keats's poem "Ode on a Grecian Urn" are sometimes called Platonic poems. Go to the library and locate them, and write an essay on one or both of them, interpreting them in the light of Plato's metaphysics. Also comment on the irony involved in the very idea of "Platonic poetry."

6. In Plato's *Republic* the healthy city is explained in terms of the same model as that of the healthy individual. Explain this congruity.

7. In the debate between Plato and Aristotle over the status of art, with which philosopher do you tend to agree? Defend your position.

8. Explain what it means to say that in the disagreement between Heraclitus and Parmenides, Plato credits both positions, but ultimately he sides with Parmenides.

9. Demonstrate the role played by teleology in the different aspects of Aristotle's philosophy.

10. In the text, the examples of an acorn and of a statue are used to illustrate Aristotle's theory of the four causes. Choose two other examples— one from nature and one from human manufacturing—and see if you can work each example through Aristotle's four causal categories.

11. First explain what Aristotle meant by describing moral action in terms of the golden mean, then show why engaging in moral action is a *necessary condition* but not a *sufficient condition* to achieve happiness, or the "good life."

12. Write an essay discussing the question of whether, in your opinion, the American constitutional system has addressed the objections that Aristotle directs toward the idea of democracy.

Notes

1. Philip Wheelwright, ed., *The Presocratics* (New York: Odyssey Press, 1966), 239.
2. Ibid., 240.
3. Plato, *Apology*, in *Plato on the Trial and Death of Socrates*, trans. Lane Cooper (Ithaca, N.Y.: Cornell University Press, 1941), 73.
4. Plato, *Republic*, in *The Dialogues of Plato*, vol. 1, trans. Benjamin Jowett (New York: Random House, 1937), 775.

5. There has been much scholarly debate concerning the best English translation of the Greek terms Plato uses in the Simile of the Line. Here is a transcription of the Greek words in question, positioned as they are on the Line:

noesis	eide
dianoia	hypothemenoi and ta mathematica
pistis	ta horomeva
eikasia	eikones

In designating *noesis* as "reason" and *dianoia* as "understanding," I am following the translations of both W. H. D. Rouse and Leo Rauch. But it should be mentioned that *noesis* has also been rendered as "understanding" (by G. M. A. Grube), as "knowledge" (by G. L. Abernathy and T. L. Langford), and as "intellection" (by Allan Bloom). *Dianoia* has been translated as "reasoning" (by Grube), as "thinking" (by Abernathy and Langford), and as "thought" (by Bloom). I have opted for Rouse's and Rauch's translation of *noesis* as "reason" because doing so best reveals the continuity between Plato and the later Western metaphysical tradition through Hegel and Kant. (We study Kant in Chapter 5 and Hegel in Chapter 6.) I have chosen to call the fourth square "formal concepts." Plato gives us two Greek terms for that slot, *hypothemenoi* and *ta mathematica.* Many interpreters choose the second phrase, "mathematical objects," as the key phrase here—and it is true that Socrates used examples from arithmetic and geometry to explain this concept. I have selected "formal concepts" because this category includes mathematical ideas but in fact encompasses more. I believe Plato did not mean to restrict *hypothemenoi* (literally "assumptions" or "postulates") to mathematical ideas. M. E. Taylor warns us against being misled by Plato's mathematical language here. He says that Plato "had before him no other examples of systematic and organized knowledge" than "the various branches of mathematics as recognized in the fifth century" (M. E. Taylor, *Plato: The Man and His Work* [New York: Meridian Books, 1960], 289). Plato is referring to organized conceptual knowledge, that is, roughly what today we would call scientific concepts. According to Plato, formal concepts are inferior to Forms both because they are copies (imitations, shadows, reflections) of the Forms and because the individual thinkers still depend on visual imagery when they operate at this level. In this sense the Forms, not the concepts, are mathematical, because they are image-free.

6. Plato, *Republic,* in *Great Dialogues of Plato,* ed. Eric H. Warmington and Philip G. Rouse, trans. W. H. D. Rouse (New York: New American Library, 1956), 305, 307.

7. Ibid., 308.

8. Ibid., 399.

9. The Greek word is *eudaimonia.* Some translators have preferred "well-being" over "happiness."

10. Aristotle, *Nicomachean Ethics,* in *A Guided Tour of Selections from Aristotle's "Nicomachean Ethics,"* ed. Christopher Biffle, trans. F. H. Peter (Mountain View, Calif.: Mayfield Publishing, 1991), 26.

11. Ibid., 30.

12. Aristotle, *Politics,* trans. Benjamin Jowett, in *The Basic Works of Aristotle,* ed. Richard McKeon (New York: Random House, 1941), 1183.

13. Ibid., 1190.

14. Ibid., 1189.

15. Aristotle, *Poetics,* trans. Benjamin Jowett, in *The Basic Works of Aristotle,* 1463–64.

16. Ibid., 1460.

3

The Hellenistic and Roman Periods

Fourth Century B.C.E. through Fourth Century C.E.

After the death of Aristotle, Greek civilization entered what historians call the Hellenistic era, a period of cultural decline. The Greek city-
states, unable to solve the problem of political disunity, were decimat-
ed by the Peloponnesian War and ravaged by the plague. First they fell
under Macedonian rule; then, after the death of Alexander the Great,
they eventually were absorbed into the newly emerging Roman Empire.
Many of the philosophies of this "decadent" period began in Greece
but received their greatest exposure in Rome, including the two major
philosophies of the period, Epicureanism and stoicism.

Epicureanism

The philosophy of Epicurus (341–270 B.C.E.) is known (not surprisingly)
as Epicureanism. If today the term hints of gluttony, debauchery,

and bacchanalian orgies, that is
not Epicurus's fault but the fault
of some of his Roman interpret-
ers. Epicurus himself led a life of
sobriety and simplicity: eating
bread, cheese, and olives; drinking
a bit of wine; napping in his hammock; and enjoying conversation

with his friends while strolling through his garden. He died with dignity and courage after a protracted battle with a painful disease.

Epicureanism was grounded in the atomic theory of Democritus, but, in fact, Epicurus, like all post-Alexandrian philosophers, seems to have been really interested not in science but in finding out about the good life. However, since

The Individual in the Roman Empire

Aristotle's time, the notion of the "good life" had suffered a setback. It no longer made sense to advocate being active, influential, political, and responsible as a way of self-improvement. Reality seemed to be unmoved by personal initiative, and the individual developed a feeling of powerlessness as he or she was about to be absorbed into the massive, impersonal bureaucracy of the Roman Empire. Like Aristotle, Epicurus believed that the goal of life was happiness, but happiness he equated simply with *pleasure*. No act should be undertaken except for the pleasure in which it results, and no act should be rejected except for the pain that it produces. This belief provoked Epicurus to analyze the different kinds of pleasure. There are two kinds of desires, hence, two kinds of pleasure as a result of gratifying those desires—natural desire (which has two subclasses) and vain desire:

I. Natural desire
   A. Necessary (e.g., desire for food and sleep)
   B. Unnecessary (e.g., desire for sex)
II. Vain desire (e.g., desire for decorative clothing or exotic food)

The Pursuit of Vain Pleasure

Natural necessary desires must be satisfied and are usually easy to satisfy. They result in a good deal of pleasure and in very few painful consequences. Vain desires do not need to be satisfied and are not easy to satisfy. Because there are no natural limits to them, they tend to become obsessive and lead to very painful consequences.

The desire for sex is natural but usually can be overcome; and when it can be, it should be, because satisfaction of the sexual drive gives intense pleasure, and all intense emotional states are dangerous. Also, the desire for sex puts people in relationships that are usually ultimately more painful than pleasant and that are often extremely painful.

One of the natural and necessary desires to which Epicurus pays a great deal of attention is the desire for *repose*. This term is to be understood both physically and psychically. The truly good person (i.e., the one who experiences the most pleasure) is the one who, having overcome all unnecessary desires, gratifies

Love is a Many-Splendored Thing
(For a Day or Two)

necessary desires in the most moderate way possible, leaves plenty of time for physical and mental repose, and is free from worry.

Notice that Epicurus's definition of pleasure is *negative*; that is, pleasure is the absence of pain. It is this negative definition that prevents Epicurus from falling into a crass sensualism. The trouble with this definition is

Cashier, do you mind!!

Sshh! She's reposing!

that, taken to its logical extremity, the *absence* of life is better than any life at all (a conclusion Freud also came to in his text *Beyond the Pleasure Principle*, where he claimed that behind the "pleasure principle" is Thanatos, the death instinct).

Beyond the Pleasure Principle

This deduction is a bit ironic because Epicurus himself claimed that his philosophy dispelled the fear of death. Democritus's atomism led Epicurus to believe that death was merely the absence of sensation and consciousness; therefore, there could be no sensation or conscious-ness of death to fear. "So long as we exist, death is not with us; but when death comes, then we do not exist."[1]

Some of Epicurus's Roman followers interpreted "pleasure" quite differently, defining it as a positive titillation. It is because of these extremists that today Epicureanism is often associated with sensu-alistic **hedonism.** Sickly Epicurus, swinging in his hammock, would have disapproved. (Though not too harshly. Polemics cause agitation, which is painful.) Epicurus's theory never constituted a major philosophical movement, but he had disciples in both Greece and Rome for a number of centuries. His most famous follower was the Roman Lucretius, who, in the first century B.C.E., wrote a long poem, *On the Nature of Things,* expounding the philosophy of his master. It is through Lucretius's poem that many readers have been introduced to the thoughts of Epicurus.

Stoicism

Stoicism was another important Hellenistic philosophy that was transported to Rome. Stoicism was founded in Greece by Zeno of Cyprus (334–262 B.C.E.), who used to preach to his students from a portico, or stoa (hence the term "stoicism," literally, "porchism"). Like

Zeno at the Stoa

Epicureanism, stoicism had its roots in pre-Socratic materialism, but stoicism too, especially in its Roman form, became less interested in physics and more particularly concerned with the problem

of human conduct. The three most interesting of the Roman stoics were Seneca (4–65 C.E.), a dramatist and high-ranking statesman; Epictetus (late first century C.E.), a slave who earned his freedom; and Marcus Aurelius (121–180 C.E.), a Roman emperor. (It's quite striking that a slave and an emperor could share the same philosophy of resignation, though probably this philosophy was easier for the emperor than for the slave!) The stoics accepted the Socratic equation that virtue equals knowledge. There exists a cognitive state that, once achieved, expresses itself as a disposition to behave in a certain dispassionate manner, and in turn it guarantees complete well-being. One should strive throughout one's life to acquire this wisdom. Human excellence is attained instantaneously once one has gained the enlightenment.

The duration of such a life of perfection is indifferent (which fact leads to the stoic advocacy of suicide under certain circumstances). To achieve this state of blessedness, one must free oneself from all worldly demands, particularly those of the emotions and of pleasure seeking. The stoic wise person is an *ascete* who has transcended the passions that create a disorderly condition in the soul. The stoic has no interest in all those objects that in normal human beings excite the passions of grief, joy, hope, or fear.

What is the content of stoic wisdom? It is similar to the Aristotelian notion that the good consists of acting in accordance with one's nature. The stoic addition to this idea is that to so act requires acting in accordance with nature itself, that is, with the totality of reality

(which the stoics take to be divine). Considered as a whole, reality is perfect. Humans will also become perfect if they learn to live in accordance with the divine plan of reality. This accomplishment requires that one make one's desires identical with the overall providential plan for the universe. In fact, a person can do *nothing but* conform to the grand design, and stoic wisdom consists in recognizing this truth. Fools are those who try to impose their own selfish desires on reality. This attempt results in unhappiness and unfreedom. If **freedom** is the unity of will and ability (i.e., being able to do what one wants), then the only way to be free is to want what the universe wants. We shouldn't wish that we could get what we desire; rather, we should desire what we get. If we could

> Just what I wanted! To be robbed while fixing a flat in a rainstorm.

Don't Try to Get What You Want— Rather, Want What You Get

THIS WAY
DOWN

learn to equate what we want with what's the case, then we would always be free and happy, because we'd always get just what we want. This is stoic wisdom.

The stoics realized that if one ever achieved this lofty state, the apparent harshness of reality might jeopardize one's inner equilibrium, and one might backslide into pain and anxiety. For this reason, and because the stoics believed that the amount of time one spent in the enlightened state was indifferent, the stoics advocated suicide in certain circumstances. If extreme conditions forced themselves upon one and if one realized that these conditions would destabilize the equilibrium of one's stoic soul and plunge one into unacceptable emotional agitation, one had every right to escape those conditions through suicide. Epictetus said of suicide, "If the smoke is moderate I will stay: if excessive, I go out. . . . The door is always open."[2] Marcus Aurelius used identical imagery: "The house is smoky, and I quit it."[3] Seneca said, "If [the wise man] encounters many vexations which disturb his tranquillity, he will release himself. . . . To die well is to escape the danger of living ill."[4] In fact, on the advice of the emperor Nero, Seneca did step into the bath and open his veins.

During the period when stoicism was exercising its greatest influence, a new social and religious form of thought was coming to the fore: Christianity. Although Christians were still a minority in the Empire, their religion had found an ever-growing number of adherents because its promises resonated with the needs of people at all levels of society. It bestowed meaning on even the most wearisome features of life; it offered a direct and personal connection to divinity through the person of Jesus, the son of a carpenter; its communal basis offered an identity that was much more concrete than that obtained by mere residence in the Roman Empire; and it offered salvation and eternal life. Although the Christians had not learned to defend their new religion with a systematic philosophy as they would in the Middle Ages, their doctrine was in competition with the philosophies of the day for the hearts and minds of men and women. All such thought systems were responding to the same problems, so it is no surprise that there are some similarities between Christianity and a philosophy like stoicism; for example, both philosophies share the doctrine of resignation, the disdain for attachment to earthly things, and the concern with conforming to the will of divine Providence. The differences cannot be overlooked, however, such as the discrepancy between stoic and Christian teachings on suicide. Whereas the stoic believed that suicide was justified to prevent oneself from going against the divine plan of the world, Christians believed that the act of suicide was prohibited by that same divine plan. Also, stoicism was inclined to be **quietistic** and acquiescent to political authority, whereas in its inception Christianity tended to be activistic and resistant to political domination.

Epictetus said, "Refuse altogether to take an oath, if it is possible; if it is not, refuse as far as you are able."[5] This attitude contrasts greatly with that of many Christians who refused to swear an oath on the divinity of the emperor and were martyred for that refusal.

Skepticism

A minor school of some interest in the period we are studying is that of skepticism. Its historical ancestor is Gorgias the sophist. Recall that Gorgias argued that nothing exists; if anything did exist, we couldn't know it, and if we did know it, we couldn't communicate it. However, Gorgias behaved as if he knew these three propositions with certainty, while the skeptics cast doubt on almost all claims to knowledge. The Greek word, *skeptikos*, from which this group derives its name, meant "inquirers." Some of the skeptics restricted the field of knowledge to immediate experience and others denied even this, claiming that, because experience gives us only appearances—which is not reality—experience therefore does not provide knowledge. The skeptics were prepared to defend their views with a number of arguments against all claims to knowledge. We will see some of these when we arrive at the philosophy of René Descartes in the seventeenth century; however, Descartes revives the skeptical arguments in order to refute them and to prove that certain knowledge is obtainable. Descartes will be interested in ontology and epistemology, while the skeptics were primarily interested in happiness—the good life—like most of the philosophers in the Hellenistic period. They seemed to believe that through an act of suspending judgment about the nature of reality—an act called an *epochê*—we could achieve a state of unperturbedness and peace of mind

THE OCCUPY IGNORANCE MOVEMENT

called *ataraxia*. The best known of the skeptics is Sextus Empiricus, partly because his writings survived while those of other skeptics did not. He lived sometime between 250 and 327 C.E. The excellence of his skills in Greek lead most scholars to believe that he was indeed Greek, but we do not know what place he called home.[6] In his writings, Sextus articulates all the reasons explaining why we should be skeptical of any claim to knowledge that goes beyond immediate sensory experience. He sets forth the contradictions into which we are led when we try to deduce the true nature of reality, stressing the conflicting claims of all philosophers who have tried to do so, and the way that any supposed foundation of knowledge can be challenged. He holds that his own view is not simply another philosophical view about reality but is a cathartic purge of all philosophical views, replacing them with a state of ataraxia.

Neoplatonism

After the death of the stoic Marcus Aurelius ("the last good emperor"), a long period of upheaval and disorder ensued. The helplessness that people felt in the face of the decadence of the crumbling empire was responded to by a religious revival. The most prominent philosophical religious competitor with Christianity during the third century C.E. was a mystical form of **Platonism** known today as Neoplatonism, espoused by Plotinus (204–270). We have already seen a deep-seated propensity toward other-worldliness in Plato, which Aristotle had criticized. Plato's claim of superiority for the other world fit in well with the world-weariness of the third century.

For Plotinus, as for Plato before him, absolute truth and certainty cannot be found in this world. Plato had taught a purely rational method for transcending the flux of the world and achieving truth and certainty, but Plotinus preached that such a vision can only be achieved extra-rationally, through a kind of ecstatic union with the One. The One was for Plotinus the Absolute, or God.

Nothing can be truly known about the One in any rational sense, nor can any characterization of the One be strictly correct. If we review Plato's Simile of the Line from a Plotinian perspective, we see that language, and therefore thought, functions by drawing distinctions (we say "this is a pen," meaning it is *not* the desk). But in the One, no distinctions exist; hence, nothing can be thought or said about it. A person can know the One only by uniting with it. That union can be achieved in this life in moments of mystical rapture, but in the long run the goal can only be achieved in death.

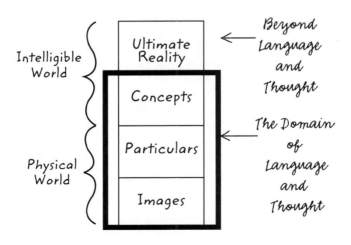

One can prepare for the ultimate union through an ascetic program of virtuous living. Plotinus's own version of the Line is based on his idea that God, or the Absolute, does not perform acts of creation (that would sully God's unchangeableness); rather, God "emanates." That is, God is

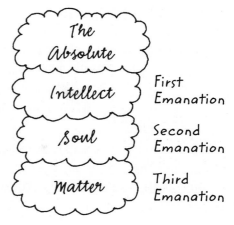

reflected onto lower planes, and these reflections represent kinds of imitations of God's perfection in descending degrees of fragmentation. (What we have here is a kind of "gooey" Simile of the Line.) This metaphysics borders on pantheism—the view that reality and God are the same. We saw in chapter 1 that the pre-Socratic philosopher Xenophanes has been interpreted by some scholars as a pantheist. The stoics too bordered on pantheism. The idea of this doctrine—that the whole universe is divine, hence perfect in its totality—crops up in the history of philosophy and religion over and over. We will see its clearest and most articulate expression in the case of seventeenth-century Dutch philosopher Baruch Spinoza, in chapter 5. In the context of the dominant religious practice in the West, pantheism has usually been condemned as a form of heresy. As we will see shortly, the problem of pantheism emerges early during the Middle Ages, again associated with neoplatonism, this time not to haunt the death scene of classicism but the birth scene of Christian philosophy.

Because the philosophy of Plotinus and his followers was the last philosophy of the classical period, his version of Platonism was the one that was handed down to the medieval world. When the early Christian thinkers faced the task of unifying and systematizing the Christian worldview, they turned to the prevailing Platonic metaphysical scheme as a framework, and the Platonism they found was already heavily influenced by Plotinus's thought.

Key Philosophical Ideas in Chapter 3

- Contrasted with the systematic philosophies of Plato and Aristotle, the philosophers of this six-hundred-year period may seem less profound, complex, and subtle: _a period of philosophical decline_.

- Philosophers primarily interested only in Socrates's question, "_How should we live?_"

- Like Aristotle, they hold that _the answer requires understanding the nature of happiness_, but their _concepts of happiness_ are _less refined and subtle than those of Aristotle_.

Epicureanism:

- According to _Epicurus, happiness is pleasure_ (_hedonism_), whose understanding requires a _theory of desire_.

- True happiness is _the fulfillment of necessary, natural desires_ and _the avoidance of vain desire_, leading to _a calm life of sobriety and simplicity_.

- A _negative definition_ of pleasure: _pleasure is the absence of pain_.

- A main cause of _unhappiness_: _the fear of death_; _but there is no death_: where I am, death is not, and where death is I am not.

- Epicurus's philosophy _corrupted by later followers in Rome_, who emphasized _gluttony, sensualism, and debauchery_.

Stoicism (especially _Seneca_, _Epictetus_, _Marcus Aurelius_):

- Accepts the _Socratic equation between virtue and knowledge_.

- A special kind of _knowledge leads to human excellence and happiness_.

- To achieve this wisdom, philosophers _control emotions_ _and desires_ that engage one in the frenzy of the demands of the world.
  - A state of _dispassionate, ascetic indifference_ is produced.

- The content of this wisdom: _One must equate one's own will with the will of nature_, which is discovered as _a divine plan_ of reality.

- One must _want exactly what the universe wants_.

- In that case, _one always gets_ exactly _what one wants_, producing a condition of pure _freedom and happiness_.

- If this state, once achieved, is threatened, _suicide_ is justified.

Skepticism (especially Sextus Empiricus):

- The skeptics cast doubt on almost all claims to knowledge, restricting knowledge exclusively to the data of the senses, or in some cases, rejecting sensorial knowledge as well.

- The goal of the rejection of the possibility of knowledge: ataraxia, unperturbed peace of mind, a particular mental and emotional state involving a suspension of judgment.

Neo-Platonism (especially Plotinus):

- A mystical form of Platonism.

- Knowledge of ultimate reality can be achieved through an extra-rational vision, an ecstatic union with the One.

- Epistemology: Nothing can be thought or said about the One because language (hence thought) can only grasp the bottom three rungs of the Simile of the Line.

- Ontology: A form of pantheism.

- Reality as seen in the Simile of the Line is composed of layers of emanations (or reflections) of the One.

- Overview: Christianity was introduced into the world in this period, and, in competition against the philosophies for intellectual recognition, borrowed considerably from neo-Platonism to structure its philosophical arguments.

Topics for Consideration

1. Show why Epicurus's decision to define pleasure negatively (in terms of a lack of agitation) produces a very different philosophy from the Roman version of Epicureanism based on a positive definition of pleasure (in terms of the experience of titillation).

2. It is often believed that desires for food and sex are based on natural (i.e., biological) needs. Epicurus too calls them "natural" but claims that the fulfillment of the desire for food is "necessary," while the fulfillment of the desire for sex is "unnecessary." Explain what he means; explain what effect acting on his philosophy would have on one's life.

3. Write a short essay defending or attacking the view that repose is a key element of the "good life."

4. Are you convinced that both an emperor and a slave could follow the principles of stoicism? Explain your position.

5. Stoic philosophers claimed that we are happy only if we are free. What did they mean by "happiness" and "freedom"? Why, if freedom is such an important virtue, did they not agonize over choices that faced them?

6. Compare and contrast stoicism with Epicureanism as practiced by Epicurus, and then again with the later followers of Epicurus in Rome.

7. Can you find any common denominators among the various philosophies of this period? If so, or if not, explain.

8. Compare and contrast Plato's version of the Simile of the Line (in Chapter 2) with Plotinus's version of it.

Notes

1. Epicurus, "Letter to Menoeceus," trans. C. Bailey, in *The Stoic and Epicurean Philosophers: Epicurus, Epictetus, Lucretius, Marcus Aurelius*, ed. Whitney J. Oats (New York: Modern Library, 1940), 31.

2. Epictetus, "Discourses of Epictetus," trans. P. E. Matheson, in *The Stoic and Epicurean Philosophers*, 267.

3. Marcus Aurelius, "Meditations," trans. G. Long, in *The Stoic and Epicurean Philosophers*, 523.

4. Seneca, *The Stoic Philosophy of Seneca*, ed. and trans. Moses Hadas (Garden City, N.Y.: Doubleday Anchor, 1958), 202–3.

5. Epictetus, "The Encheiridion," in *The Discourses of Epictetus*, ed. and trans. George Land (Mount Vernon, Va.: Peter Pauper Press, n.d.), 22.

6. An English translation of the writings of Sextus Empiricus are found in four volumes translated from Greek by R.G. Bury called Sextus Empiricus (London: Loeb Classical Library, 1917–1955).

4
Medieval and Renaissance Philosophy
Fifth through Fifteenth Centuries

All three of the main Western religions—Judaism, Christianity, and Islam—had their birth in the land that was home to the ancient Mediterranean desert cultures, in today's Egypt, Israel, Palestine, Jordan, and Saudi Arabia. By the beginning of the period now known as the Middle Ages, Islam had not yet appeared on the scene (I will speak more of Islam shortly), and Christianity was barely 400 years old. But the main books of the Hebrew Bible on which Judaism was based already dated back 1,200 years. Judaism itself developed out of earlier, tribal polytheistic religions from which Judaism distinguished itself when it proclaimed that there was but one God, Jehovah, who had chosen the natives of ancient Judea—the Jews—with whom to establish a special

**The Creation of the World
(After an Anonymous Medieval Painting)**

covenant. This covenant was the basis of a law that not only lays out moral strictures (the Ten Commandments), but also provides rituals governing dietary habits, marriage and funerary rites, prayers, sacrifices, and almsgiving. The Jewish Bible, or Torah (later called the Old Testament by Christians), describes God's creation of the world, assigns humans a place in it, contains God's commandments, expresses his will, and relates a history of the Jews. It explains both the triumphs and the many sufferings of the Jews, whose homeland unfortunately lay on one of the major military crossroads of the world; therefore, Judea suffered numerous invasions and brutal conquests. These holy writings also contain the fiery words of great prophets who are said to have recorded divinely inspired visions of God's will and of the future. Among other prophecies, one foretells the coming of a messiah (or "anointed one") who will liberate the Jews from their oppressors and establish a kingdom of Glory.

Christianity derived from precisely this Jewish prophetic tradition, when an initially small band of Jews—then later increasing numbers of non-Jews—claimed to recognize an individual named Jesus of Nazareth (ca. 4 B.C.E.–ca. 29 C.E.) as the "Christ," a Greek translation of the Hebrew word "messiah." The story of Jesus is told in four gospels (proclamations of good news): Matthew, Mark, Luke, and John. These books tell of the annunciation by angels to Jesus's virgin mother, Mary; of her pregnancy; of Jesus's humble birth in a stable; of his family's flight to Egypt to escape the wrath of the jealous King Herod; and of the miracles and cures Jesus performed. The gospels also tell of his teachings, which involve a reinterpretation of the Jewish law that de-emphasizes those features governing ritualistic practices and dietary habits and instead underscores an interiorization of the law. This reinterpretation produces a doctrine of compassion and aid for one's fellow human being, particularly for the downtrodden, despairing, and disadvantaged. Jesus's teachings also contain a strong element of **eschatological** prophecy that urges people to prepare for the Kingdom of God, which is at hand. Furthermore, these gospels tell the story of Jesus's betrayal by one of his disciples, of his arrest

**The Annunciation
(After Fra Angelico)**

by the Roman authorities—who forcibly included a rebellious Judea in their empire—of Jesus's trial and condemnation by the Jewish court, of his crucifixion by the Roman soldiers, of his burial and miraculous resurrection, and of the ascension to heaven of the living Christ. All these events were viewed by Jesus's followers, and by the Christian Scriptures themselves, as fulfillment of the prophecies of the Old Testament and therefore as proof that, indeed, Jesus was the Christ, the messiah foretold by the ancient prophets.

The Christian communities in Palestine immediately after Jesus's execution were composed mostly of Jews who saw Jesus's message as directed primarily toward Jews, but at the same time the doctrine was spreading to the broader Greek-speaking and Latin-speaking world. Indeed, after the first four gospels, the bulk of the rest of the New Testament is dominated by the letters of Christian leaders to communities of believers in the Greek-speaking parts of the Mediterranean world. Foremost among these writings are the letters of Saint Paul, Christianity's greatest missionary and organizer.

In these letters he developed and clarified the doctrines of love and servitude and the spritualization and interiorization of the Hebrew law; he emphasized Jesus's suffering and death as an atonement for the sins of the whole human race and as a guarantee that this atonement meant an eternal life for those who believe in Jesus as the Christ and who live according to his teachings.

The New Testament concludes with an apocalyptic vision of the end of the world based on the writings of a Christian prophet called Saint John the Divine, not to be confused with Saint John, the author of the Fourth Gospel. John the Divine was indeed confused with Saint John during the Middle Ages, and this misunderstanding bestowed great authority on John the Divine's writing, known as the Book of Revelation. In his vision John sees a great battle between the forces of God and those of the devil, Satan, that results in the return of Christ, the Final Judgment of the living and the dead, the admission of the blessed into the New Jerusalem (heaven), and the consignment of the damned to hell.

During the 300 years after Jesus's death, Christianity spread throughout the Roman Empire, but tumultuously so, because of the sometimes bloody repression of it by the Roman authorities and because of internal debates among its leaders concerning the correct form that Christian **dogma** should take. Its **canon** did not take form until the fourth century after the birth of Jesus.

The Damned Dragged Down to Hell by Demons (After Luca Signorelli)

Saint Augustine

In the year 313 C.E. an important event occurred. The Roman emperor Constantine was converted to Christianity, and even though only one in ten citizens of the Empire was a Christian, Christianity became the official religion of the realm. During the next couple of centuries, the early Church fathers turned to the prevailing Neoplatonic philosophical tradition in their search for intellectual foundations for their still relatively new religion. The first truly important philosopher in this Christian Platonic tradition was Augustine of Hippo (354–430). He had one foot squarely planted in the classical

world and one in the medieval world, and he straddled the abyss that separated these two worlds.

As a young student of rhetoric in Rome, acutely aware of his own sensual nature, Augustine was concerned with the problem of good and evil. He became attracted to **Manicheanism** (founded by Mani of Persia in the third century), which was a philosophy that combined certain Christian and Persian elements and that understood reality in terms of an eternal struggle between the principle of light (Good) and the principle of darkness (Evil). The strife between these two principles manifested itself as the world. The soul represented the good and the body represented evil. As a Manichee, Augustine could attribute his many sins to a principle somehow outside himself.

But Augustine soon became dissatisfied with this "solution" to the problem of evil, and he became attracted to Neoplatonism and its conception of an *immaterial reality*. It was from Neoplatonism that Augustine got his idea of evil not as a real feature of reality, but as a lack, an incompleteness, a privation. (Recall the Simile of the Line: the more goodness a thing has, the more real it is. Conversely, the less reality it has, the worse it is. Just as a

dental cavity is a *lack* of calcium [a hole is not a *thing*, it is an absence of being], so is a sin not a thing, but an absence of goodness.) In 388, after a minor mystical experience, Augustine converted to Christianity and never again vacillated in his intellectual commitment. Though Augustine returned to the religion of his mother (she was eventually designated by the Catholic Church as a saint, Saint Monica), his understanding of Christianity remained influenced by Neoplatonic ideas. But he would now admit that sin was not simply a privation of goodness, but the result of excessive self-love on the part of the sinner and the lack of sufficient love for God. In 391 Augustine was ordained a priest and in 396 he became the Bishop of Hippo, on the North African coast. During this period, Christianity was still seeking to achieve

Evil as the Absence of Being

focus on its own identity, and Augustine spent an enormous amount of energy combating a series of heresies: **Donatism, Priscillianism, Arianism,** and of course, his former persuasion, Manicheanism. But at the same time, he had to combat a new and especially difficult heresy, that of **Pelagianism.** Pelagius's heresy was that of overaccentuating the role of free will in salvation and minimizing the role of God's grace. Much to Augustine's embarrassment, Pelagius had been using Augustine's book on free will to defend his own view.

So Augustine found himself walking a tightrope. He had to attack the Manichees for minimizing free will and attack the Pelagians for overemphasizing it. This problem occupied him in some very subtle philosophical reasoning.

The problem: If God is all-wise (omniscient), then he knows the future. If he knows the future, then the future must unfold exactly in accordance with his knowledge (otherwise, he does *not* know the future). If the events in the future *must* occur according to God's foreknowledge of them, then they are *necessary,* and there is no freedom. If there is no freedom, then humans are not responsible for their acts, in which case it would be immoral to punish people for their sins. (If God knew millions of years before Judas was born that he would betray Jesus, how could God send Judas to hell for his betrayal?) So the conclusion seems to be: Either God is omniscient but immoral, or he is benevolent but ignorant. How can Augustine avoid this unpalatable dilemma? He does so with a number of sophisticated arguments. One is that, for God, there is no past or future, only an eternal present. For him, everything exists in an eternal moment. To say "God knew millions of years before Judas's birth that he would betray Jesus" is to make the *human error*

Does God's Foreknowledge Determine Our Actions?

of believing that God is in time. In fact, God is outside of time. (That's what it means to say that God is eternal.) Another tack of Augustine's is to admit that God's knowledge of the world entails **necessity,** but to deny that necessity is incompatible with freedom. Like the stoics, Augustine believed that freedom is the capacity to do what one wants, and one can do what

Judas

one wants even if God (or anyone else) already knows what that person wants. Augustine pointed out that God's foreknowledge of a decision doesn't *cause* the decision, any more than my own acts are caused by my knowledge of what I'm going to do.

I have just presented a sample of Augustinian thought. His philosophy is a profound meditation on the relation between God and the human being. It was addressed to a troubled and expiring world. The old order was crumbling. In fact, on the same day Augustine succumbed to the infirmities of old age in the cathedral at Hippo, the barbaric Vandals were burning the city. Even though they left the cathedral standing out of

God Is Not in Time

respect for him, the fires that consumed Hippo were the same ones that consumed the Roman Empire. The classical period was over, and that long night, which some call the Dark Ages, had commenced.

At the death of Augustine, Western philosophy fell into a state of deterioration that was to last for 400 years. This period, the advent of the medieval world, truly was the dark night of the Western soul. The Roman legions could no longer control the frontiers of the Empire, and the Teutonic tribes from the eastern forest swarmed over the old Empire.

Rome was sacked twice within a thirty-five-year period. The new "barbarian" emperors no longer bore Latin names but had Germanic ones. They were not interested in culture as it had been known in classical times. Philosophy as the Greeks and Romans had under-stood it was in danger of perishing.

The Encyclopediasts

During this long dark night, philosophy flickered only as individual candle flames at distant corners of the old, dead empire. Certain isolated monasteries in Italy, Spain, and Britain and on the rocky crags of islands in the Irish Sea produced what are known as the encyclopediasts, who systematically compiled and conserved whatever remnants of classical wisdom they could lay their hands on. The three salient figures in

this tradition are Boethius (480–525) in Italy, Isidore (570–636) in Spain, and The Venerable Bede (674–735) in England. (St. Isidore's encyclopedia is particularly revealing. Under the letter "A" can be found both an entry on the atomic theory and an entry on the Antipodes, a people who were supposed to inhabit the rocky plains of southern Africa and who, Isidore believed, had their big toes on the outside of the feet, thereby allowing them more maneuverability among the rocky fields where they dwelt!) Isidore's hodgepodge is emblematic of the state of philosophy during the Dark Ages.

An Antipode Showing Off in Rocky Terrain

John Scotus Eriugena

Suddenly, after four centuries of relative silence, philosophy blossomed forth in the work of the first great metaphysical system builder of the Middle Ages, the redundantly named John Scotus Eriugena ("Sean the

Irishman, the Irishman" [ca. 810–ca. 877]). John had been called from Ireland to the Palatine School of King Charles the Bald to translate the Greek document known today as the Pseudo-Dionysius (a work falsely believed to have been written by St. Paul's Christian convert St. Dionysius but believed today to have been written by a Neoplatonic philosopher sympathetic to Christianity). John's own book, *On the Divisions of Nature*, was greatly influenced by his reading of the Pseudo-Dionysius and is a confusing combination of Christian dogma and Neoplatonic pantheism. Through his book and his influential translation, Platonism gained an even greater foothold in Christianity.

John's goal was the categorization and understanding of the totality of reality (what he calls "Nature"). The first categorical distinction he drew was between

John Scotus Divides Up Nature

This distinction involves the Platonic supposition that there is a hierarchy of being, that some things are more real than other things. "Things that are not" are those entities that on a Neoplatonic scale contain a lesser degree of reality. For example, a particular tree or horse contains less being than the form "tree" or the form "horse";

hence, particulars are subsumed under this negative category. So are all "lacks" or "deprivations," such as sinful acts or acts of forgetting. The most surprising thing we find in this category is what John called "super-reality"—that which cannot be grasped by the human intellect, that which on the Neoplatonic scale is "beyond being." Apparently, John was talking about God.

What is left? What can be called the "things that are"? Only those entities that can be comprehended by pure human intellect, namely, the Platonic Forms! All else is beyond being.

So we find this Christian scholar in the apparently awkward position of claiming that God is among those things classified as nonexistent—in the same class where we would expect to find centaurs, griffins, round squares, and mountains made of gold. Why doesn't John's writing end all discussion of God once and for all? Because John's method of the "vias affirmativa and negativa" (borrowed from the Pseudo-Dionysius) allowed him to make sense of the nothingness of a being beyond being.

This affirmation and its negation do not lead to a self-contradiction; rather, they serve as thesis and antithesis and are **dialectically** reconciled in a (Hegelian-like) synthesis that will lead us to realize that God is somehow superwise. The same method will show us why John said that God does not exist but that he [super] exists.

VIA AFFIRMATIVA	VIA NEGATIVA
We affirm:	We deny the affirmation:
"God is wise."	"God is not wise."
↑	↑
This affirmation is true only as metaphor. "Wisdom" is a word that gets its meaning from *human discourse*. We can apply it to God only analogically to give us a hint of his nature.	This negation is literal. Because "wisdom" gets its meaning from human discourse, it cannot literally apply to God.

There is yet another way in which John Scotus Eriugena divided Nature:

1. Nature that creates and is uncreated (i.e., God)
2. Nature that creates and is created (i.e., the Platonic Forms)
3. Nature that is created and does not create (i.e., the physical world)
4. Nature that is not created and does not create (i.e., God)

(Remember, in this Neoplatonic schema, to say that something "X" creates is to say that there is something below X in the hierarchy of reality that is dependent upon X. Conversely, to say that something "Y" is created is to say that Y is dependent on something above it for its existence.)

In this system, God is both Alpha and Omega, Beginning and End, Creator and Goal of Creation. God issues out into the world and comes back to himself. John's philosophy looks suspiciously like Plotinus's pantheistic system of emanations, and though many attempts were made to defend *On the Divisions of Nature* against the charge of heresy, eventually it was condemned as heterodoxical, in 1225 by Pope Honorius III.

Alpha and Omega

Saint Anselm

After John Scotus Eriugena, there were no great system makers for the next 350 years. From the ninth to the thirteenth centuries, philosophy would be done in a more piecemeal manner than it had been done by Augustine or John Scotus, or than it would be done in the thirteenth century by Thomas Aquinas. It was confined to a kind of philosophical grammar of theological terms. A piecemeal approach, however, does not mean that philosophy was always unimpressive. One of the most striking pieces of philosophical logic produced in the medieval period is the demonstration of God's existence created by Anselm of Canterbury (1033–1109), later Saint Anselm. Today this demonstration is known as the **ontological argument** because it is derived not from observation but from the very idea of being ("ontology" equals "theory of being").

Anselm's argument began with a reference to the fool (of Psalms 53:1) who "says in his heart, 'There is no God.'" But, said Anselm, even the fool

is convinced that something exists in the understanding at least, than which nothing greater can be conceived. For when he hears of this he understands it. . . . And assuredly that than which nothing greater can be conceived, cannot exist in the understanding alone. For suppose it exists in the understanding alone: then it can be conceived to exist in reality, which is greater. . . . Hence, there is no doubt that there exists a being than which nothing greater can be conceived, and it exists both in the understanding and in reality … and this being thou art, O Lord, our God.[1]

Psalms 53:1

Try out Anselm's argument. Conceive in your mind the most perfect being you can think of. (Anselm believed it will look very much like the conception of the traditional Christian God—a being who is all-good, all-knowing, all-powerful, eternal, and unchangeable.) Now ask yourself, does the entity you conceived exist only in your mind? If it is even possible that it exists only there, then it is not the most perfect entity conceivable because such an entity who existed both in your mind and extramentally would be even more perfect. Therefore, if it's possible even to conceive of a most perfect being, such a being necessarily exists.

This argument is a slippery one, and it immediately found detractors. A contemporary of Anselm's, Gaunilon, a monk by profession, made the following objections on behalf of the fool.

1. It is, in fact, impossible to conceive of "a being than which nothing greater can be conceived." The very project boggles the mind.
2. If Anselm's argument were valid, then it would follow that the mere ability to conceive of a perfect tropical island would logically entail the existence of such an island.

Anselm's response was as simple as Gaunilon's rebuttal:

1. If you understand the phrase "most perfect being," then you already have conceived of such a being.

Gaunilon's Objections

2. There is nothing in the *definition* of a tropical island that entails perfection, but the very definition of God entails that he be all-perfect, so it is impossible to conceive of God as lacking a perfection; and since it is obviously more perfect to be than not to be, the bare conception of God entails his existence.

This argument is both more difficult and more ingenious than it may appear to you. It is, in fact, a very good argument (which is not to say that it is flawless). Its genius is its demonstration that the sentence "God does not exist" is a self-contradictory sentence. That is why only a fool could utter it.

Take note of how very Platonic Anselm's argument is. First, it is purely **a priori**—that is, it makes no appeal whatsoever to sensorial observation; it appeals exclusively to pure reason. Second, it makes explicit the Platonic view that the "most perfect" equals "the most real." (Recall the Simile of the Line.)

The ontological proof has had a long and checkered history. We shall see it again more than once before this narration ends. Many philosophers think that Immanuel Kant finally put it to rest in the eighteenth century (by showing that the flaw in the argument was not one of logic but of *grammar*); but even today, 900 years after it was written, the argument has astute defenders.

Muslim and Jewish Philosophies

During the eleventh and twelfth centuries the growing influx into
Europe of Latin translations from Arabic and Hebrew manuscripts
had a dramatic effect on the directions that philosophy would take.
Many of these works entered the Christian monastic world by way
of Spain. From the ninth through the twelfth centuries the courts
of the Muslim caliphs of Spain were the most cultured in Europe.
The "Moors" (Arab, Berber, and other Muslim groups) had invaded
Christian Spain in the year 711 C.E. as part of the militant expansion
of Islam. Islam is the third of the three dominant Western religions,
all of which derive from roughly the same area of the Middle East. The
key figure in Islam is Muhammad, who was born at Mecca in today's
Saudi Arabia in 570 and died in Medina in 632 C.E. According to the
tradition, when he was forty years old he received a direct revelation from the angel Gabriel while meditating in a cave on a desert
mountain. Over the next twenty years Muhammad continued to
receive revelations that designated him as the latest in a long line of
prophets of God that were to be accepted by the new religion, including all the great prophets from the Jewish Bible, but also Jesus of
Nazareth. Muhammad copied the words that were revealed to him,
and they became the Qur'an (or Koran), the holy book of the Islamic
religion. The main idea in this religion is monotheism, just as it is
in Judaism and Christianity (though Jews and Muslims often see
the Christian **doctrine of the Trinity** as a backsliding into polytheism). Even more than Judaism or Christianity, Islam preaches the
power of God (Allah) over the world and in everyday life. The words
"Islam" and "Muslim" both derive from the Arabic word for "submis-
sion" or "surrender." Like the other two religions—but unlike the
tribal religions of Muhammad's native Arabia—Islam forbids the
use of idols. Like Judaism and Christianity it sees its patriarch in
the biblical figure of Abraham. Islam preaches the brotherhood of all
believers, and it requires charity to the poor. In addition, it stresses
prayer (five times daily), purification, and fasting during holy days

(Ramadan), and it enjoins the faithful to make a holy pilgrimage to Mecca at least once during one's lifetime.

Islam had tremendous appeal because of its theological simplicity, its ability to address the spiritual and material needs of great numbers of people who lived in chaotic times, its capacity to transcend tribal rivalries, and its offer of community and personal salvation. Its survival against

The Court of the Lions
The Alhambra—Granada

great odds and bloody oppression in its first years gave it a militant cast. Its leaders believed in the idea of holy war (*jihad*), and through conquests and conversion Islam spread rapidly in all directions. In the West, by the year 732—a little more than 100 years after Muhammad's first revelations—Muslim armies had penetrated deeply into France, where they were finally defeated at the Battle of Tours by Charles the Sledgehammer, Charlemagne's grandfather. The Arab-dominated Muslim army retreated behind the Pyrenees, where the Moors developed a splendid Islamic culture in Spain that contained beautiful cities, magnificent gardens with flowing water everywhere, great architectural monuments, and spacious centers of learning. There Muslim, Christian, and Jewish scholars worked side by side studying the manuscripts of the Greek philosophers, whose surviving copies were slowly being discovered and gathered in the great libraries of Seville, Granada, Cordoba, and Toledo. These libraries had no match in the Christian world. The products of the Muslim schools of translators slowly worked their way into Catholic-dominated Europe and caused a great stir, especially the translations of Aristotle and many commentaries on his works, most of which had been lost to the Christian world.

Averroës

One of the most influential of the Muslim philosophers in both the Islamic and Catholic worlds was Abul Walid Muhammad ibn Ahmad ibn Muhammad ibn Rushd, better known in the West as Averroës (1126–1198), who was born in Cordoba, Spain. His most impressive writings were his careful explications and analyses of Aristotle's philosophy. Aristotle's rediscovery had sent shock waves through the Muslim intellectual community. Averroës's commentaries were written in the context of a debate among Arab-speaking theologians as to whether the claims of Aristotle's philosophy were compatible with Muslim dogma. The Arab theologian al-Ghazali (1058–1111) had written against Aristotle, and the Persian Avicenna (980–1037) had defended the Greek philosopher. Averroës rejected the arguments of both al-Ghazali and Avicenna, claiming that they had both mis-read Aristotle. There still exists today a scholarly debate as to how Averroës himself should be read. According to one group of interpret-ers, Averroës wrote two types of commentary: one for more general consumption in which he asserted that all of Aristotle is compatible with Islam and that Aristotle's ideas can be used to explore and clarify Muslim belief, and another for a more sophisticated audience in which he defended Aristotle *against* Islam. According to a second group of scholars, Averroës's message is consistent throughout and is somewhere between the two extremes demarcated by the other two groups.[2] Averroës's commentaries came into the Christian world appearing to claim that there were two kinds of opposing truths, philosophical truth (i.e., Aristotelian) and religious truth, yet also claiming that the contexts of philosophical and theological dis-course were so distinct that both truths could be accepted at the same time. Averroës's writings had a dizzying effect on the philoso-phers of the monasteries and newly established universities of the

Catholic world. On the one hand, Averroës's work was indispensable for the understanding of Aristotle, but on the other, it was felt that his theory of the discrepancy between religion and philosophy would have to be refuted in the name of Christian dogma. Thomas Aquinas (whom we will study shortly) wrote a book called *On the Unity of the Intellect against the Averroists*, yet he so respected Averroës's explanations of Aristotle that he simply called him "the Commentator." Some Western theologians, led by Siger of Brabant (ca. 1240–ca. 1284), went against the grain (and got in trouble for it), defending what they took to be Averroës's **doctrine of double truth.** They were called the Latin Averroists.

Maimonides

What Averroës was to Muslim philosophy and Thomas Aquinas was to Catholic philosophy, Moses Maimonides (1135–1204) was to Jewish philosophy. Like his contemporary Averroës, Maimonides was born in Cordoba and also was most influential in the Catholic world for his insights into the philosophy of Aristotle. Thomas Aquinas revered Maimonides, and Thomas's demonstrations of God's existence were clearly influenced by those of Maimonides. In fact, Maimonides' first book, *A Treatise on Logic,* is a compendium of the categories of Aristotle's logic and an analysis of them. It was written in Arabic when Maimonides was sixteen years old.

Maimonides' most celebrated book is called *Guide of the Perplexed.* It purports to conduct educated but intellectually confused Jews through the labyrinth of philosophy and Judaic theology in their quest to resolve the conflicts between science and religion. The problem is, the *Guide* itself needs a guide, for it is a very difficult work, and it

Moses Maimonides

raises questions about its author's intentions similar to those raised about Averroës's. The most common way of understanding the book is to treat it as an attempt to reconcile Aristotelian philosophy with Jewish theology, showing that the Greek's theories provide tools for exploring and expanding on Judaism. Maimonides calls Aristotle "the chief of the philosophers" and calls Moses "the master of those who know."[3] But there have been very respectable scholars who see the book as subversive of religious values. Despite appearing to support religious values, the book in fact undermines them in a subtle and sophisticated way. For instance, Maimonides insists on what he claims to be the primary commandment of Judaism, to know God. Yet his theology is a *negative theology*, apparently showing that God cannot know us (an idea of Aristotle's, as you may recall) and that we can only know what God is not (a Neoplatonic idea that we have already seen in the work of John Scotus Eriugena). One Maimonidean scholar states the problem like this: Maimonides "records the duty to know God as the very first commandment.... Yet when we examine it in the total context and full development of his own analysis, we seemingly must conclude that this ideal is not only impossible, but empty of content and meaning."[4]

But if some scholars have seen Maimonides as a heretic destroying Jewish doctrine with Aristotelian logic, others have seen him as an anti-Aristotelian rabbi whose intention was to demonstrate the incoherence of so-called philosophical wisdom. Still others have seen him as holding a version of the doctrine of double truth attributed to Averroës, whose work he knew and admired. Whatever Maimonides' true intentions were, his astute clarification of Aristotelian categories and the use of Aristotelian arguments in his books left the impression in the world of Latin-speaking scholars that he was indeed a guide for those readers perplexed by Aristotle.

Despite the small minority of vociferous critics calling Maimonides a heretic, Jewish culture has for the greatest part been very proud of him from his day to ours. When Christian troops under Ferdinand and Isabella conquered the Moors in 1492 and expelled the Jews from Spain, there emerged this adage in Ladino, the Spanish spoken by the exiled Jews: "De Moisés a Moisés no ha habido nadie como Moisés" (From Moses to Moses there has been nobody like Moses).

The Problem of Faith and Reason

The problem being dealt with by Maimonides and Averroës, the problem of faith versus reason, was one that plagued the whole of medieval philosophy. In the Christian world it received its best medieval solution at the hands of Thomas Aquinas in the thirteenth century, as we shall soon see. The problem concerned the question of whether to emphasize the claims of divine revelation or the claims of philosophy in one's conception of reality, and among Christians there were extremists in both camps. We've seen that philosophers like John Scotus Eriugena had purely conceptual schemes in which there seemed to be no room for mere religious belief. Even St. Anselm's God seemed primarily philosophical and a far cry from the Stern Father and Vengeful Judge of the Old Testament. At the other end of the spectrum was the antiphilosopher Tertullian (169–220), whose famous cry was *"Credo quia absurdum"* ("I believe that which is absurd"), with the implication that he believed it *because* it was absurd.

Credo Quia Absurdum

The debate between these two groups reached a high pitch and produced a number of startling claims, such as the view that we have seen attributed to the Latin Averroists, who produced the doctrine of double truth. Recall that according to this doctrine there are two mutually contradictory truths, one produced by faith and one by reason, but both valid from their respective points of view. So, for example, from the anatomical perspective, the human being is a compilation of organs that, when they cease to function, bring about the termination of the person; but from the theological perspective, the human being is a soul that is, through God's grace, immortal.

This theory, though logically unsatisfactory, did for a short time play the historically positive role of allowing science to develop without having to conceive of itself in theological terms.

The Problem of the Universals

The other vexing problem of the day, the problem of the **universals,** was the question concerning the referents of words. Augustine had inaugurated a concern about language that dominated philosophical thought throughout the Middle Ages. Remember that according to Augustine, God sees his creation as an eternal present—that is, past, present, and future all rolled up into one. If language represents reality, and if humans experience reality so differently from God, then the true "word of God" can be nothing like the language of humans, who perceive the world in terms of a temporal sequence in finite space. Human language, then, must be a kind of degradation of Godly language. (Notice that this situation is probably another one in which medieval thought is haunted by Plato's Simile of the Line, in which each level of the hierarchy of being is a poor copy of the one above it.) Yet human language can aspire to the truth, being God-given, so theological concerns necessarily overlapped linguistic ones. The specific version of the problem that would obsess Christian, Jewish, and Muslim philosophers for several centuries had been introduced by Boethius, who had been deeply influenced by Augustine and who had translated from the Greek an essay about Aristotle by the Neoplatonic author Porphyry (232–304). The latter had queried the ontological status of genera and species. We know that there exist individual things that we call "whales"; but does the genus *Balaenoptera,* or the species *Balaenoptera physalis* (fin whale), or the species *Balaenoptera musculus* (blue whale) exist in nature, or are these only artificial categories existing merely in the mind? (The same problem appears in sentences like "This dog is brown." Do the words "dog" and "brown" name only the individual, or do they name the *classes* of canines and brown things, and are those classes real or artificial?)

The debate that ensued was, of course, similar to the debate between Plato and Aristotle over the status of the Forms, but the original works of the Greeks were lost to the philosophers of the early Middle Ages, and it took them 900 years to arrive at the point that Aristotle had gained in one generation. The issue reached such a state of confusion that John of Salisbury (ca. 1115–ca. 1180) claimed that in his day there were as many ideas on the subject as there were heads. The extremes in this debate were represented, on one side, by the strict **Platonic realists** (today

Whales exist only in the mind.

called "exaggerated realists"). They held that classes were not only real but *more* real than individuals. Anselm himself was a representative of this view. The other extreme, represented by Roscelin (ca. 1050–1120) and William of Ockham (ca. 1280–ca. 1349), was the doctrine known as **nominalism,** from the Latin word for "name" (*nom*). According to this view, which was eventually found unacceptable by the Church, only particulars are real, and words denoting classes are *merely* names.

According to the nominalists, the system of names creates differences and similarities that exist only in the mind of the speaker or in the system of language itself.

You and I may smile when we are told by anthropologists that an Amazonian tribe includes in the same class toads, palm leaves, and armpits (namely, the class of entities that are warm and dry on top and damp and dark underneath), but the nominalist asks us if this classification is any more arbitrary than our claim that whales and moles are members of the same class (namely, the class of entities with mammary glands).

Saint Thomas Aquinas

As I mentioned earlier, it is Thomas Aquinas (1225–1274) who is generally credited with working out the best medieval solution both to the problem of faith versus reason and to the problem of the universals.

Thomas was an Italian nobleman who ran away from his family's castle to join the Dominican order (where, by the way, he was so well fed that a niche eventually had to be carved out of the dinner table to accommodate his ample girth). Before I talk about his philosophy, let's look at the world he inhabited, thirteenth-century Europe.

More than 100 years had elapsed between Anselm's death and Thomas's birth. In that century, as we have seen, European scholars were becoming more and more acquainted with the "lost" works of the classical age, particularly the writings of Aristotle. Though the theories of Aristotle were found to be shocking by some, his philosophy

Prima mangiare, poi filosofare!

was actually more com-
patible with the new this-
worldly attitude of the
thirteenth century than was
the now somewhat stale
other-worldliness of Platonic
thought. The human race
had survived the millen-
nium. The year 1000 had
passed without the world
ending, as many people had
expected.

The old apocalyptic
prophecies faded further
into the future, and as
Europe emerged from the darkest moments of the Dark Ages, interest in the world of here and now was revived. Aristotle surfaced as
the champion of these new interests. It fell to Thomas Aquinas to
"Christianize" him—no easy task considering that Aristotle held
such un-Christian views as

  A. The earth is eternal. (There never was a creation.)
  B. God, the Prime Mover, knowing only his own perfection, is
      indifferent to human affairs. (He doesn't even know we exist.)
  C. The soul is not immortal.
  D. The goal of life is happiness.
  E. Pride is a virtue and humility a vice.

No surprise that Aristotle's works were banned by the University of Paris in 1210. (Indeed, Thomas's works themselves were condemned at Paris and at Oxford just after his death.)

Thomas Aquinas wrote more than forty volumes. His leading
works are two encyclopedic projects, the *Summa theologica* and the
Summa contra gentiles. These tremendously systematic works comprise a whole structure that has often been compared to the Gothic
cathedrals, which were the new architectural style of his day. Like

them, Thomas's work is not only
a mirror held up to late medieval
society but also a beacon unto it.

Thomas's main job was that
of reconciliation, not only the
reconciliation of Aristotle with
Christendom but also that of reason with faith and of the warring
sides in the debate over the status of universals. Concerning the
latter, Thomas was able to take
advantage of the Aristotelian
solution: Universals are neither

autonomous forms nor mere mental states. They are "embedded" in
particular objects as their "whatness." The human mind has the power
of *abstraction* based on its ability to recognize real similarities that
exist in nature. These abstractions become *concepts.* This solution
came to be known as **moderate realism.** It had been anticipated
120 years earlier by Peter Abelard (1079–1142), whose view is called
conceptualism. The only difference between the two views seems to
be one of emphasis. Both are grounded in Aristotle's insistence that
essences do not exist apart from individual substances, even though
as an intellectual act one can abstract the essence from the substances that exhibit essential similarities. For example, I can mentally
and linguistically isolate the "dogness" that all dogs have in common,
even though in fact that dogness exists only *in* real dogs. Abelard appears to concentrate more than Thomas does on the *conventionality*
of the concepts in the human mind and therefore holds that there is
a slight discrepancy between the concept in the mind and the essence
(i.e., the real similarity existing among all dogs) that that concept is
meant to represent. This view pushes Abelard a bit closer to nominalism than Thomas would be willing to go. The distinctions I am discussing here are subtle; nonetheless, precisely these kinds of fine points
caused passionate intellectual battles in the Middle Ages.

Concerning the problem of reason versus faith, Thomas began by distinguishing between *philosophy* and **theology.** The philosopher uses *human reason alone.* The theologian *accepts revelation as authority.*

Then Thomas distinguished between *revealed theology* (accepted purely on faith) and *natural theology* (susceptible of the proof of reason). That is, he showed where philosophy and theology overlap.

Thomas admitted that sometimes reason cannot establish the claims of faith, and he left those claims to the theologians (e.g., the claim that the universe has a beginning in time).

Most of Thomas's system is concerned with natural theology. Nevertheless, in order to establish that form of theology, he first developed a whole metaphysical system based on Aristotelian philosophy. Thomas agreed with Aristotle that there is nothing in the human mind that does not begin with observation and experience. Even though there are no innate ideas that explain how knowledge is possible (as in Plato's philosophy), according to Thomas, the soul does have the capacity for abstraction, contemplation, and reasoning. This ability allows humans to arrive at principles and causes that can explain the observable world even if those principles and causes are themselves unobservable. To arrive at these principles—which will also be the principles of his natural theology—Thomas first employed the Aristotelian conception of the world as a plurality of substances, which, you will recall, can be analyzed in terms of form and matter, or actuality and potentiality. Thomas stressed even more than did Aristotle the idea of actuality, which he called "act" (*actus* in Latin), and associated it strongly with the idea of "being" (*esse* in Latin). *Esse* is the *actus* whereby an essence or a form (*what a thing is*) has its being. "There is no essence without existence and no existence without essence."[5] In other words, chimeras and griffins do not have essences because they do not have being. They do

(After Sir John Tenniel)

not exist and never have existed. They are just fanciful constructions based on imaginative abstraction.

Aquinas placed this idea of "acts of being" in a context that is clearly more Platonic than Aristotelian, the context of a hierarchy of being. Reality is a system of "acts of being" in a hierarchical framework with God at the top and the lowliest "acts of being" taking place at the bottom. The word "being" (*esse*) here does not mean the same thing at each level of the hierarchy. The word has an **analogical** meaning rather than a single meaning. That is, *esse* at the bottom of the scale is *something* like *esse* at the top, but not identical to it. For example, according to Thomas, God is a *pure* act of being. He is, like Aristotle's Prime Mover, pure actuality with no potentiality to be anything other than what he is, whereas things farther down the ladder have less actuality (they are lesser "acts of being") and have more potentiality to be something other than what they are at the moment. A tree can become lumber for a house, or it can rot, dry up, and turn into powder. It follows from this line of thinking that some substances have no physical matter, because matter has the most potentiality for change, according to Aristotle and Thomas. This lack of physical matter is true for God *and* humans, according to Aquinas. Here is where Thomas and Aristotle part company, because Aristotle called the human soul "the form of the body," implying thereby that the soul, along with the body, is mortal. But Thomas said that the soul is the form of the *subject*, the human individual, and therefore the soul is possibly immortal. (Thomas could not logically *prove* that the soul is immortal, but as a theologian he accepted Christian revelation as establishing the truth of immortality.)

Thomas also believed that from this metaphysical scheme of reality as a hierarchy of substances one could deduce a priori that angels *must* exist to fill the gap between human souls—which are embodied—and God, who is pure, unembodied *esse*. Indeed, there have to be different levels of angels in the hierarchy, some more spiritual than others. The seraphim, for example, are higher than the cherubim. This deduction, for which Saint Thomas's followers gave him the title of the Angelic Doctor, shows not only how far the mind's capacity for abstraction can carry us beyond the confines of direct observation, but also provides

**The Cherubim and the Flaming Sword Block
the Garden of Eden (Genesis 3:24)**

a good example of a theological idea whose truth can be known both philosophically (natural theology) and by revelation (see Genesis 3:24 and Isaiah 6:2), according to Aquinas. Another, even more important, example of a truth that can be known both philosophically and through revelation is that of God's existence. In the *Summa theologica* Aquinas provided five philosophical arguments for God's existence. They are called **cosmological arguments,** as opposed to Anselm's ontological argument, because they all begin with observations derived from the natural world. (Remember, *kosmos* is the Greek word meaning "world.") Three of Thomas's "five ways" are very similar. I present here the second of the five as representative of Thomas's natural theology:

> In the world of sensible things we find there is an order of efficient causes. There is no case known (neither is it, indeed, possible) in which a thing is found to be the efficient cause of itself; for so it would be prior to itself, which is impossible. Now in efficient causes it is not possible to go on to infinity. . . . Now to take away the cause is to take away the effect. Therefore if there be no first cause among efficient causes, there will be no ultimate, nor any intermediate cause. . . . Therefore it is necessary to admit a first efficient cause, to which everyone gives the name of God.[6]

THE BUCK STOPS HERE

In the simplest reading of his demonstration, Thomas seems to be giving us a domino theory and merely saying that if there is a series of causes and effects, such a series must be caused by a being who is itself uncaused; otherwise we will have an infinite regress, which Thomas found intellectually repugnant. This version of the argument was submitted to careful scrutiny (e.g., by David Hume in the eighteenth century). Thomas's alleged knowledge of an order of causes was challenged, as was his claim that an infinite series of causes is impossible. However, Thomistic scholars have demonstrated that Thomas's second way is more complicated than it appears to be, because it involves a horizontal system of causes (in which an infinite series cannot be disproved) and a hierarchical system of dependencies (which, according to Thomas, cannot admit of an infinite regress).

Horizontal Structure

Whatever their validity, the five Thomistic proofs have some historically notable features. Unlike the ontological proof of Anselm, they all begin with an **a posteriori** claim, that is, with an appeal to observation. This is one of the Aristotelian characteristics of the argument, and in its commitment to the reality of the observable world, it contrasts greatly with the Platonism of Anselm's a priori proof. Still, there are vestiges of Platonism in the five ways, including their appeal to a *hierarchy* of causes.

Like Aristotle's philosophy, all of Thomas's thought is teleological, especially his ethics. Human activity is viewed as a means-end structure. We choose desired goals and then choose among acts that lead to those goals. The acts are relative to the ends, but the ends (health, beauty, duty) are themselves relative to some absolute ends that give meaning to the relative ends; otherwise, every series of actions would lead to an infinite regress.

If we want to make correct choices, we must know what the ultimate goal is. Aristotle said it was happiness. Thomas agreed but thought he now knew what the Greeks did not—that happiness itself must be eternal to be an absolute. To be an absolute goal is to be a goal in and of itself and not be merely a goal relative to some other goal (the way that taking aspirin is a goal relative to the goal of getting rid of a headache, which is a goal relative to the higher goal of maintaining health). The argument for God's existence looks backward to a first, aboriginal *efficient cause* (in the language of Aristotle, which Thomas expressly employs), and the argument for meaning looks forward to a *final cause*. The argument claims that if there is no final cause (that is, no ultimate goal) that bestows meaning on each of the actions leading to that goal, then no action has any real meaning and human life itself is meaningless—"a tale told by an idiot, full of sound and fury, signifying nothing," in the words of Shakespeare's Macbeth (act V, scene v). Our happiness, hence our correct choices and acts, depends on knowledge of God—not just on philosophical knowledge of God but on the expectation of that full and final knowledge, the **Beatific Vision.** This possibility, when achieved, fulfills the Eternal Law of God, which is the law that sustains the universe—a divine ordering that governs nature. Just as this divine law that directs natural substances is obviously consistent with the essences of those substances and is reflected in their behavior, so is it reflected in human nature. "Natural law" is the term chosen by

Thomas to designate the eternal law as it applies to humans. God also gave human beings freedom; therefore they are free to obey the natural law or not. (Notice that Aquinas's use of the phrase "natural law" is not related to modern science's application of it. In the scientific sense, humans are *not* free to disobey natural law.) Obedience to natural law is "a rational participation in the eternal law of God."[7] Thomas argued that individuals have a sufficient knowledge of their own human nature to understand generally what is morally correct and to be able to regulate their own actions in the light of that understanding. They know, for instance, that they should seek to preserve themselves and that suicide is therefore wrong. They know that they should, as a species, reproduce. (I say "as a species" because individuals, such as nuns, monks, and priests, may choose to guard their virginity without going against the natural law.) Humans also know that they should care for their fellow humans. But just in case self-knowledge is not strong enough in a weak-minded person to lead to these moral insights, revelation has also provided humans with the Ten Commandments. Thomas's moral philosophy, then, is yet another example of "natural theology," in which both philosophy and biblical revelation lead to the same conclusion.

Thomas himself seems to have experienced some kind of ecstatic realization two years before his death (a prefiguring of the Beatific Vision?), which caused him to cease writing. He said that in the face of that experience, all his words were like mere straw.

The work of Saint Thomas Aquinas represents the apogee of scholastic philosophy. But at the very moment when **scholasticism** was being articulated by Thomas Aquinas and by other thirteenth-century philosophers such as John Duns Scotus (1265–1308) as the most excellent statement of the high medieval mind, currents were already developing that would begin to undermine the scholastic synthesis, foreshadowing as they did the birth of a new, more secularly oriented world. These currents were the voices of individuals who, intentionally or unintentionally, separated the theological from the philosophical in ways that prepared the path for the "new science" of the Renaissance. Such was the thought of Roger Bacon (ca. 1212–ca. 1292), whose disdain for speculative metaphysics and whose curiosity about the natural world influenced other philosophers to move along the new path— philosophers such as John Buridan (ca. 1300–ca. 1358), Nicholas of Oresme (1320–1382), and Nicholas of Autrecourt (ca. 1300–?).

William of Ockham

The most influential of these antischolastic late medieval philosophers was William of Ockham (ca. 1280–ca. 1349), who has already been mentioned here for his nominalistic stance in the debate concerning the status of universals. William's name comes from his birthplace, the town of Ockham in Surrey, in the south of England. After entering the Franciscan order he studied theology at Oxford, where he proved himself to be a superb logician. His philosophy—if not his theology—is unabashedly empiricist. According to William, all knowledge other than revealed knowledge must be derived *directly* from sensorial observation of particular objects and events. Therefore, strictly speaking, there is no such thing as metaphysical knowledge (knowledge that goes beyond the physical). From the narrow epistemological foundation constructed by Ockham, Thomas Aquinas's metaphysical inferences are unwarranted. The search for knowledge must be governed by a methodological principle of simplicity according to which "plurality is not to be assumed without necessity." This principle, now known as Ockham's razor (or Occam's razor, after the Latinate spelling of William's name), would in later years come to be accepted as a guiding rule by all empiricists, and indeed, it seems to have become a component of the scientific method itself. Its modern form has usually been worded as "Do not multiply entities beyond necessity," meaning that whenever a phenomenon can be equally well explained by a theory containing fewer elements rather than many, the simpler theory is to be chosen over the more complicated one. (Contrast these two theories: Your watch is powered by an electronic battery;

Ockham Wielding Razor

or, your watch is powered by a workforce of invisible fairies.) William's principle of simplicity raised some ecclesiastical hackles. There were suspicions that his "razor" could be used to reduce the Holy Trinity to one, or even to shave God out of the picture. But William's goal was almost certainly not to attack religion. He was interested in ejecting universals and essences from metaphysical theories and, indeed, in shaving metaphysics itself from the realm of possible knowledge.

Ockham's razor also eliminates Aristotle's formal and final causes, concepts used extensively by the scholastic philosophers of the thirteenth century. In reducing causality to what Aristotle had called "efficient causes," William helped usher in the **mechanistic** conception of causality that would characterize modern science from the seventeenth through the nineteenth centuries. William's tight empiricist program also disallows the traditional proofs of God's existence, whether Anselmian or Thomist, depending as they do on the idea of a hierarchy of degrees of perfection or on the impossibility of an infinite series of efficient causes. According to Ockham, these ideas are illegitimate metaphysical notions that cannot be justified by empirical observation.

William's nominalism is such that only individual objects and events are real, and universality is a feature of language, not of the world. That is, we can talk about "vegetables," for example, as a universal concept, but the universality inheres pragmatically in the linguistic category we use rather than in some universality actually existing in the various organic entities we call vegetables. William assumed that it is possible to create universal categories in language because of actual similarities between real individual objects in the world—individual carrots are similar not only to one another, but also to beets and to spinach—so his nominalism is not as radical as some later philosophers would carry it when they argued that even the concept of "similarity" is arbitrary, a conventional invention imposed on objects that are basically different from one another.

The genuine similarities and dissimilarities that exist among real objects and events permit a science of natural things, according to Ockham, including the cataloging of causal laws, but causality cannot be an absolute. There can be no *necessary connections* found among objects and events in the world. The reason for our failure to find necessity in the world is not the fault of our sensory apparata (as it will be in the radical empiricism of David Hume in the eighteenth century), but because of theological considerations. If God is omnipotent but inscrutable, as William thought Christians must believe, then all events in the natural world must be radically **contingent,** because divine omnipotence has the capacity to interrupt any series of events whatsoever, even those that we humans think are the most necessary. Indeed, there is historical and revelatory proof that such interruptions do happen, according to William, namely, the miracles recounted in the Bible.

In dealing with William of Ockham, we must constantly remind ourselves that in his own mind his radical philosophy did not undermine theology; rather, it strengthened it by preventing metaphysical ideas from claiming to impose constraints on God's ability. God's infinite freedom, inscrutable grace, and perfect omniscience are not limited by any human principles except the law of noncontradiction, according to William. Indeed, these divine powers can even overturn the principles of empiricist philosophy, for God has the capacity to produce at will in the minds of his subjects appearances that are uncaused by any actual events in the world and yet that seem to be caused by such events. The proof of this claim is found in the visions that God allowed some of the biblical prophets to have of the future as if that future were contemporary with them.

St. John the Divine Sees the End of the World

Also, revealed theology presents some paradoxes that cannot be resolved logically or philosophically, such as the compatibility of divine foreknowledge and human freedom. William rejected as sophistic the solutions to this problem of predestination that were offered by Saint Augustine, but he was unable to suggest a solution of his own.

Not surprisingly, a number of religious figures of his day found William's views to be heretical. His degree of Master of Theology from Oxford was blocked by the chancellor of the university, who sent to the pope a complaint concerning the danger of allowing William's ideas to be circulated. Ockham was called to the papal palace in Avignon to be investigated. (This period in Catholic history—between 1309 and 1377—was later called by some theologians the "Babylonian captivity" of the papacy,[8] because the French cardinals had managed to outmaneuver the Italians and forced the papacy from the Vatican in Rome to Avignon in southern France.) William stayed in Avignon for four years without any judicial decision being reached.

At Avignon William got caught up in a controversy about the role of poverty among the clergy, because he supported the Franciscan doctrine of poverty against the stance of the pope. When he realized that the pope was about to issue a condemnation of his defense of apostolic poverty, William escaped to Bavaria and sought the protection of Emperor Ludwig, the antipapal regent there. Pope John XXII excommunicated William in absentia. William probably died in Bavaria in 1349 of the Black Plague, which was ravaging Europe at that time. The epidemic deprived Europe of many of its most creative minds and contributed to a deterioration of culture that lasted well into the next century.

Renaissance Philosophers

The historical period that marks the transition between the Middle Ages and the modern world took place approximately between 1450 and 1600. It is called the Renaissance, meaning the "rebirth," which refers not only to the recovery of classical Greek and Roman art, ideas, styles, and forms but also to a renewed enthusiasm for the more sensual aspects of life as the ancient Greeks and Romans were imagined to have lived it. The exploration and exploitation of the "New World" by navigators and conquistadores such as Christopher Columbus, Ferdinand Magellan, and Hernan Cortés, along with the opening of trade routes to Asia, produced new economics, new classes of wealth, and demands for education outside the Church-dominated cathedral universities and cloisters. The culture that emerged put down its first and deepest roots in Italy, where the arts and literature were liberated from what the late-fifteenth-century citizens felt were the artificial strictures of the medieval world. Innovative and highly talented artists flourished, including painters (for example, Fra Angelico, Raphael,

Michelangelo, and Leonardo da Vinci), sculptors (Donatello and Verroc-chio), and architects (Giotto and Brunelleschi). In politics, the erosion of papal power opened channels for ambitious monarchs (for example, Charles I of Spain, Francis I of France, and Henry IV of England) and for influential religious reformers (such as Martin Luther, John Calvin, John Knox, and Jonathan Wycliffe). The works of the artists and writers of the period, as well as translations of the Bible into local languages, were made available for mass consumption for the first time because of the invention of the printing press and of engraving procedures.

Closer to the specific interests of this book, attention should be directed toward the end of the Renaissance, when some of the fields that we now recognize as the modern sciences began to establish inde-pendence from their philosophical and theological moorings, and a gen-eration of scientific heroes emerged—men such as Nicolaus Copernicus (1473–1543), the Polish astronomer who articulated the modern ver-sion of the heliocentric (i.e., sun-centered) theory of the planets; Tycho Brahe (1546–1601) of Denmark, who gathered the astronomical data that would later be formulated into the laws of planetary motion by Johannes Kepler (1571–1630) of Germany; Galileo Galilei (1564–1642), the Italian physicist, mathematician, and astronomer who laid the foundations of contemporary science; and the English physician William Harvey (1578–1657), who discovered the circulation of blood.

Renaissance philosophers are in general not remembered today as well as the artists, scientists, politicians, and explorers who were their contemporaries. But there are in the Renaissance two related philosophical developments that should be reported: the emergence of humanism, and the battle between a newly articulated Neoplaton-ism and a revised Aristotelianism.

The word "humanist" was used in the Renaissance to desig-nate those scholars whose interests were the *studia humanitatis*, the humanities. These philosophers were keenly interested in human affairs: politics, institutions, art, and mores as well as human free-dom and dignity. In general, they were more concerned with moral philosophy than with metaphysics. They removed philosophy from the hands of ecclesiastical professionals and turned it into a fitting study for laypersons. To this end, they promoted translations of the Graeco-Roman masterpieces into modern European languages and experimented in writing their own works in those same vernacular languages—the language of the people. Although several important humanists were clergymen, they too participated in freeing philosophy from the institutional control of Christian authority. Their eventual power was such that even a number of popes were designated as humanists, most notably, Nicholas V (pope from 1447 to 1455).

The poet Petrarch (Francesco Petrarca, 1304–1374) is usually regarded as the founder of Italian humanism. Inspired as he was by the rhetorical skills and aesthetic qualities of the Roman poets and orators such as Cicero and Seneca, he objected not only to the content but also to the style of the works of the scholastic philosophers, which he found "barbaric, tediously pedantic, arid and incomprehensible." He had "nothing but contempt for what he regarded as their empty loquacity and their addiction to disputation for its own sake."[9] He attacked the scholastic addiction to Aristotle and touted Plato over Aristotle as the superior philosopher.

Important Renaissance humanists were Desiderius Erasmus (1466–1536) of Holland, whose *In Praise of Folly* cleverly satirized the overintellectualizing of the scholastics and called for a return to a simpler and happier Christianity; Thomas More (1478–1535) of England, whose *Utopia* combines Platonic, Epicurean, and Christian theories in a depiction of an ideal human life; the Italian Giovanni Pico della Mirandola (1463–1494), whose *Oration on the Dignity of Man* lauds human freedom and the human power of self-creation; and Michel de Montaigne (1533–1592) of France, whose influential *Essays* set forth in a witty manner his philosophy of skepticism. Even Niccolò Machiavelli (1469–1527) has been called a humanist, despite the fact that his book *The Prince* seems to be less "in praise of folly" than in praise of the manipulation of political power.

The big philosophical debate in the early Renaissance was over the question of which ancient *auctor* (author), Plato or Aristotle, was the truer *auctoritates* (authority). To the Renaissance philosophers, was it Plato or Aristotle who had more genuinely anticipated the truths of Christianity? Which of the two had offered a better framework for a philosophical defense of Christian dogma?

So we see that despite the Renaissance reaction against medieval scholasticism, there was nevertheless a strong Aristotelian tradition throughout the period, but it was Aristotle in a new style as humanists tried to claim him for their own. If the scholastics had produced a perversion of the true Aristotle, then he must now be reclaimed for the new age. The Italian universities taught philosophy as a preparation for medicine, and in these teachings Aristotle's natural philosophy played a very different role from the role it had played at Oxford and Paris in the Middle Ages. Still, numerous empirically oriented philosophers continued to argue that Aristotle's philosophy—especially in its new, humanized guise—was better than Platonism for defending Christian dogma. However, as one Renaissance scholar noted, "even the most advanced Aristotelians did not progress from empiricism to

experimentalism. They remained content to observe nature passively in order to confirm established doctrines rather than trying to devise methods of active intervention or validation."[10]

Renaissance Neoplatonism, especially that of the Florentine Academy, founded by Marsilio Ficino (1433–1499), was nevertheless not identical to its earlier incarnation. It was more humanized, yet it was also more entirely Christianized. The early Church fathers had speculated that Plato had learned of the Hebrew Bible during a visit to Egypt. This connection explained what the Platonized Christians took to be striking similarities between Plato's philosophy and Christianity, which to them was the fulfillment of biblical prophecy. Ficino translated all thirty-six of Plato's dialogues, plus the *Enneads* of Plotinus, into Latin. Furthermore, he translated a manuscript attributed to Hermes Trismegistus, an Egyptian priest, that purported to show how Mosaic wisdom had been transmitted to Plato. This document was later discovered to be a forgery from the early Christian period, but in the Renaissance it added considerable stature to Plato's religious credentials.

The Neoplatonic Christians of the early medieval period had found it advantageous to interpret passages of the Bible not only literally but also allegorically and esoterically (finding layers of hidden meaning). The Platonism espoused in the Renaissance by Ficino and his teacher, Cardinal Bessarion (ca. 1403–1472), and by Nicholas of Cusa (1401–1464) in Germany applied the same technique to the writings of Plato himself. This interpretation allowed them not only to find in Plato's writings cryptic allusions to biblical truth but also to explain away certain awkward features of Plato's philosophy, such as his apparent approval of homosexuality, his communism, and his doctrine of **metempsychosis** (according to which the soul exists in a heaven of souls before the body is born and enters the body at birth). Despite the mystical tendencies in Neoplatonism, in its Renaissance version it avoided Plato's apparent other-worldliness by seeing each individual object in the visible world as a microcosmic replica of the whole of reality. So, rather than viewing the physical world as disgusting, ugly, and sinful, humans could appreciate and even spiritualize the beauties of the material realm. The influence of humanism on Neoplatonism even permitted the glorification of pleasure and sensuality. This feature of Neoplatonism is perhaps best manifested in Renaissance art and allows that art to be paradoxically Platonic, despite Plato's own suspicions about art and particularly about art's sensuous aspects.

Giordano Bruno (b. 1548)—whom we could call the last man of the Renaissance—was burned at the stake by the Inquisition on February 17, 1600, for refusing to treat philosophical issues from the perspective that the religious authorities had deemed orthodox. At his trial he said that he pursued his ideas "according to the light of nature, without regard to any principles prescribed by faith."[11] Among his crimes was his espousal of the Copernican heliocentric theory of planetary motion.

Key Philosophical Ideas in Chapter 4

- Overview: The one thousand years of the <u>medieval philosophy dominated by religious concerns</u>.

St. Augustine of Hippo:

- Christianity still hammering out an official orthodoxy; <u>Augustine combats</u> a number of <u>heresies</u>: Manicheanism, Donatism, Priscillianism, Arianism, and Pelagianism.
- Augustine's attempt to <u>solve philosophical problems in Christian theology</u>.
- <u>The problem of predestination</u>: Does God's omniscience entail predestination? If an individual's future is predetermined, how can the individual be blamed for his sin?
- <u>Solutions</u>:
  - <u>God is not in time</u>, therefore to say that God knows the future is inaccurate.
  - <u>God's knowledge does not cause sin</u>.
  - God only punishes sins of free will: <u>if a person can sin, wants to sin, and does sin, that sin is a free act</u>.

The Encyclopediasts:

- Groups of philosophically oriented scribes who <u>preserved ancient Greek and Roman texts</u> from the outrages of barbarian invasions

John Scotus Eriugena:

- First metaphysical system builder in four centuries
- <u>On the Divisions of Nature</u>, <u>Christian metaphysics</u> deeply <u>influenced by Neo-Platonism</u>
- The Divisions of Nature:
  - <u>First</u> method of <u>division</u>: "<u>Things that are</u>" (Platonic Forms) and "<u>Things that are not</u>" (everything else, including God!)
  - The "<u>Via affirmativa</u>" and the "<u>Via negativa</u>," the dialectic between literal and metaphorical meaning, determining how we can talk about God
  - <u>Second</u> method of <u>division</u>: <u>(1) God</u>, <u>(2) the Platonic Forms</u>, <u>(3) the</u> physical <u>World</u>, and <u>(4) (again) God</u>
  - <u>God as Beginning and End</u>, Creator and Goal <u>of creation</u>

St. Anselm of Canterbury:

- The <u>ontological argument</u> for God's existence.
- If the fool who says in his heart "there is no God" can conceive of God, then God must exist.
  1. "Existence is a perfection."
  2. If God lacks existence he is imperfect.
  3. But, by definition, God is all-perfect.
  4. Therefore, God exists (by definition).
- The <u>Platonic features</u> of the <u>ontological proof</u>:
  - The <u>argument is</u> purely <u>a priori</u> (based purely on logic, not on observation).
  - Makes the assumption that "<u>most perfect</u>" equals "<u>most real</u>" (<u>as in the Simile of the Line</u>).

Muslim and Jewish Philosophies:

- The Muslim occupation of Spain, 711–1492
- Great libraries and learning centers attracting Muslim, Jewish, and Christian scholars, restoring to Europe copies of Greek and Roman philosophical, medical, and scientific manuscripts destroyed by the Dark Ages in Europe

Averroës

- Most influential of Muslim philosophers: commentator on the meaning of the newly recovered books of Aristotle.
- Source of the "doctrine of double truth": Religious truth does not have to agree with scientific truth.

Maimonides

- Most influential of Jewish philosophers: also an important commentator on Aristotle.
  - Tries to demonstrate compatibility between Aristotelian philosophy and Judaic theology—The Guide of the Perplexed.
  - With Christian philosophers, the Muslim and Jewish philosophers enter the debate over faith vs. reason, with extremes such as St. Anselm (no faith required, only reason), St. Thomas (reason usually supports faith), and Tertullian (no reason needed, only faith).

The Problem of the Universals:

- Impelled by religious concerns, the medieval world was fascinated by the question of language: What are the referents of words? In the sentence, "This dog is brown," or "A whale is beached," do the words refer to (A) individual things, (B) universal things, or (C) nothing?
- Plato would choose (A): Words denote universal forms—which are the most real things.
- Common sense would choose (B): Words denote individual objects— which are the most real things.
- The sophists would choose (C): Words are just noises that motivate us.

Medieval solutions:

- Exaggerated realism: an extreme version of (A) (e.g., Anselm)
- Moderate realism: Essences (universals) exist in things, and not beyond them, and can be abstracted from things by the mind. Language does a fine job of performing this abstraction (e.g., Thomas Aquinas).
- Conceptualism: same as moderate realism, but language does only an OK job of performing this abstraction (e.g., Abelard).
- Historically, Thomas's moderate realism was the most influential.

St. Thomas Aquinas:

- Averroës reconciled the bold "new" philosophy of Aristotle with Islamic theology; Maimonedes reconciled it with Judaic theology; Thomas will reconcile it with Christian theology.

- Thomas is interested in "natural theology," where philosophy and theology overlap.

- Thomas borrows from Aristotle the doctrine of "substances" as beings with actuality and potentiality.

- Thomas borrows from Plato the hierarchy of being, and places each "act of being" higher on the hierarchy (God, angels, humans) or lower (dogs, trees, insects).

- The higher up the ladder, the more "being" (esse) a thing has: the more being it has, the more spirit.

- Thomas traces observable causes and effects to a "first cause"—God.

- If there were no first causes, there would be no effects at all.

- Therefore, God's existence can be logically deduced from observable causes and effects.

- Thomas's ethics:
  - Thomas borrows from Aristotle's teleological theory of action as a system of means and ends (the meaning of an act is its goal).
  - If there is no ultimate goal (eternal happiness), then no act has meaning.

The Last Stage of Medieval Philosophy ("Anti-Scholasticism")

- Post-systematic philosophy; revolts against Thomism and other metaphysical schemes

William of Ockham:

- Nominalism, empiricism, Ockham's razor, skepticism.

- Nominalism: Universals are only abstractions; only universals are real; words name individuals, not "essences."

- Empiricism: all knowledge (except revealed knowledge—biblical, angelic, or Godly) derived solely from the senses.

- "Ockham's razor": an appeal to simplicity in explanation (the simplest theory that accounts for all features of the phenomenon is the correct explanation of the phenomenon).
- Skepticism: We have mostly faith, not knowledge.

Renaissance Philosophy:

- Humanism: relaxing the grip of clerical authority, studying the human world, emphasizing human dignity and freedom.
- The renewal of the debate over whether Plato or Aristotle should dominate philosophical studies, but with a new, humanized Aristotle and a new, more sensual neo-Platonism.
- Neo-Platonism was thoroughly Christianized, but now the Platonism was more worldly, sensuous, and humanized, and the Christianity more allegorical and symbolic.

Topics for Consideration

1. According to the information in this chapter, what is the relationship among the three major religions in the West: Judaism, Christianity, and Islam?

2. Write a short essay setting forth your own views about what is called in this chapter the problem of God's foreknowledge. If you agree with Augustine's solution, defend it. If you disagree with Augustine, criticize his solution.

3. Explain how the Christian philosopher John Scotus Eriugena could assert that God belongs in the category of "things that do not exist."

4. Explain why the opposite of a self-contradictory statement (i.e., the negation of such a statement) is necessarily true. Then explain why Saint Anselm asserted that the statement "God does not exist" is self-contradictory.

5. Describe the similarities that you find among the philosophies of Averroës, Maimonides, and Thomas Aquinas.

6. Explain what the problem of the universals is. Detail your explanation by analyzing the concept "dog" from the perspective of (a) the exaggerated realists, (b) the moderate realists, and (c) the nominalists. (Begin by looking up the words "dog" and "canine" in the dictionary.)

7. Compare and contrast Saint Anselm's ontological argument with Saint Thomas's cosmological argument.

8. Explain the ways in which the philosophy of William of Ockham, if true, would undermine the philosophy of Thomas Aquinas.

9. In your library find a book with reproductions of paintings from Renaissance Italy. Select a few and analyze each of them first from the point of view of Plato himself (see Chapter 2), then from the perspective of the Neoplatonic Renaissance philosophers.

Notes

1. Anselm of Canterbury, *Proslogium*, in *The Age of Belief*, ed. Anne Fremantle (New York: New American Library, 1954), 88–89.

2. This debate is discussed by Oliver Leaman, *Averroës and His Philosophy* (Richmond, England: Curzon Press, 1998). Leaman espouses the second of the two views.

3. Moses Maimonides, *The Guide of the Perplexed*, trans. Shlomo Pines (Chicago: University of Chicago Press, 1966), 29, 123.

4. Marvin Fox, *Interpreting Maimonides: Studies in Methodology, Metaphysics, and Moral Philosophy* (Chicago and London: University of Chicago Press, 1990), 21.

5. Frederick Copleston paraphrasing St. Thomas, in *A History of Philosophy*, vol. 2, *Medieval Philosophy*, part 2 (Garden City, N.Y.: Image Books/Doubleday and Co., 1962), 53.

6. Thomas Aquinas, *Summa theologica*, in *The Age of Belief*, 153.

7. Vernon J. Bourke paraphrasing Saint Thomas, in *The Encyclopedia of Philosophy*, vol. 8, ed. Paul Edwards (New York and London: Macmillan, 1972), 112.

8. The term "Babylonian captivity" refers by analogy to the enslavement of the Jews by the Babylonians between 579 and 338 B.C.E. Parts of the story of the complications of the Avignon papacy are nicely dramatized in Umberto Eco's best-selling novel *The Name of the Rose*, whose main character, William of Baskerville, is an amalgamation of William of Ockham and Sherlock Holmes.

9. Jill Fraye, "The Philosophy of the Italian Renaissance," in *The Routledge History of Philosophy*, vol. 4, *The Renaissance and Seventeenth-Century Rationalism*, ed. G. H. R. Parkinson (London and New York: Routledge, 1993), 17.

10. Ibid., 42.

11. Quoted by Fraye, 49.

5

Continental Rationalism and British Empiricism
The Seventeenth and Eighteenth Centuries

Descartes

René Descartes

Though there were a number of lesser philosophers during the Renaissance, the first truly magnificent philosophical system of the modern period was that of the Frenchman René Descartes (1596–1650). Descartes may not have been very good looking, but he was *smart!*

Descartes first carved a niche for himself in the pantheon of intellectual giants by discovering analytical geometry, thereby fulfilling the old Pythagorean dream of demonstrating the relation between plane geometry and pure algebra.

Having made his contribution to math, in 1633 Descartes was about to publish his manuscript on physics, but when news reached him that Galileo Galilei had been arrested by the Inquisition for teaching views about the physical world that were very close to Descartes's own views, Descartes ran, did not walk, to his publisher to withdraw his manuscript.

Galileo's crime had been to peer through his newly invented telescope and discover that the planet Jupiter had four moons.

Why should anybody care? Least of all, why should the Brothers of the Inquisition care?

Because the Renaissance mind had inherited from the medieval world the view that the Garden of Eden was the belly button of the universe and that God had created the rest of the cosmos in concentric layers around the stage of the human drama.

Of course, there had been rumors floating around that the sun and not the earth was the center of the planetary system, but the scientific evidence against that view was the undisputed fact that the moon orbits the earth. If the sun is the center of everything, then why doesn't the moon orbit the sun instead of the earth?

So, if Galileo proved that Jupiter has four moons that orbit it, then he had pulled the last strut out from under the geocentric theory of the universe. As Freud was to say later, this discovery was the first of the three major blows against humans' conception of their own self-importance. (The other two were Darwin's revelation that we are only animals and Freud's discovery that we are sick animals.)

It was too much for the Brothers of the Inquisition, so Galileo was arrested and sentenced to life imprisonment. He was confined to his home, which he was not allowed to leave and where he died five years later, in 1642, but not before managing to smuggle out a new defense of the heliocentric theory that was published in Holland.

Descartes was a practicing Catholic, but he believed that religion as it was conceived and followed by some of his fellow Catholics—including some powerful ones—was riddled with contradiction and superstition. He disapproved of what he saw as the Church's reactionary stance in its confrontation with the newly emerging sciences, including Galileo's astronomical writings, and he thought that a correct picture of humans would include both spiritual values and the capacity for rigorous scientific investigation. He correctly saw that if religion tried to stem the tide of science, religion would be swept away. But Descartes did not want to have to go to jail to prove it.

So he decided to ease his ideas about physics onto an unsuspecting

Stemming the Tide

I don't think I can take any more revelations, Doc.

religious establishment by smuggling them into a book of philosophy called *Meditations,* which, in a groveling and self-effacing manner, he dedicated to "the Most Wise and Illustrious Doctors of the Sacred Faculty of Theology in Paris."

Meanwhile, to his friend he wrote, "the six Meditations contain all the fundamental ideas of my physics. But please keep this quiet."[1] Descartes hoped that the theologians would be convinced by his arguments before they realized that their own views had been refuted.

To discover a firm foundation of absolute certainty upon which to build his new objective system of knowledge, Descartes chooses a method of "radical doubt," whose motto is *De omnibus dubitandum*—everything is to be doubted. Descartes will doubt away anything that can possibly be doubted, no matter how weak the grounds are for doubting, until he can discover a proposition that is logically indubitable. This proposition, if it exists, will be the absolutely certain foundation of all knowledge.

He writes:

I must once for all seriously undertake to rid myself of all the opinions which I had formerly accepted, and commence to build anew from the foundation if I wanted to establish any firm and permanent structure in the sciences.[2]

This radical project requires him to tear down the old "house of knowledge," riddled as it was with rotten beams and unsupportable planks, and rebuild it from the ground up. Descartes realizes that such a project could take forever if, one by one, he challenges each of what seems like an infinite number of beliefs in the attempt to "rid himself of all his former opinions," so, like a termite inspector operating on the assumption that if a main bottom support beam is rotten, the whole building is in danger, Descartes immediately scrutinizes a structure that supports most of what passes for knowledge, namely, information about the outside world supplied by the five senses. He writes: "All that up to the present time I have accepted as most true and certain I have learned either from the senses or through the senses" (166). Amazingly, his method of radical doubt eliminates the primary source of information in one fell swoop. He announces that the senses are known deceivers, and it is not prudent ever to trust a known liar.

Descartes's point is clear. We all know about optical illusions (the "bent oar" in the pond, the "water" on the road, the tracks that "meet at the horizon") as well as illusions associated with the other senses. So, suddenly, radical doubt has deprived Descartes of all sensory information.

But Descartes immediately feels he has gone too far. He writes:

And how could I deny that these hands and this body are mine, were it not perhaps that I compare myself to certain persons, devoid of sense, whose cerebella are so troubled and clouded by the violent vapours of black bile, that they constantly assure us that they think they are kings when they are really quite poor, . . . or who imagine that they have an earthenware head or are nothing but pumpkins, or are made of glass. But they are mad, and I should not be any the less insane were I to follow examples so extravagant. (166)

If you can cut through the wonderfully Baroque language here, you'll see that Descartes is saying that anyone who can stare at his hands and *wonder* if they are his hands is not a philosopher, but a lunatic. Radical doubt, in telling us that we should never trust the senses, has suddenly become a form of insanity.

Descartes realizes that perhaps the only way to keep his method from leading us away from the "house of knowledge" and into a madhouse is to acknowledge that simple commonsense judgments such as "This is my hand" are the legitimate foundations of knowledge. But remember, the philosophical game Descartes is playing ("radical" or "methodological" doubt) requires that the *slightest* ground for doubt be accepted as canceling out any claim of certainty. Therefore, Descartes proceeds to scrutinize his thoughts about his hand as he stares at it, trying to see if he can detect a weakness in these thoughts; he discovers a major debility that has since come to be called "the problem of dreams." Descartes writes:

> I am in the habit of sleeping, and in my dreams representing to myself the same things or sometimes even less probable things, than do those who are insane in their waking moments. How often has it happened to me that in the night I dreamt that I found myself in this particular place, that I was dressed and seated near the fire, whilst in reality I was lying undressed in bed! (166–67)

He comes to what he calls an "astonishing" realization: that there is no test to prove with absolute certainty that at any given moment one is not dreaming. (Any test you can *think*, you can *dream*, so it's no test at all.)

Therefore, consistent with radical doubt, Descartes assumes that it is always possible that he *is* dreaming. This assumption totally undermines the possibility that the senses can provide us with certain knowledge. (Imagine someone saying, "This is a table" but then having to qualify her assertion by adding, "However, I may be dreaming, so maybe there is no table here.")

What about mathematics? Perhaps it can be a candidate for absolute certainty. Descartes says, "For whether I am awake or asleep, two and three together always form five, and the square can never have more than four sides, and it does not seem possible that truths so clear and apparent can be suspected of any falsity or uncertainty" (168). But radical doubt requires Descartes to suspect even the simplest propositions of arithmetic if there is *any* reason for doing so. Well, what if the Creator of the universe was not the benevolent God of Catholicism about whom Descartes had learned in his childhood, but an Evil Genius, a malevolent demon whose sole purpose was that of deception, so that even the simplest mathematical judgment would always be false? (Again, imagine a math teacher saying to her class, "two plus three equals five . . . unless there is an Evil Genius, in which case maybe two plus three is not five.") Could Descartes know for sure that such a demon did not exist?

No, he could not! It is logically possible that Descartes's mind is being controlled externally by a malevolent force. So, following the rules of radical doubt, Descartes assumes that all the world is nothing but the diabolical fiction of the Evil Genius.

Well, then, is there any thought that would be certain to Descartes even if his senses are deceiving him, even if he is dreaming, even if an all-powerful demon is exercising its full might to deceive him? Is there any truth that is correct and certain, even to a lunatic? Yes, there is one, and only one, such truth: "I think, therefore I am."[3] Even if his senses deceive him, even if he is dreaming, even if he is mad, even if an evil genie is set on deluding him, this proposition is true for as long as he asserts it or holds it in consciousness. It and it alone cannot be doubted under any circumstances.

Having discovered certainty in selfhood and having established that his self is identical to his consciousness (for it is possible to doubt that you have a body, but it is impossible to doubt that you have a mind; therefore, your self and your mind must be the same), Descartes now has a foundation upon which to build his new "house of knowledge": the certainty of selfhood, or of consciousness, or as he calls it in his more religious moments, of the soul. But what can he build upon that foundation? Descartes now must find a way of escaping **solipsism,** that is, of escaping the confines of his own **subjectivity** and establishing the existence of an external world. To do so, he looks inward and carefully examines the contents of his own mind—because, at this point,

Solipsism

working under the strictures of the rules of radical doubt ("anything that *can* be doubted *must* be doubted"), the contents of his mind are all that Descartes has to work with. In addition to the absolutely certain knowledge of selfhood, Descartes also finds what philosophers today call **sense data,** the immediate sensations of perception: colors, sounds, odors, tastes, and tactile textures (hard, soft, cold, hot, etc.). These sense data too are *certain* as long as we merely describe them and do not make causal inferences to the external world. "I am experiencing red, white, and blue now" is certain, but "There is a French (or American, or British, or Dutch) flag out there" is not certain. (I may be dreaming; an Evil Genius may be deceiving me.) At least the existence of mental sense data and the possibility that they are caused by a physical world outside my consciousness gives Descartes hope of making progress. But Descartes's survey of the contents of consciousness provides him with a much firmer bridge to external reality, even if that bridge's connection to the outside physical world is rather indirect. Descartes discovers that besides sense data, the mind also contains four **innate ideas** (shades of Plato) that are not derived from sense data. In fact, the very idea of selfhood is such an idea, according to Descartes. The other innate ideas are the idea of *identity,* that is, the idea of "sameness"; the idea of *substance,* that is, the idea of "thingness"; and the idea of an all-perfect being (that is, God). Descartes demonstrates that the idea of substance (thingness) and the idea of identity (sameness) are innate by grasping a piece of wax in his hand, describing all of the sense data he associates with the wax (sweet taste, odor of flowers, yellow, hard, cold, tube-shaped, emits a hollow sound when tapped), then holds the wax to the fire and every sense datum changes (taste and odor change, it is white, soft, hot, and soundless). Yet, despite all the changes it has undergone, he knows that it is the *thing* (substance) we call wax, and it is the *same* (identity) wax as before. This knowledge is not derived from the external world, which can provide only sense data; rather, it is what Descartes calls "an intuition (*inspectio*) of the mind," his language designating an innate idea.

Now, the idea of selfhood is not only innate but veridical—as you saw, it *can't* be wrong. The problem is that the ideas of identity and substance are not proved true just because they are innate. The Evil Demon could have placed them in our minds in order to deceive us, in which case the "knowledge" of which I spoke above might be false knowledge. What about the idea of God? How does Descartes

"SELF"
"IDENTITY"
"SUBSTANCE"
"GOD"

know that his apparently innate idea of God was not placed in his mind by the Evil Genius? Descartes has to *prove* God's existence and has to do so using only those data that he can deduce logically from the one certainty afforded him—the immediate states of his own consciousness. (Critics point out that Descartes overlooks the fact that the process of logical deduction is exactly the kind of reasoning that the Demon could distort. If it can distort math, it can distort logic. They are roughly the same thing.) Nevertheless, Descartes does prove—to his own satisfaction, at least—God's existence. He offers two arguments to achieve this result. Here's the first:

> [E]xistence can no more be separated from the essence of God than can having its three angles equal to two right angles be separated from the essence of a [rectilinear] triangle, or the idea of a mountain from the idea of a valley; and so there is not any less repugnance to our conceiving a God (that is, a Being supremely perfect) to whom existence is lacking (that is to say, to whom a certain perfection is lacking), than to conceive of a mountain which has no valley. (204)

This argument is clearly a version of the ontological argument of Saint Anselm, whom Descartes fails to acknowledge as the author of this demonstration. (To be fair to Descartes, we could say that it is precisely Descartes's appeal to reason rather than to authority that makes him a modern thinker.)

Here's a paraphrase of the second argument in four steps. (Such a condensation of his proof may be unfair to Descartes. The argument may be more convincing in all its detail. But Descartes takes four pages to develop it! Philosophy is long; life is short.)

(A) The fact that I doubt proves that I am an imperfect being. (A perfect being would know everything, hence would have no doubts.)

(B) I can only know that I am imperfect if I already understand the idea of perfection.

(C) My idea of perfection could only be caused in me by something perfect. (Nothing can be more perfect than its cause, and nothing in my actual experience is perfect enough to cause the idea of perfection in my mind.)

(D) Therefore, a perfect being (God) exists.

Notice that *doubting* is a form of *thinking*—indeed, it has so far been Descartes's main form of thinking, given his method. Therefore the two main **Cartesian** philosophical arguments so far could be stated as

1. I doubt, therefore I exist.

       and

2. I doubt, therefore God exists.

Also notice that both proofs presuppose the Platonic hierarchy of being, in which "most real" equals "most perfect," and vice versa.

If valid, Descartes's proof of God's existence disposes of the Evil Genius. (If a secret universal deceiver exists and causes me to err, and if God has given me no way to know of its existence, then my error must be blamed on God. But a perfect Being is by definition faultless. Therefore, if God exists, the Evil Demon does not exist.)

Descartes's discovery of the logical impossibility of an Evil Genius restores mathematics to his system (the only objection to math had been the Evil Genius hypothesis). Descartes applied math not to the world as known by the senses (the senses are never

**The End of the Evil Demon
(Or Is It?)**

fully rehabilitated in Descartes's system) but to his innate concept
of corporeal substance, introducing him to a world not of colors,
sounds, tastes, smells, and heat and cold—for Descartes, these
qualities exist only in the mind, *caused by material substance*—but
of objects of size, shape, location, and three-dimensionality moving
through space at different velocities. *These* ideas can be treated
mathematically, and mathematical laws describing their nature and
behavior can be discovered, in fact—*quelle surprise!*—are exactly
the kind of mathematical laws developed by Galileo and soon to be
developed by Johannes Kepler, Isaac Newton, and a host of others.
The *real* world is not the world as known by the senses but the world
as known by mathematical physics. Yet, in Descartes's system, none
of these conclusions would be possible if Descartes did not base science on the certainty of self (self equals soul) and God's existence.

Ce ne sono quattro!

Without God there is only confusion and solipsism; with God, science can happen. Descartes has pulled it off. He has shown that you can have both God and Galileo!

However, Descartes does leave himself with a few problems. First, he has replaced the commonsense view of the relation between self and world (what philosophers call **"naive realism"**), but he replaces it with a most circuitous route, indeed. Second, he assigns all perceivable qualities ("red," "blue," "sweet," "warm," "melodious") to

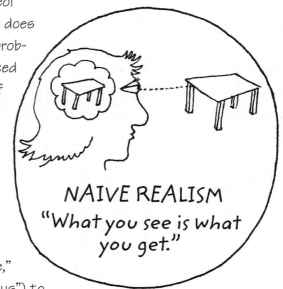

NAIVE REALISM
"What you see is what you get."

the mind and leaves only mathematically measurable quantities in the external world—a cold, colorless, odorless, soundless, tasteless world of matter in motion.

Furthermore, Descartes's picture of the world is hopelessly divided into substances that are defined in ways that mutually exclude each other. How could the

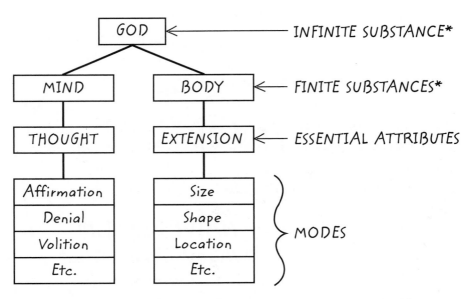

CARTESIAN REALISM
"What you see is _not_ what you get."

GOD ←————————— INFINITE SUBSTANCE*

MIND · BODY ←—— FINITE SUBSTANCES*

THOUGHT · EXTENSION ←—— ESSENTIAL ATTRIBUTES

Affirmation	Size
Denial	Shape
Volition	Location
Etc.	Etc.

} MODES

* Substance is defined as "that which can exist by itself, without the aid of any other substance."[4]

mental world (a nonspatial, purely spiritual sphere) have any effect on the physical world of crass matter, and vice versa, in this radically dualistic scheme of things? Descartes tries to solve the problem by claiming that *mind* meets *body* at the center of the brain, in the pineal gland.

It should be obvious that this solution does not work. No matter *where* mind meets body, at that place it *becomes* body, because it then has *location,* which is a mode of physical substance. At this point, Descartes conveniently dies of the common cold while visiting his benefactress, Queen Christina of Sweden, in order to explain to her the function of the pineal gland. So, he left to his followers the legacy of his radical dualism.

Having mentioned Queen Christina of Sweden (1628–1689), I will remind you of what must be obvious: few women appear in the ranks of the philosophers in the period covered by this chapter. Indeed, until the twentieth century, women were given very little voice in the intellectual world. Yet, they often made their influence felt—especially in cases when they were rich enough, independent enough, or aristocratic enough to ignore the social prejudice against intellectual women. Queen Christina probably taught Descartes very little; she had an immense curiosity but no real formal education. But the same cannot be said of Princess Elizabeth of Bohemia (1618–1680), who sought political asylum in Holland while Descartes was living there

and read the *Meditations* with great care. She established a correspondence with Descartes and sent astute questions to him about
all aspects of his philosophy. His answers to her show that she had
made him aware of weaknesses in parts of his argument. She posed
what some critics still think is the most crucial question: if we cannot
account for the mind's effect on the body in the analogy of one body's
causal effect on another body, what analogy can we use to explain it?

Descartes had intellectual exchanges with another woman,
Anna Maria van Schurman (1607–1678), though in the end, he
claimed to disdain her mental abilities. (According to his most
recent biographer, Descartes's attitude was probably provoked
by the fact that she sided with one of his adversaries, Gisbertus
Voetius, in a theological debate.) Van Schurman "attended theology lectures given by Voetius at the university, while hiding behind
a curtain, since women were not allowed to register officially for
university studies."[5]

Despite having to hide behind a curtain to attend university courses—or perhaps *because* of it—van Schurman wrote a

Anna Maria Attends Classes at the University of Utrecht

sophisticated tract on the need for women's education called *Dissertation on the Aptitude of Women's Intelligence for Learning and Advanced Studies* (Clarke, 251) and published it in 1641, the same year as the publication of Descartes's *Meditations*.

Other women in this same time frame whom today we would call philosophers—even if their contemporaries did not—include Émilie du Châtelet (died 1689) and, in the next century, Mary Wollstonecraft (1759–1797), who was married to the philosopher William Godwin and was mother of Mary Shelley, who wrote *Frankenstein*.

Spinoza

Back on the Continent, the Dutch-born Jewish philosopher Baruch Spinoza (1634–1677) was trying to resolve the dilemmas of Descartes's legacy while remaining within the rationalistic tradition that Descartes exemplified. (Rationalists believe that the true source of knowledge is reason, not the senses, and that the correct philosophical model must be an a priori one, not one based on empirical generalizations.) Spinoza was, according to Bertrand Russell, "the noblest and most lovable of the great philosophers,"[6] because Spinoza, more than any other philosopher, *lived* his philosophy, even though he realized that doing so would result in his alienation from both the Jewish and the Christian communities. Spinoza accepted his excommunication from synagogue, church, and society without rancor, and he never sought fame or riches, or even a professorship, living out his life philosophizing and grinding lenses to earn a meager living. He accepted as his reward the state of tranquility afforded to him by his philosophy, and his

Baruch Spinoza

motto could well have been his own epigram, "All excellent things are as difficult as they are rare."[7]

Spinoza tried to submit Cartesian metaphysics to a geometric method even more rigorous than that used by Descartes himself. Like Descartes's, Spinoza's philosophy is centered on a definition of substance, but Spinoza had detected a contradiction in Descartes's account. Descartes had said, "By substance, we can understand nothing else than a thing which so exists that it needs no other thing in order to exist." Then Descartes had gone on to say, "And in fact only one single substance can be understood which clearly needs nothing else, namely, God,"[8] which he called "infinite substance." Despite this admission that by definition there could exist only one kind of being that was absolutely independent, Descartes (in a contradictory manner, according to Spinoza) proceeded to distinguish between "infinite substance" and "finite substances"—the latter were called corporeal substance (body) and mental substance

FIRST SUBSTANCE

There ain't room enough in this cosmos for both of us!

2nd. SUBSTANCE

(mind). This radical dualism led Descartes to his notorious mind-body problem and his universally scorned pineal gland solution.

Spinoza avoided this embarrassment by accepting Descartes' definition of substance (as that which is absolutely independent) and taking deadly seriously the inference that there could be only one such substance. (If there were two, they would limit each other's independence.)

Furthermore, because finiteness would constitute a limitation on God's absolute independence, Spinoza defined God as having infinite attributes. So once again, the conclusion is that there can be but one substance because any substance other than God would have to possess attributes that have already been defined as belonging to God.

Let's look at a schematized comparison of the systems of Descartes and Spinoza:

*An <u>attribute</u>, for Descartes, is a characteristic that is the <u>essence</u> of a substance (i.e., that which is essential to it). For Spinoza, an attribute is a characteristic that to the human intellect <u>seems</u> to be an essence. A <u>mode</u> is a specific modification of an attribute (i.e., a characteristic of a characteristic).

Like Descartes, Spinoza equated "infinite substance" with God, but he also equated it with nature. The equation "Nature equals God" makes him a pantheist. (It is also this equation that got him into trouble with both the Jewish and Christian theologians.) There are two human perspectives on reality (i.e., on God): one viewed through the attribute of mind (resulting in idealism, the claim that only mind exists) and one viewed through the attribute of body (resulting in materialism, the view that only matter exists). In theory, there are an indefinite number of other perspectives on reality, but only these two are open to the human intellect. A completely consistent idealistic or materialistic account of reality can be given, but no consistent dualism is possible. Dualism involves a confusion of perspectives. (So much for Descartes's pineal gland.)

The true philosopher attempts to transcend the purely human perspective and view reality *sub specie aeternitatis*, that is, from the perspective of reality itself. From this perspective, one comes to realize that the human has no privileged position in the cosmos, that the human has no more and no less dignity than anything else in nature. One must come to love everything, which is to say, to love God (because one must either love everything or nothing at all). The *love of God* is tantamount to the *knowledge of God*, which is to say, a philosophical knowledge of reality. This difficult intellectual love of God is a form of rationalism

> Mais Monsieur Descartes, est-ce que vous avez mal à la glande pinéale?

> I'm sure it's due to substance abuse.

that, like Platonism, is tainted with mysticism. It also contains a stoic component, insofar as knowledge of reality leads one to realize that everything that happens, happens of necessity. There is no **randomness** and no freedom of the will. But the realization that there is no such thing as free will, neither for God nor for humans, can itself be a liberating realization because one is thereby freed from the demands of desire and passion, both of which were seen by Spinoza as murky emotions that manage to control us only because of our fail-

The Unrequited Love of Nature

ure to grasp the rational structure of reality. With knowledge, these emotions can be transformed into clear and distinct ideas leading to a kind of blessedness and joy. Spinoza wrote, "There cannot be too much joy: it is always good: but melancholy is always bad."[9]

Leibniz

The third of the great Continental rationalists was the German Gottfried Leibniz (1646–1716). He was a universal genius who made significant advances in symbolic logic and who created a plan for the invasion of Egypt that may have been used by Napoleon 120 years later. Leibniz also invented a calculating machine that could add, subtract, and do square roots. Furthermore, he discovered infinitesimal calculus simultaneously with Sir Isaac Newton (and got into a squabble with him concerning who had stolen the idea from whom).

Like Spinoza, Leibniz wished to correct the errors of Cartesian metaphysics without rejecting its main structure, but Leibniz was not satisfied with Spinoza's pan-theistic monism nor with his naturalism (i.e., his view that all is nature and that the human being has no special status in reality). Leibniz wanted a return to a Cartesian system with real individuals and a transcendent God—as opposed to the **immanent** God of Spinoza. Leibniz's system, as set forth in his *Monadology* and *Essays in Theodicy*, can be summarized in terms of three principles: the **principle of identity**, the **principle of sufficient reason**, and the **principle of internal harmony.**

Gottfried Leibniz

"Leibniz was one of the supreme intellects of all time, but as a human being he was not admirable."[10]
Bertrand Russell

In his *principle of identity*, Leibniz divided all **propositions** into two types, which later philosophers would call **analytic propositions** and **synthetic propositions.**[11] Take a look at the following table:

ANALYTIC	SYNTHETIC
A. True by definition (They are true merely by virtue of the meanings of the words in the sentences.)	A. Not true by definition (Their truth or falsity depends not on <u>meanings</u> but on facts in the world.)
B. Necessary (Their opposites are self-contradictions. They <u>cannot</u> be false.)	B. Not necessary; rather, contingent (They <u>could</u> be false if facts were different.)
C. A priori (Their truth is known independently of observation.)	C. A posteriori (Their truth or falsity is known by observation.)

Following are some examples of *analytic sentences:*

A. All bachelors are men.
B. 2 + 3 = 5
C. Either A or not–A

This category includes definitions and parts of definitions (example A) and arithmetic and the principles of logic (examples B and C). Analytic propositions were said by Leibniz to be based on the principle of identity in the sense that this principle is the positive counterpart of the principle of non-contradiction (which says that it cannot be the case that A and not–A at the same time) in that the negation of every analytic sentence is a self-contradiction (e.g., "*Not all bachelors are men*" implies the contradictory assertion "Some men are not men" because the definition of "bachelor" is "unmarried man").

Following are some examples of *synthetic sentences:*

A. The cat is on the mat.
B. Caesar crossed the Rubicon in 49 B.C.E.

Now, having drawn what many philosophers believe to be a very important distinction, Leibniz made the surprising move of claiming that all synthetic sentences are really analytic. *Sub specie aeternitatis,* that is to say, from God's point of view, it is the case that all true sentences are *necessarily* true, even though it doesn't seem to be the case to us humans. For Leibniz, Tuffy the cat's characteristic of "being on the mat at time T" is a characteristic necessary to that specific cat in the same way that "being a feline" is necessary to it.

This line of reasoning brings us to the *principle of sufficient reason.* According to Leibniz, for anything that exists, there is some reason why it exists and why it exists exactly as it does exist. Leibniz claimed that this second principle is the main principle of rationality and that anyone who rejects this principle is irrational. If the cat is on the mat, then there must be some reason why the cat exists at all, and why it is on the mat and not, for example, in the dishwasher.

Both these reasons should be open to human scientific inquiry,
though perhaps only *God* can know why the cat exists *necessarily*
and is necessarily on the mat.

What is true of the cat is true of the whole cosmos, said
Leibniz. There must be a reason why the universe exists at all, and
this reason ought to be open to rational human inquiry. The deepest
question, according to Leibniz, is "why there exists something rather
than nothing."[12] Like Saint Thomas, he concluded that the only possible answer would be in terms of an uncaused cause, an all-perfect
God whose being was itself necessary. So if Leibniz was right, we
can derive the proof of the existence of God from the bare notion of
rationality plus the self-evident proposition that something rather
than nothing exists.

This conclusion leads us to the *principle of internal harmony*. If
there is a God, God must be both rational and good. Such a divinity, Leibniz told us, must desire and be capable of creating the
maximum amount of existence possible ("metaphysical perfection")
and the maximum amount of activity possible ("moral perfection").
Therefore, at the moment of creation, God entertained all possibilities. He actualized only those possibilities that would guarantee the

maximum amount of metaphysical and moral perfection. For example, God did not just consider the individual "Caesar" in all of Caesar's ramifications (would write *The Gallic Wars*, would cross the Rubicon in 49 B.C.E., would die on the Ides of March) before actualizing him. Perhaps God considered actualizing (i.e., creating) in Caesar's place "Gaesar" and "Creasar," who, as potential actualizations, were identical to Caesar in all respects except that Gaesar would cross *not* the Rubicon but the Delaware River in 49 B.C.E., and Creasar would cross the Love Canal. God saw that *only* Caesar was compatible with the rest of the possibilities that he would activate, and therefore he actualized him and not the others. A similar thought experiment could be performed with God's creation of Brutus (as opposed, perhaps, to "Brautus" and "Brutos"). So the relation between Caesar and Brutus is not a causal one but one of *internal harmony*. And the same holds true of the relations among all substances. God activates only substances that will necessarily harmonize with each other to the greatest extent possible. This principle now explains why all true sentences are analytic. If Tuffy is on the mat at 8 P.M., that is because *this cat must* be on the mat at 8 P.M. (otherwise it is not Tuffy, but another cat). It also explains Leibniz's notorious claim that *this is the best of all possible worlds*. His actual words are "Hence the world is not only the most admirable machine, but in so far as it consists of minds, it is also the best Republic, that in which the minds are granted the greatest possible happiness and joy."[13] The world may appear very imperfect to you, but if you knew what the alternative was, you would be very grateful indeed to God. (It is this feature of Leibniz's philosophy that was to be lampooned by Voltaire in *Candide*.)

Every philosopher in the 250-year period after the publication of Descartes's *Meditations* conceived of reality in terms of substances. Leibniz called these substances **monads,** which he defined as units of psychic force. They are "substances" in that they are the simplest and realest "things" that can exist independently of one another. They are not *material* substances, however, as were both

Candide Inspects the Ruins of Lisbon after the Earthquake of 1755

the "atoms" of Democritus and the "corporeal existence" of Descartes, because materiality is not an irreducible substratum but a quality that is a product of the relation between certain monads—the way that liquidity is a product of relationships between certain molecules of hydrogen and oxygen, even though neither hydrogen nor oxygen is itself liquid. Monads are simple (i.e., they have no parts), and each is "pregnant"[14] with all its future states. Each monad is a mirror of the entire universe (God actualized only those monads that *would* mirror the rest of the universe), but they perceive the rest of reality only as features of their own inner states. "The

monads have no windows."[15] All
monads have a psychic life,
but some have a higher
degree of psychic life
than others. These
monads (or com-
munities of monads
clustered around a
"dominant monad")
are conscious. Some
conscious clusters
of monads are also
free, and these are

The view's lousy, but they've got great video!

The Monads Have No Windows

human beings. (Of course, in Leibniz's theory, as in the theory of
Saint Augustine, God already knows how these human beings will
spend their freedom.)

Perhaps it can be said that Leibniz's philosophy solves the
problems of Descartes's dualism, but it does so at the expense of
common sense and seems to be fraught with as many problems as
Descartes' theory, taking us on what must seem to some to be a
flight of fancy far from common sense.

Hobbes

Meanwhile, across the Channel, Thomas Hobbes (1588–1679) was
dealing with problems similar to those addressed by his contemporary René Descartes. Hobbes was a contentious old codger who
dabbled in everything. (His experiments in math led him to claim that
he had squared the circle and cubed the sphere.) At one point or
another he managed to antagonize every political party in Britain and
had to flee to France.

Hobbes solved Descartes's dualistic dilemma simply by
dismantling dualism. He loudly proclaimed a form of mechanistic
materialism reminiscent of Democritus's atomism, thereby rejecting

one side of Descartes's diagram; and Hobbes's thinly disguised atheism rejected Descartes's "infinite substance" as well. For Hobbes, the only things that existed in reality were bodies in motion. Despite his claim that "there exist everywhere only bodies," Hobbes did not actually deny the existence of thoughts. He simply held them to be "phantasms," shadows of brain activity, mere **epiphenomena** that had no practical effect on the physical system. Similarly, though he was a determinist, he was, like the stoics and St. Augustine, a "soft determinist." (A soft determinist believes that freedom and determinism are compatible.) It was okay to talk about freedom as long as all one meant by it was "unimpeded movement." (Water flows down a channel both necessarily and freely.)

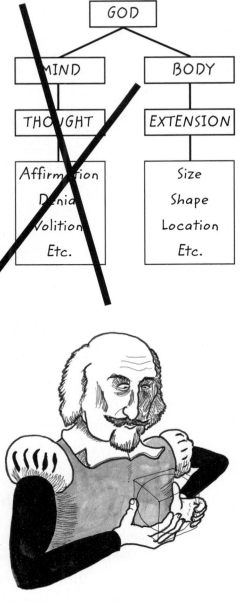

Thomas Hobbes Squares the Circle

Hobbes's psychology is very pessimistic. Every living organism obeys laws of individual survival; therefore, all human acts are motivated by self-interest and the quest for power. Altruism is not just a bad idea; it is impossible. Far from being immoral, *egoism* is the only show in town: "Of the voluntary acts of every man, the object is some good to himself."[16]

What makes Hobbes's **psychological egoism** pessimistic, in my opinion, is that if it is true, then it is impossible for individuals to act except in ways that they take to be in their own interest. Anyone who makes a claim to the contrary is lying or is in a state of self-delusion, ignorance, or stupidity.

Hobbes is best known for his political philosophy, which is influenced by his egoistic theory of motivation. He recognized the state as an artificial monster (the "Leviathan") that restricts what little freedom there is in nature and flaunts its power over the individual,

but Hobbes justified the existence of the political state by con-
trasting it to the notorious "state of nature," dominated by scarcity and fear, where "every man is enemy to every man" and where life
is "solitary, poor, nasty, brutish and short."[17] In the state of nature, there is no law, no morality, no property, and only one "natural
right"—the right to protect oneself using any means at one's dis-
posal, including violence and slaughter. If two people are on a desert
island and there isn't an abundance of coconuts to eat, then neither
dares turn a back nor sleep lest the other bash him or her with a

rock in order to get all the coconuts. However, if both are rational, they will realize that the most likely way of surviving is to agree with each other to forswear violence and share the coconuts. The trouble is, given the selfish nature that Hobbes attributes to all of us, there is no reason at all for either party to keep the agreement if he or she can figure a way to break it with impunity. So there is every reason for them to distrust each other. Despite their "agreement," neither dares yet to sleep a wink. The solution requires that a third party be found. The first two parties give to the third party all the rocks (and perhaps an army), and they give up their right to violence. In exchange, the third party promises to use her absolute power to guarantee that the first two parties honor their agreement with each other. ("She" may be either a monarch or a parliament—in either case she is the source of all authority.)

The Sovereign

This is Hobbes's famous "social contract." He realized that there is nothing to prevent the new sovereign from abusing her power (indeed, given *her* egoistic nature and innate lust for power, it is almost inevitable that she will *do* so), but he believed that the state, even with its necessary abuse of power, was better than the alternative—the horrors of anarchy in "the state of nature."

(It should be mentioned that, typically, Hobbes's political theory managed to please no one in Britain. The parliamentarians didn't like it because of its absolutist implications, and the king didn't like it because of its denial of the divine right of monarchs.)

Locke

John Locke (1632–1704) was the first of the classical British empiricists. (Empiricists believed that all knowledge derives from experience. These philosophers were hostile to rationalistic metaphysics, particularly to its unbridled use of speculation, its grandiose claims, and its epistemology grounded in innate ideas.) In his *Essay Concerning Human Understanding,* Locke began his attack on Descartes' "innate ideas" by threatening them with Ockham's razor. (Recall that Ockham's razor is a principle of simplification derived from William of Ockham. It cautions, "Do not multiply entities beyond necessity." Given two theories, each of which adequately accounts for all the observable data, the simpler theory is the correct theory.) If Locke could account for all human knowledge without making reference to innate ideas, then his theory would be simpler, hence better, than that of Descartes. He wrote, "Let us then suppose the mind to be, as we say, white paper, void of all characters, without any ideas: How comes it to be furnished? . . . To this I answer, in one word, from *experience.*"[18] So the mind at birth is a *tabula rasa,* a blank slate, and is informed only by "experience," that is, by sense experience and acts of reflection. Locke built from this theory an epistemology beginning with a pair of distinctions: one

John Locke

between simple and complex ideas and another between primary and secondary qualities.

Simple ideas originate in any one sense (though some of them, like "motion," can derive from either the sense of sight or the sense of touch). These ideas are simple in the sense that they cannot be further broken down into yet simpler entities. (If a person does not understand the idea of "yellow," you can't explain it. All you can do is point to a sample and say, "yellow.") These simple ideas are Locke's primary data, his psychological atoms. All knowledge is in one way or another built up out of them.

The Tabula Rasa Being Marked by Experience

Complex ideas are, for example, combinations of simple ideas. These result in our knowledge of particular things (e.g., "apple"— derived from the simple ideas "red," "spherical," "sweet"), comparisons ("darker than"), relations ("north of"), and abstractions ("gratitude"). Even abstractions, or general ideas, are nevertheless particular ideas that stand for collections. (This doctrine places Locke close to the theory known in the medieval world as "nominalism." All the empiricists share with the nominalists the anti-Platonic thesis that only particulars exist.)

Locke's distinction between primary and secondary qualities is one that he borrowed from Descartes and Galileo, who had in turn borrowed it from Democritus. Primary qualities are characteristics of external objects. These qualities really do inhere in those objects. (Extension, size, shape, and location are examples of primary qualities.) Secondary qualities are characteristics that we often attribute to external objects but that in fact exist only in the mind,

The Problem: To Construct Knowledge from Simple Ideas

yet are *caused* by real features of external objects. (Examples of secondary qualities are colors, sounds, and tastes.) This view of the mind has come to be known as *representative* **realism.** According to it, the mind *represents* the external world, but it does not duplicate it. (Naive realism, the view that the mind literally duplicates external reality, was discussed earlier in this chapter.) The mind is something like a photograph in that there are features of a photo that very accurately represent the world (e.g., a good picture of three people correctly depicts the fact that there are three people and that each of them has two eyes, one nose, and one mouth), and there are features of the photograph that belong exclusively to the photo (its glossiness, its two-dimensionality, the white border around its content). So in Locke's system, as in Descartes's system, there is a real world out there and it has certain real qualities—the primary qualities. Now, these qualities—what are they qualities of? In

What Appears to Be Out There   **What Is Out There**

answering this question, Locke never abandoned the basic Cartesian metaphysics of substance.

A real quality must be a quality of a real *thing*, and real things are *substances*. (Once again, everything in the world is either a substance or a characteristic of a substance.) Well then, what is the status of this pivotal idea of "substance" in Locke's theory? Recall that Descartes had claimed that one cannot derive the idea of substance from observation precisely because perception can only generate qualities. For this very reason, it was necessary to posit the idea of substance as an *innate idea*. But Locke was committed to the rejection of innate ideas and to defending the claim that all knowledge comes in through the senses. So what did he say about the idea of substance? Rather amazingly, he said the following:

> So that if anyone will examine himself concerning his notion of pure substance in general, he will find he has no other idea of it at all, but only a supposition of he knows not what *support* of such qualities which are capable of producing simple ideas in us.[19]

So, having claimed that he could account for all knowledge purely in terms of experience and having arrived at the concept that had dominated philosophy for the last several generations, Locke proclaimed it a mystery and even joked about it. (He compared the philosopher trying to explain substance to the Indian who explained that the world was supported by a great elephant, which in turn was supported by a tortoise, which in turn was supported by— "something, he knew not what.") Locke's conclusion is a bit embarrassing, and it is either a rather inauspicious beginning for empiricism or the beginning of the end of the metaphysics of substance. (We will soon see that it is the latter.)

John Locke concerned himself not only with epistemology but with politics as well. In his theory, developed in *Two Treatises on Government*, Locke, like Hobbes, drew a distinction between the "state of nature" and the "political state." However, what he meant by "state of nature" was very different indeed from what Hobbes meant by it. Far from being a condition in which there is no justice nor injustice, no right nor wrong, "no mine and thine distinct,"[20] Locke's "state of nature" is a *moral* state—the state into which we are all born as humans, where we are all bestowed with certain *God-given* natural rights, the right to "life, health, liberty and possessions."[21] Recall that for Hobbes, there was only one natural right, the right to try to preserve one's life. Hobbes seems to have believed that a kind of instinct for survival authorized that right. Locke's theory contains several natural rights, all of which are moral rather than instinctual, and they derive their authority from God. Hobbes purposely left God out

The State of Nature according to Hobbes

of his theory because he was trying to escape medievalism, where all philosophy presupposed God's existence. Hobbes was particularly insistent that there was no such thing as a "natural right to property," because in nature there is no property, only possession ("only that to be every man's, that he can get; and for so long as he can keep it").[22] Locke, on the contrary, claimed we have a natural right to whatever part of nature we have "mixed our labor with."[23] So if I till the soil, or cut down a tree and

The State of Nature according to Locke

make a house from it, then this garden and that house are *mine* (and will be my children's when they inherit them from me). Locke did put qualifications on this natural right to property. One can accumulate as much "natural property" as one can use, as long as:

A. It does not spoil in its accumulation.
B. Enough has been left for others.
C. Its accumulation is not harmful to others.

Locke's wealthy friends were probably glad to hear that "gold and silver may be hoarded up without injury to anyone."[24]

(It is noteworthy that Locke's theory presupposes a state of abundance in nature, whereas Hobbes's presupposes a state of scarcity. It may be true that human nature would express itself very differently in these vastly dissimilar "states of nature.")

According to Locke, individual political states are to be evaluated in terms of how well they protect the natural rights of the individuals living in those states. A good state is one that guarantees and maximizes those rights; a bad state is one that does not guarantee them; and an evil state is one that itself assaults the natural rights. Locke's version of the "social contract" is that all citizens consent to be ruled by a government elected by a majority for just as long as that government protects the natural rights. But a tyrannical government is illegitimate and *ought* to be revolted against. Note that, unlike Hobbes, Locke is

able to distinguish between a legitimate and an illegitimate government and provides a theory of justifiable revolution. It is clear that
the Founding Fathers used Locke's theory to justify the American
Revolution, and they incorporated his ideas into our Declaration
of Independence and Constitution. Perhaps what is best in the
American system derives from what is best in Locke's theory, and
some social critics claim that what is worst in the American system
is derived from what is worst in Locke's theory. America can be seen
as a great Lockean experiment.

Berkeley

The second of the British empiricists was the Irishman George Berkeley
(1685–1753), a teacher at Trinity College in Dublin who eventually
became the Anglican Bishop of Cloyne. As a philosopher, he was very
impressed by Locke's work and wanted to correct what he took to
be its errors and inconsistencies while remaining true to the basic

platform of empiricism ("blank slate" theory, **psychological atomism,** nominalism, commitment to Ockham's razor). In fact, he applied Ockham's razor to the idea of material substance so scrupulously that he shaved it clean away and was left with a type of subjective idealism—the view that only minds and ideas exist.

Early in his *Principles of Human Knowledge,* Berkeley attacked Locke's distinction between primary and secondary qualities. Recall that the former were said to inhere in material substance that existed independently of the mind, whereas the latter existed only in the mind (or, as Berkeley put it, their *esse* is *percipi*—their "being" is "to be perceived"). Berkeley pointed out that our only access to so-called primary qualities is through secondary qualities. The only way we can know the size, shape, location, or dimensionality of an object is by feeling it or seeing it (i.e., through the secondary qualities of tactile or visual sensation). Berkeley's conclusion was that

George Berkeley

descriptions of primary qualities are really only interpretations of secondary qualities—different ways of talking about colors, sounds, tastes, odors, and tactile sensations. Therefore, primary qualities too exist only in the mind. Their *esse* is also *percipi*.

To explain how this translation of secondary qualities into primary qualities is possible, Berkeley drew a distinction between direct perception and indirect perception. Direct (or immediate) perception is the passive reception of basic sense data (Locke's secondary qualities and simple ideas). Indirect (or mediate) perception is the interpretation of those sense data. Consider the process of learning to read. The small child confronts a written page and sees only black "squigglies" on a white background. (This is direct perception.)

Through a process of acculturation, the child eventually learns to see these markings as words loaded with meanings. (This is indirect perception.) It is an interesting fact that once we've learned to read, it is very difficult to recover the child's "innocent eye" and see the words again as mere squigglies. This distinction explained to Berkeley why we adults perceive the world as groupings of things rather than as sense data. Nevertheless, claimed Berkeley, the things we see in the so-called external world are really only collections of ideas, philosophically analyzable into their component sense data. Said Berkeley,

> As several of these [sense data] are observed to accompany each other, they come to be marked by one name, and so to be reputed as one thing. Thus, for example, a certain color, taste, smell, figure and consistence having been observed to go together, are accounted one distinct thing, signified by the name "apple"; other collections of ideas constitute a stone, a tree, a book, and the like sensible things.[25]

What's true of the component parts of a stone is true of the whole stone. Its *esse* is also *percipi*.

Notice that the notion of material substance (Locke's "something, I know not what") has simply disappeared in Berkeley's system. And the role played by the rationalists' innate idea of substance in explaining how we come to know the world as a concatenation of individual physical objects has been taken over by language. We teach our children words, which organize the ideas in their minds into "things." Berkeley's subjective idealism holds that each of us lives in his or her own subjective world composed of the sense data of the five senses. This is the same world we entered into as infants. But we were taught a language, which is to say, taught to "read" our sense data. Language is also the cement of intersubjectivity. I am able to bridge the gap between my private world and yours through the shared use of conventional symbols. Without language I would be stuck solipsistically in the echo chamber of my own mind.

Berkeley believed that with these two categories (sense data and language) he could account for all possible human knowledge—all except the knowledge of God. (Berkeley was a bishop, after all, so don't be surprised to find God playing a key role in Berkeley's philosophy, even if it was a bit embarrassing to him that God's *esse* is not *percipi*.) God's existence can be deduced from the regularity and predictability of sense data. If the so-called physical world's "being" is to "be perceived" and hence is dependent on the mind, then why is it that when I return to an empty room that I had vacated earlier, everything is just as I left it? Why didn't the room disappear when I stopped perceiving it? Because God was perceiving it while I was out. God is the guarantor of the laws of nature. When the Bible says that God created the world, it means that he created sense data and minds (spirits, selves) to perceive them. God did *not* cause there to be some unperceivable, mysterious stuff—"material substance"— which in turn causes ideas. Believing in the existence of such a "stuff" was the error of Locke's representative realism. Locke failed to see that the representation *is* the reality. Berkeley has merely eliminated

Why Doesn't the Room Disappear When We Leave It?

the "middleman." His theory explains everything that Locke's does but is more economical; hence, according to Ockham's razor, it is *better* than Locke's. So Berkeley believed.

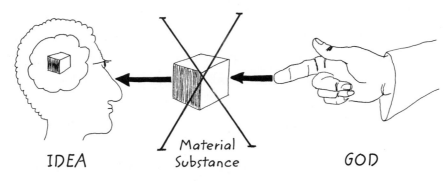

IDEA   Material
            Substance   GOD

Berkeley Eliminates the Middleman

Hume

The third of the "Holy Trinity" of British empiricism is the Scot, David Hume (1711–1776). He published his first book, A *Treatise of Human Nature*, when he was twenty-seven, and he hoped to achieve fame and fortune from it, but by his own reckoning, it "fell dead-born from the press." Ten years later he rewrote it and published it as An *Inquiry Concerning the Human Understanding*. This book was considerably more successful than its predecessor, possibly because it was a bit more moderate. Today Hume is recognized as the most acute, if the most perplexing, of the British empiricists.

David Hume

Hume's philosophy began with a revival of Leibniz's analytic-synthetic distinction, or in Hume's words, a distinction between "relations of ideas" and "matters of fact." It will be recalled that analytic propositions are expressed by sentences

A. whose negation leads to a self-contradiction,
B. that are a priori,
C. that are true by definition, and therefore,
D. that are necessarily true.

Synthetic propositions are expressed by sentences that are the opposite of sentences expressing analytic propositions; that is, they are sentences

A. whose negation does *not* lead to a self-contradiction,
B. that are a posteriori,
C. that are *not* true by definition, and
D. that, when they are true, they are not necessarily true (they *can* be false).

Now, in accepting this distinction, Hume was admitting that there are such things as *a priori necessary truths*. It would seem that any empiricist who accepted such truths was jeopardizing the program of empiricism by recognizing the legitimacy of the rationalists' dream, but Hume defused this situation by adding one more characteristic to the list of features of "relations of ideas." He said that they are all *tautological*; that is, they are all redundant, repetitive, merely verbal truths that provide no new information about the world, only information about the meaning of words. Thus, given the conventions of the English language, it is certainly true that "all sisters are siblings," but this statement tells us nothing about any particular sister that wasn't already known by calling her a sister in the first place. Similarly, anybody who really understands the concept "five" and the concepts "three," "two," and "plus" already knows that three plus two equals five. So the rationalistic dream of a complete description of reality that is a priori and necessarily true is a will-o'-the-wisp because a priori truths aren't descriptions of *anything*, according to Hume. Only synthetic claims—"matters of fact"—can correctly describe reality, and these claims are necessarily a posteriori. Therefore, all true knowledge about the world must be based on observation. This is, of course, the central thesis of all empiricism.

What Hume was claiming was that there are basically only three categories of analysis. Any proposition whatsoever is either analytic, synthetic, or nonsense. Hume said:

> When we run over libraries, persuaded of these principles, what havoc must we make? If we take in our hand any volume—of divinity or school metaphysics, for instance—let us ask, *Does it contain any abstract reasoning concerning quantity or number* [i.e., analytical truths]? No. *Does it contain any experimental reasoning concerning matter of fact and existence* [i.e., synthetic truths]? No. Commit it then to the flames, for it can contain nothing but sophistry and illusion.[26]

(No wonder Hume lost his job as a librarian.)

There is, then, very clearly a "Humean method" of philosophizing. One takes any claim that one would like to test and asks a series of questions about that claim:

David Hume—Librarian

1. *Is it analytic?*
    (This is determined by negating the sentence in which the claim is expressed. If the resultant negative sentence is a self-contradiction, then the original sentence is analytic.)
    ☐ YES (If the answer is YES, the claim is *true* but philosophically trivial.)
    ☐ NO (If the answer is NO, go to the next question.)

2. *Is it synthetic?*
    This question is posed by Hume in the following way: "When we entertain . . . any suspicion that a philosophical term is employed without any meaning or idea (as is but too

frequent), we need but inquire, *from what impression is that supposed idea derived?* And if it be impossible to assign any, this will serve to confirm our suspicion."[27]

In other words, question 2 can be answered affirmatively only if it is possible to trace its ideas back to sense data ("impressions"). For example, all the ideas in the sentence "This stone is heavy" can be traced back to sense data; hence, it passes the empirical criterion of meaning.

☑ YES

But what if, in a particular case, the answer to question 2 is negative?

☑ NO

That is, what if a particular idea cannot be traced to a sense impression? In that case, according to Hume, we must be dealing with vacuous ideas, that is to say, with *nonsense*.

Now, with Hume's method in hand, if we turn to some of the traditional philosophical topics, such as God, world, and self, we arrive at some pretty startling conclusions. Let's start with the sentence "God exists."

1. Is this proposition analytic?

That is to ask, is its negation ("God does not exist") a self-contradiction? Most people would answer no. Of course, some would answer yes—namely, all those defenders of the "ontological proof of God's existence" (e.g., Anselm, Descartes, Spinoza), but Hume would respond to them by saying that if the sentence "God exists" is analytic, then it is tautological and tells us nothing about reality. The true sentence "A being whose existence is necessary would be one that necessarily exists" still doesn't tell us whether there is a necessary being.

☑ NO

So if we assume that "God exists" is not analytic, the next question is,

2. Is this proposition synthetic?

Hume believed that it was impossible to trace the idea of God back to sense data. He said, "Our ideas reach no farther than our experience: We have no experience of divine attributes and operations; I need not conclude my syllogism. You can draw the inference your-self."[28] So although Hume didn't actually say so, his method seems to imply that the idea of God is vacuous and that statements about God are literally nonsense.

So much for God in Hume's system. What about the world? Berkeley, using Ockham's razor, had already eliminated "material substance" from empiricism. Material substance was *one* of the key concepts philosophers had used to explain the world. Hume now turned to another, one that was employed not only by philosophers but also by scientists and by ordinary people of common sense— that of **causality.**

Let's take the sentence "X causes Y," where X and Y are both events. (We'll use Hume's example: X is the event of billiard ball A striking billiard ball B, and Y is the event of ball B moving after being struck.)

1. Is the sentence "X causes Y" analytic?
   (That is to say, is the sentence "X does not cause Y" a self-contradiction? Obviously not, because it is perfectly possible to conceive of A striking B and B *not* moving.)

   ☑ NO

2. Is the sentence "X causes Y" synthetic?

Now, it seems that the answer will be affirmative because there should be no difficulty in tracing back the idea of "cause" to sense data. But Hume *found a difficulty.* When he analyzed the concept of causality, he broke it down into three components: (a) priority, (b) contiguity, and (c) necessary connection. Priority (the fact that X precedes Y) can be traced to sense data. So can contiguity (the fact that X touches Y). But no matter how many times Hume observed ball A strike ball B, he could not find any

Hume Observing Causality

necessary connection (the fact that if X happens, Y *must* happen), yet this was exactly what needed to be found if the concept of causality was to be sensible.

So the concept of "causality" proved to have the same status as "material substance" and "God." This embarrassment has far-reaching consequences. It means that whenever we say that event A causes event B, we are really only reporting our own *expectation* that A will be followed by B in the future. This statement expresses a psychological fact about us and not a fact about the world. But if we try to show the rational grounding of our expectation, we cannot do so. Even if A was followed by B innumerable times in the past, that does not justify our claim to know that it will *do* so again in the future. Hume did not, however, conclude that no causality exists in the world. He never doubted that objects and events stand in causal relations to each other, but he did doubt that an adequate philosophical account of causality was available.

Hume's discovery has come to be known as the problem of **induction.** What makes us so certain that the future will behave like the past? If we answer "because it has always done so in the past," we are **begging the question,** because the real question is, Must it do so in the future just because it has always done so in the past? Nor can we appeal to the "laws of nature," because then the question is, What guarantees that the laws of nature will hold tomorrow? There is no analytic or synthetic guarantee of the laws of nature. The concept of causality is one of the key ideas that are needed to understand the world. Hume concluded that neither reason nor experience could justify the idea of "necessary connections," which is the main component of the notion of causality.

"Hume's fork" (the analytic-synthetic distinction) has equally disastrous results for the concept of self. There is no sense datum to which the concept can be traced. Far from finding the self to be the simple, indubitable, absolutely certain, eternal soul that Descartes had claimed it to be, Hume found, according to his method, that "there is no such idea" as "self." The so-called self proves to be "a bundle or collection of different perceptions [. . . heat or cold, light or shade, love or hatred, pain or pleasure . . .] which succeed each other with an inconceivable rapidity, and are in a perpetual flux and movement."[29]

David Hume had consistently and vigorously followed the program of empiricism to its logical conclusion. The results were disastrous for the philosophical enterprise. The sphere of rationality was found to be very small

Hume Discovers the Self— Such As It Is

David Hume—Shepherd

indeed, reduced as it was to verbal truths and descriptions of sense data; yet nearly everything that interested people as philosophers or nonphilosophers fell beyond those limits. Hume believed he had shown that human life was incompatible with rationality and that human endeavors always extend beyond philosophical justification. (Rationally, I can never know that the loaf of bread that nourished me yesterday will nourish me today; hence, I can never be *rationally* motivated to eat.) But Hume knew perfectly well that the human being could not be sustained by the meager fruits of philosophy. Even while writing his philosophical manuscript Hume knew that, once he put down his pen, he too would revert to the normal, unfounded beliefs of humanity—namely, beliefs in self, world, and causality (if not in God). He even suggested, maybe with tongue in cheek, that perhaps we should abandon philosophy and take to tending sheep instead.

Kant

It would be fair to say that the history of philosophy would have ended with Hume if his views had prevailed. To survive Hume's attack, philosophy needed a powerful, subtle, and original mind to come to its defense. It found such a protector in the German Immanuel Kant (1724–1804). Kant spent the whole of his life in the old Hanseatic city of Königsberg in the northeastern corner of Prussia (today, Kaliningrad, Russia), where, at least until his fiftieth year, he passed his days complacently in the bourgeois

Herr Professor Immanuel Kant on His Daily Walk

life of a respected professor of the university. This old bachelor, whose personal life was so methodical that his neighbors used to set their clocks by his afternoon walks, had been trained in the rationalistic metaphysics of Christian von Wolff, an undistinguished disciple of Leibniz, and Kant had found no reason to doubt any of its tenets—that is, not until one fine day in his late middle age when a copy of Hume's *Inquiry* crossed his desk. Kant's reading of it "awakened him from his dogmatic slumber," as he later reported. He realized that Hume's powerful argument undermined everything Kant had believed and that no honest progress in philosophy could be made until Hume's skeptical arguments had been refuted.

Kant's response to Hume, and his attempt to synthesize what he took to be the best of Hume's philosophy with the best of what was left of rationalism after Hume's full-scale frontal assault on it, is found in *The Critique of Pure Reason*. There Kant accepted Hume's analytic-synthetic distinction as the key philosophical tool of analysis. Kant agreed with Hume that all analytic propositions are a priori and that all a posteriori propositions are synthetic, but he disagreed with Hume's claim that all synthetic propositions are a posteriori and that all a priori propositions are analytic (hence tautological). That is to say, according to Kant, there is such a thing as a **synthetic a priori** *truth,* a meaningful statement about reality whose truth is known independently of observation.

Kant believed that only by demonstrating the existence of such truths could Hume be refuted and philosophy, science, and common sense (and perhaps religion) be made respectable again. This demonstration would be done by showing that the knowledge that Hume denied was, in fact, grounded in synthetic a priori truth, as were the very arguments that Hume had mustered against such claims of knowledge. Kant began by dividing the mind into three "faculties"— intuition (i.e., perception), understanding, and reason—and then performing what he called a "transcendental" analysis of each faculty.

Kant first dealt with the faculty of intuition. Here the primary question that concerned Kant was not "What is perception?" nor

"Is perception possible?" Rather, it was "*How* is perception possible?" That is, he began with the commonsense view that we *do* perceive the world and asked what conditions must hold for that to be possible. For example,

he wanted to know how it was possible that we are able to utter true sentences about the height of the Matterhorn if the empiricists were right to say we never perceive space, only sense data. And he wanted to know how it was possible that we are able to utter true sentences about the amount of time it takes to get to Berlin if the empiricists were correct to say we never perceive *time*, only sense data. Kant's solution was to demonstrate that space and time are the synthetic a priori foundations of the faculty of perception. An a posteriori sentence like "The cat is on the mat" *presupposes* the truth of the sentence "Objects exist in space and time." According to Kant, we sometimes know the first sentence to be true, yet *it* cannot be true unless the second is also true. The latter is not analytic, and it is not a posteriori (there is no sense datum of space or time—Hume was right about that), so it must be a synthetic a priori truth.

Kant called this method of analysis a "transcendental **deduction**" because it transcends direct observation or, better, gets behind and underneath it to discover its necessary conditions. This analysis led Kant to conclude that space and time were not features of external reality. Rather, they were features of the *structure of the mind*. The human mind analyzes the data it receives in terms of space and time. Space and time are the "irremovable goggles" through which we perceive the world. They are not like pieces on a chess board (things in the world); rather, they are like the rules according to which we play chess and in whose absence chess would not exist.

The Irremovable Goggles

Having discovered the synthetic a priori foundations of the faculty of intuition, Kant then turned to the faculty of understanding. This faculty enables us to understand facts about the world (that Mt. Whitney is higher than Death Valley, that the cat is on the mat). Once again, Kant began not by asking "Can there be knowledge of the world?" Instead, he began with the commonsense assumption that we *do* have such knowledge and asked how such knowledge was possible. He found that it was grounded in the synthetic a priori foundations of the faculty of the understanding, which he called "the categories of the understanding." These categories included those of unity/plurality/totality, causality, and substantiality. These concepts are not deduced by the mind from reality; on the contrary, the mind brings them to reality. This is why Hume had been unable to find them "out there" when he looked for them. A sentence such as "Every event is caused" (which to Hume was neither empirical nor true by definition) is, according to Kant, a synthetic a priori truth.

Kant also claimed that mathematics belonged in the category of the synthetic a priori. First, math has an a priori status because our knowledge of it is independent of observation. (Your first grade teacher, Miss Green [you remember her!] was wrong when she pointed to two piles of chalk and said, "Two pieces of chalk plus three pieces of chalk is five pieces of chalk. *Therefore, two plus three equals five."* No, two plus three would equal five even if chalk had never been created.) But math also has a synthetic status. It tells us something about the world. A mathematical proposition is not merely an empty tautology in the way that definitions are.

Obviously, Kant's theory of the synthetic a priori is reminiscent of the Platonic-Cartesian doctrine of innate ideas, but there is a major difference. Kant did not claim that we are born with a group of *ideas* but that the mind is structured in such a way that it analyzes its data in terms of a particular set of synthetic *a priori rules,* which are like a permanent program in a computer and which produce ideas when fed information by the senses. If you are a human being, then you make sense of the world in terms of such concepts as time/space/substantiality/causality. The mind *must* order the world in terms of "thingness," though there is nothing "out there" corresponding to our idea of substance. The mind *must* understand the world in terms of causal series even though there is nothing out there that could correspond to our idea of *the* cause of any event.

Kant's position was meant to represent a compromise between the warring rationalists and empiricists. His famous assertion "thoughts without content are empty, intuitions without concepts are blind"[30] was meant to grant to the rationalists that sense

Uninterpreted
Data

Ordering
Principles of
the Mind

The Idea of One
Event Causing
Another

data alone could not provide knowledge and to grant to the empiricists that there could be no knowledge in the absence of sensorial contribution. To many philosophers, Kant's solution seemed to be successful; however, it had the consequence of putting him in the disconcerting position of admitting that there does exist some kind of ultimate reality (what he called the **noumenal world,** or the "thing-in-itself" [*das Ding-an-sich*]) but that the human mind is incapable of knowing it. The noumenal world (from a Greek word meaning "the *thing* that appears," as contrasted with "phenomenon," from a Greek word meaning "the *appearance* of a thing") is the reality behind appearances, and we can know that such a reality *does* exist because appearances must be appearances *of* something. But we humans of necessity have no access to this noumenal world; rather, we are limited to knowledge of what Kant called the "phenomenal world"—

Kant Peers beyond the Curtain of the Phenomenal World and Sees Nothing

the world as perceived, conceived, imagined, interpreted, analyzed, and theorized about by the human mind. That is, we can only know a world that has passed through the human mind, through the gridwork of space and time and the categories of the understanding. Contrary to Hume's conclusion, Kant's conclusion was that common sense and science are valid but only insofar as their claims are about the phenomenal world. But nothing positive can be said about ultimate reality, other than that it exists. The concept of a noumenal world is what Kant calls a *limiting* concept. We can say *that* a noumenal reality exists, but not *what* that existence comprises. This limiting concept meant that traditional metaphysics of the type attempted by philosophers from Plato through Leibniz was impossible. Kant deduced this conclusion from his transcendental analysis of the faculty of reason.

The faculty of reason was supposed by Kant to be the faculty that produced the "pure" concepts (i.e., concepts uncontaminated by the senses) such as "God" and "soul." Were there any synthetic a priori foundations for this faculty? (Which is another way of asking, can we hope to know any "higher truths" about ultimate reality?) Kant's notorious answer—which was so scandalous to the metaphysicians and theologians—was *no!* Traditional metaphysics

The House of Metaphysics
before and after The Critique of Pure Reason

was impossible because it was always the result of illegitimately applying notions of space, time, and causality to the noumenal world when in fact these concepts can be applied only to the observable world. Therefore, all proofs of God's existence must fail, along with all attempts to describe ultimate reality in terms of that mysterious category "substance." We humans must therefore despair of ever knowing of God, justice, immortality, or freedom, because all these ideas overreach the human capability for knowledge.

If Kant had concluded *The Critique of Pure Reason* at this point, he would have satisfied the Humean critics of metaphysics and theology while pleasing the defenders of common sense and science, but he would not have satisfied those impulses in the human heart toward higher sentiments. To these stirrings, Kant addressed the rest of his *Critique*. There he claimed the following: There is no logical necessity to conceive of the world in terms of God, immortality, justice, and freedom (in the way that there *is* a logical necessity of conceiving of the world in terms of time, space, and causality); nevertheless, without such inspirational concepts, many humans would lose their enthusiasm for life. If one could not believe, for example, that the human soul is free and that ultimately justice will triumph, then one might well lose the motivation required for the engagement in the day-to-day world. Therefore, according to Kant, one has the right to *believe* (but not to claim to know) that God, soul, immortality, justice, and freedom exist, not as *metaphysical*

No God, no immortality, no justice. I can't stand it! Barkeep, bring me another.

necessities, but as *practical* (i.e., moral) necessities. We have the right to treat these topics as if they were synthetic a priori truths if doing so will make us better, more successful human beings.

Kant's attempt to distinguish knowledge from belief, yet ground belief in moral necessity, was acceptable to many people who were tired of the extravagant claims made by metaphysicians and theologians but who were also looking for a legitimate role for *belief* in the modern world. Kant's critics, however, accused him of merely "kicking God out the front door in order to let him in through the back door."

After *The Critique of Pure Reason*, Kant wrote a number of other important philosophical works, including *The Critique of Practical Reason* and *The Foundations of the Metaphysics of Morals*, both of which addressed specifically the problem of ethics. In its emphasis on intention and duty, Kant's theory demonstrated Christianity's influence on him, and in its attempts to ground duty in reason, Kant's theory showed him to be a thinker of the Enlightenment. By positing freedom as if it were grounded in a synthetic a priori truth (for without freedom there can be no moral acts), one can derive an ethical code from its foundations in reason. Being a rule-guided activity, reasoning itself is based on a respect for rules and laws. From such respect, Kant deduced a moral command, which he called the *categorical imperative*: "Act only according to that maxim by which you can at the same time will that it should become a universal law."[31] All moral acts are modeled on principles that may be universalized without contradiction. Kant thought that, as creatures of reason, we are duty-bound to obey such principles, or "maxims," as he calls them, meaning subjective rules of conduct—subjective in that we must choose to submit ourselves to them. Here, I am going to oversimplify this idea a bit to see what Kant was talking about.

Let's suppose that you owe a friend five dollars, and to your annoyance, he pressures you to repay. So you say to yourself, "If I kill him, I won't have to repay the debt." But as a true Kantian, you first check to see if you could universalize the maxim governing the

LAW OF THE LAND
Everyone must kill someone

proposed action. You ask yourself, What if everyone accomplished his or her goals by killing someone? Could there exist a universal law that states, "Everyone ought to kill someone"? This law would be an impossible law because if everyone complied with it, there would be no one left to comply with it. Therefore, we are duty-bound not to kill as a way of solving problems. Okay, then, what if you lie to your friend, telling him that you already repaid the debt? Can the principle behind this proposal be universalized? Could there be a general law that states, "Everyone ought always to lie"? Obviously not, because it would be impossible even to state the law without breaking it. Furthermore, if everyone always lied, then there would be no such thing as a lie, or, lies would

Where Theft Is the Law of the Land

be the truth. (For the same reason, if all money were counterfeit, then there would be no such thing as counterfeit money. Counterfeit money would be real money.) This law would be self-contradictory. Therefore, we are duty-bound not to lie. Well, what if you repay the five dollars and then steal them back? Can the principle behind this act be universalized? Imagine a general law that states, "Everyone ought always to steal."

This too is an impossible law because the concept of stealing is parasitical upon the concept of *property*. But if everyone always steals, there can be no property; there can be only temporary possession, that is, stuff passing from person to person. So we are also duty-bound to refrain from stealing. (If you are a true Kantian, it's beginning to look as though you will have to pay your debt!)[32]

You may have noticed a similarity between Kant's categorical imperative and Jesus's Golden Rule, "Do unto others as you would have them do unto you." Both are meant to force individuals to look at their behavior in nonegotistical ways. But there are interesting differences as well. It appears that Jesus's maxim appeals to feelings and desire, whereas Kant—who does not trust feeling and desire—claims to appeal only to reason. Jesus's intentions (and those of countless generations of parents who have demanded of their mean little kids, "How would you like it if someone did that to you?") can be thwarted by sadistically oriented masochists who might be very pleased to be humiliated or slapped around a bit. The categorical imperative gives them no such leeway.

Kant formulated the categorical imperative in a number of ways, not just in terms of the principle of universalizability. One such formulation was this: "Act so that you treat humanity, whether in your own person, or in that of another, always as an end and never as a means only."[33] By saying we should treat people as ends and not merely as means, Kant was, of course, admonishing us against *using* other people as a means to our own ends. He thought that morality entailed the recognition of the *dignity* of each person as a person. If there were no *persons* in the world, only *things*, there would be no *values*. Nothing would be worth anything more or less than anything else. But there are persons in the world—that is, individual entities having not only desires (because animals, too, have desires) but also rationality and freedom. Therefore, as the source of values, humans have *dignity*, which Kant defines as something so valuable that nothing could transcend it in worth. To claim our status as humans—that is, to claim our dignity—we must value above all else that which bestows dignity and humanity, namely, rationality, freedom, and autonomy. We must value these qualities in ourselves, but also in other individuals as well. Or, in Kant's words, we must treat other individuals as *ends* and not as *means*. The principle of universalizability behind the categorical imperative makes this our duty as rational beings. This side of Kant's ethics has widespread practical implications for such issues as sexual relationships, discrimination, informed consent, and death with dignity.

If we dwelt solely on the first formulation of the categorical imperative (the one based on universalizability), Kant's ethics might seem quite bloodless; but this second formulation adds some warmth to his moral doctrine. Nevertheless, there is a *bit* of coldness at the heart of his view. He was so intent on making morality a question of *duty* that he refused to grant any worth to *inclination*.

According to him, if a person who was motivated by feelings of empathy toward humanity rendered assistance to a helpless, needy person, this act would be of less moral value than would be the same act performed by someone who actually loathed humanity but who was motivated purely by a sense of duty.

Kant's ethical conclusions, like his metaphysical conclusions, were essentially conservative in nature. His theory rationalized all the virtues that his Protestant upbringing had extolled. (Protestants had always known that a human's relation to God was one of belief, not of knowledge; and they had always known that they were duty-bound not to murder, lie, or steal.) Nevertheless, it is striking that Kant derived his principles from reason and not from divine commandment. Here he was more of an Enlightenment figure than a Christian. And many philosophers believe that Kant, in saying that certain kinds of metaphysical speculation are a waste of time, revealed something essential about the limits of human reasoning, and in saying that morality requires acts to be viewed from a perspective other than that of self-interest, he revealed something essential about ethics.

Key Philosophical Ideas in Chapter 5

- Overview: Much philosophical innovation in Europe during the seventeenth and eighteenth centuries. Especially the articulation and defense of the rationalist and empiricist schools.

- Postures are each primarily epistemological but with ontological implications.

The Continental rationalists, René Descartes, Baruch Spinoza, and Gottfried Leibniz, and their followers claim that the foundation of knowledge is Reason:

- The workings of the mind on the innate ideas of mathematics and logic.

- Therefore, the most important kind of knowledge is a priori.

- A divine being, whose idea was innate to every human mind, plays a large role in rationalist philosophy.

René Descartes:

- Searches for the absolutely <u>certain foundations of knowledge</u>
- Method: <u>radical doubt</u> (digging down)
  - <u>skepticism of the senses</u>; the <u>problem of dreams</u>; the problem <u>of the</u> "Evil Genie."
  - The discovery of <u>certainty</u>: "<u>I think, therefore I am</u>."
- Solution (discovery of the <u>foundation of knowledge</u>): Certainty of <u>consciousness, self, soul</u>.
- Construction of the House of Knowledge (building up):
  - The <u>(ontological) proof of God's existence</u>.
  - The recovery of <u>mathematics</u>.
  - The proof of <u>the existence of the material world</u>.
- Only <u>mathematical science</u>, not the senses, <u>can explain</u> the nature of <u>the material world</u>.
- Defends <u>the new sciences</u> (such as Galileo's).
- But <u>science cannot explain the nature of consciousness</u> and selfhood.
- <u>Defends the new sciences from religious meddling</u>.
- <u>Defends consciousness (the soul) from scientific reductionism</u>.
- Descartes's legacy: an unsustainable <u>radical dualism</u>.

Baruch Spinoza:

- Discovers a <u>logical error on Descartes's part</u> which, when corrected, <u>solves the problem of dualism</u>, replacing it with a form of <u>pantheism</u>.
- Descartes's error: defining substance as "absolutely independent," and claiming there are two substances.
- <u>Spinoza's correction: there is one substance, God</u> (= nature, <u>= pantheism</u>).
- Spinoza's solution won him few friends but provided him with the kind of <u>peaceful bliss that many of the ancients had sought</u>.

Gottfried Leibniz:

Like Spinoza, Leibniz <u>critiques Descartes's dualism</u>, doing so <u>using three logical principles</u>.

- The principle of identity (A = A):
  - Every proposition, whether _analytic_ or _synthetic_, _is_ ultimately (i.e., from God's perspective) _a version of "A = A."_
  - Therefore, _every true proposition is a priori, necessarily true_.
  - Therefore, _every fact is related necessarily to every other fact, and every event that happens does so necessarily_.
  - _Reality_, then, must be _composed of monads_ as ultimate substances, _containing_ within them all _their past and future states_.
- The principle of sufficient reason: _For everything that exists, there is a reason why and how that thing exists_.
  - If we ask _"Why is there a universe?"_ the only possible reason would be _an all-intelligent, all-powerful being created the universe_.
  - Therefore _God exists_.
    - _The principle of internal harmony_:
    - If there is such a God, he must be _omnibenevolent_.
    - Such a divine creator would have created the best possible universe.
    - Therefore, _ours is "the best of all possible worlds."_
    - This seems to leave us with a _determinism that defies free will_.

Philosophy in the British Isles during this period is represented by Thomas Hobbes, a contemporary of Descartes, and later by the Empiricists, John Locke, George Berkeley, and David Hume.

Thomas Hobbes:

- Hobbes's philosophy _is neither_ a form of _rationalism nor empiricism_, but tends more toward the latter than the former.
- _Replaces Descartes's dualism with monism_: a _thoroughgoing materialism_ that would be anathema to the rationalists and a _form of "soft determinism"_ that is even more rigorous than that of Leibniz.
- _Moral theory: Psychological egoism (selfishness) as the motive of all individual action_.
- _Political theory: Also presupposes psychological egoism as the only political motive_.
- _Contrasts the "state of nature" with civil society_.
- In the "state of nature" life is "solitary, poor, nasty, brutish, and short."
- Any form of _civil society is better than the "state of nature."_
- One _escapes the "state of nature" with a "social contract"_:

- Each citizen agrees to surrender her "natural right" to self-protection (right to violence) if all others also agree.
- Each citizen agrees to transfer his right to violence to the "sovereign" (monarch or parliament).
- The sovereign establishes a police force/army to enforce the social contract.
- The sovereign is likely to abuse its power, but even with such abuse of power, society under the contract is better than the "state of nature."

The British Empiricists: "Employing Ockham's razor," they reject rationalism's innate ideas, and its broad metaphysical speculation, positing experience (reception of sensory data) as the foundation of knowledge.

John Locke:

- Epistemology (representative realism): Explanation of knowledge in terms of primary qualities (e.g., size, shape, location) and secondary qualities (sensations in the mind produced by the impact of primary qualities: e.g., yellow, hard, sweet).
- Ontology: Secondary qualities exist only in the mind, and primary qualities are real characteristics of material substance. ("Substance" proves to be a rather mysterious concept in Locke's philosophy.)
- Political theory: Like Hobbes, a political philosophy based on "the state of nature."
- Unlike Hobbes's "war of each against all," Locke's "state of nature" is a moral condition with God-given natural rights to "life, liberty, and possessions"
- American Declaration of Independence and Constitution use Locke's philosophy as a model, but change "life, liberty, and possessions" to "life, liberty, and the pursuit of happiness."

George Berkeley:

- Eliminates Locke's idea of physical substance with Ockham's razor.
- Explains the whole of human knowledge in terms of sense data and linguistic constructs, replacing "physical substance" with permanent relations among sense-data (Ockham's razor).
- So-called physical objects are "collections of ideas."
- Only God is more than sense-data: His *esse* is not *percipi*.

David Hume:

- To his empiricist principles (<u>blank slate theory of the mind, nominalism, application of Ockham's razor, and sense data as the foundation of all knowledge</u>), <u>Hume added Leibniz's distinction between analytic and synthetic propositions</u>.

- Unlike Leibniz (who held that a priori analytic propositions provide the most important kinds of truth), <u>Hume held that analytic propositions are</u> true but <u>tautological</u>.

- <u>Synthetic propositions are meaningful</u> only <u>if</u> they can be <u>derived</u> directly or indirectly <u>from sense data</u>. <u>All other propositions are meaningless</u>.

- Concepts such as <u>God</u>, <u>soul</u>, and <u>immortality are nonsense</u>, but so are concepts such as <u>selfhood</u> and <u>causality</u> ("necessary connection"), <u>time, and space</u>.

- Not only was <u>the foundation of religious belief lost but also the foundation of our faith in science and in common sense</u>.

- <u>Hume's radical empiricism leaves us with</u> very <u>little</u> we can call certain <u>knowledge</u>.

Immanuel Kant:

- <u>A German synthesis of rationalism and empiricism</u>?
- <u>Epistemology</u>:
  - "Awakened from his dogmatic slumber" by reading Hume, Kant <u>tries to salvage</u> the best <u>of empiricism and</u> the best of <u>rationalism</u>.
  - The key: the proof of "<u>synthetic a priori truths</u>" (i.e., truths about reality that are not derived from sense data).
  - <u>Synthetic a priori truths are universal structural components of the human mind</u>.
  - Time and space are the synthetic a priori foundations of all perception (every perception is in terms of time and space).
  - Causality is the synthetic a priori foundation of understanding (all understanding of events and actions is in terms of causality).
- Thus <u>Kant recovers</u> the foundations of <u>common sense and science</u>.
- <u>But he admits that there are no synthetic a priori foundations for concepts such as God, soul</u>, and <u>immortality</u>.
- However, in the name of psychic and moral health, <u>individuals have the right to posit these items as objects of faith</u>.

- Ontology:
  - Kant's solution <u>leaves us with two worlds</u>:
    - The <u>phenomenal world</u>: the world as known by the human mind, and . . .
    - The <u>noumenal world</u>: the world impenetrable by the human mind.
- If there is a <u>God, freedom, an immortal soul, and eternal justice</u>, these must be located <u>in the noumenal world, never to be known in this life</u>, but only posited as possibilities and made <u>objects of faith</u>, not knowledge.
- Ethics:
  - Only by <u>positing human freedom as if it were a synthetic a priori truth</u> can Kant also <u>develop</u> a complicated <u>ethical system based on the "categorical imperative."</u>
  - Derived from <u>the logical implications of the concept of human dignity</u>, Kant deduced that <u>every truly human act should be motivated by a principle of universalizability</u>: The "categorical imperative": "So act that you could will the maxim of your action as a universal law."
  - An act is <u>universalizable if</u> there would be no <u>logical or material contradictions</u> in an imagined world in which <u>all human beings engage</u> in <u>the act that one is entertaining</u>.
  - <u>This thought-experiment</u> justifies philosophically our <u>condemnation of the traditional vices, such as lying, theft, and intentional homicide</u>.
  - However, the <u>absolutism</u> to which Kant's system commits us seems like <u>moral extremism</u> when it tells us, e.g., that we could never lie even to save someone's life.

Topics for Consideration

1. Discuss the role that God plays in Descartes's philosophy. Based on the evidence provided in this chapter, defend one of these views:

    A. Descartes was an atheist who used the idea of God to disguise the true nature of his enterprise from religious authorities who were hostile to the new mechanistic sciences.

    B. Descartes gave God so much power in his system that without God the system would collapse, which proves that Descartes was a religious philosopher as well as a supporter of science.

2. Discuss Descartes's method of radical doubt, which he used to establish an absolutely certain foundation for his philosophy. Are you

convinced that Descartes's method achieved that goal? If so, say why. If not, explain what you think goes wrong.

3. Explain why Descartes's philosophy leaves us with what has been called the "mind-body problem," and briefly show how Hobbes, Spinoza, and Leibniz, respectively, dealt with that problem.

4. State the thesis of Hobbes's psychological egoism, and then either defend it or criticize it.

5. Explain how Hobbes justified the legitimacy of governments and the absolute power of sovereigns within governments.

6. Replace the word "God" as used in Spinoza's philosophy with the word "nature," and report what differences, if any, such a change makes in his philosophy.

7. Central to the theories of both Leibniz and Hume is the distinction between analytic and synthetic propositions. What differences exist in their respective treatment of these categories that can explain why their general philosophies are so much in opposition to each other?

8. Explain the different views that Descartes, Spinoza, and Leibniz had of the idea of "substance," and show the consequences that these differences produced in their respective philosophies.

9. Show the further development of the idea of "substance" in the philosophies of Locke and Berkeley.

10. Contrast the idea of the "self" in the theories of Descartes and Hume.

11. It was suggested on page 200 that in conditions of abundance, Locke's optimistic view of human nature may be correct, and in conditions of scarcity, Hobbes's pessimistic view may be correct. If this suggestion is valid, what are the implications for the idea of "human nature"?

12. Critically discuss Berkeley's claim that descriptions of so-called primary qualities (size, shape, location, etc.) are really only interpretations of secondary qualities (colors, sounds, tastes, etc.).

13. Explain the idea of "necessary connection" in Hume's discussion of causality. Why do you think Hume held that necessary connections are required in true causal relations, and why did he hold that propositions attempting to describe necessary conditions are neither analytic nor synthetic?

14. Using examples from the text, explain why Descartes, Spinoza, and Leibniz are all called rationalists, and why Locke, Berkeley, and Hume are called empiricists.

15. What, in your opinion, does Kant's theory of knowledge have in common with rationalism? What does it have in common with empiricism?

16. Try to construct an argument showing that the following maxim is ultimately self-contradictory and that willing it as a universal law would therefore be impossible: "Everyone desiring to escape an onerous obligation should kill the person to whom he or she is obligated." (See note 32.)

Notes

1. René Descartes, *Essential Works of Descartes*, trans. Lowell Blair (New York: Bantam Books, 1966), x.

2. René Descartes, *Meditations on First Philosophy*, in *The Essential Descartes*, ed. Margaret D. Wilson, trans. Elizabeth S. Haldane and G. T. R. Ross (New York: Mentor, The New American Library: 1969), 165. Subsequent references to this book appear in parentheses in the text.

3. Descartes's version of this idea as expressed in the *Meditations* is simply, "I am, I exist" (35). I have used "I think, therefore I am," the version from the *Discourse on Method*, because it is better known than the other. Indeed, it may be the most famous line from the history of Western philosophy. See *Discourse on Method*, in *The Essential Descartes*, 127.

4. Descartes, *Objections and Replies*, in *The Essential Descartes*, 274.

5. Desmond M. Clarke, *Descartes: A Biography* (Cambridge and New York: Cambridge University Press, 2006), 251. Subsequent references to this work appear in parentheses in the text.

6. Bertrand Russell, *A History of Western Philosophy* (New York and London: Simon and Schuster, 1972), 569.

7. Baruch Spinoza, *Ethics and On the Correction of the Understanding*, trans. Andrew Boyle (New York: Dutton/Everyman's Library, 1977), 224.

8. Descartes, *The Principles of Philosophy*, in *The Essential Descartes*, 323.

9. Spinoza, 171. I have tampered a bit with Boyle's translation of the Latin word *hilaritus*, which Boyle renders as "merriment" and I have changed to "joy." The word "mirth," chosen by R. H. M. Elwes, is, to my ears, even less Spinozistic than "merriment."

10. Russell, 581.

11. Leibniz called his two propositions simply "necessary" and "contingent" judgments, but Immanuel Kant in 1781 gave them the name they now have. Propositions whose predicate is embedded in the subject and can be "analyzed out" of the subject are analytic. (In the sentence, "A bachelor is male," the subject "bachelor" already contains the predicate "male.") Propositions whose predicate is not embedded in the subject are synthetic, originally meaning "brought together." (In the sentence, "The cat is on the mat," the subject "cat" does not contain the predicate "on the mat," so the sentence brings together the subject and the predicate.)

12. Gottfried Wilhelm von Leibniz, *Monadology and Other Philosophical Essays*, trans. Paul Schrecker and Anne Martin Schrecker (New York: Bobbs-Merrill, 1965), 87.

13. Ibid., 90–91.

14. Ibid., 151.

15. Ibid., 148.

16. Thomas Hobbes, *Leviathan: On the Matter, Forme and Power of a Commonwealth Ecclesiasticall and Civil* (New York and London: Oxford University Press, 1998), 88.

17. Ibid., 84.

18. John Locke, *An Essay Concerning Human Understanding* (Cleveland and New York: Meridian Books, 1964), 89.

19. Ibid., 185.

20. Hobbes, 102.

21. John Locke, *The Second Treatise of Civil Government*, in *Two Treatises of Government* (New York: Hafner, 1964), 124.

22. Hobbes, 85.

23. Locke, *The Second Treatise*, 134.

24. Ibid., 144.

25. George Berkeley, *A Treatise Concerning the Principles of Human Knowledge*, in *Principles, Dialogues, and Philosophical Correspondence*, ed. Colin Murray Turbane (Indianapolis and New York: Bobbs-Merrill, 1965), 22.

26. David Hume, *An Inquiry Concerning Human Understanding* (Indianapolis: Hackett, 1993), 114.

27. Ibid., 13.

28. David Hume, *Dialogues Concerning Natural Religion*, in *Focus on "Dialogues Concerning Natural Religion,"* ed. Stanley Tweyman (London and New York: Routledge, 1991), 108.

29. David Hume, *A Treatise of Human Nature* (Oxford: Clarendon Press, 1941), 252–53.

30. Immanuel Kant, *Critique of Pure Reason*, trans. Norman Kemp Smith (New York: Humanities Press, 1950), 93.

31. Immanuel Kant, *Foundations of the Metaphysics of Morals*, trans. Lewis Beck White (Indianapolis: Bobbs-Merrill, 1976), 39.

32. When I said in the text that I had oversimplified the presentation of Kant's theory of universalizability, what I meant is that I was going to ignore for the moment some of the problems related to interpreting this theory. For example, there is a debate concerning the generality or specificity of the maxim to be universalized. Some Kantian scholars believe that the correct rendition of the categorical imperative requires adding the phrase "similarly circumstanced," for example, to each of the laws I mentioned in my examples. For instance, when you think about killing your friend to avoid repaying your debt, rather than testing the morality of your action by suggesting a law that states, "Everyone ought to kill someone," you should propose the maxim "Everyone desiring to escape an onerous obligation should kill the person to whom he or she is obligated." (There would be similarly circumstanced maxims in the case of lying to the lender or stealing from him.) These formulations stressing circumstance would make it harder for Kant to demonstrate the self-contradictoriness of these maxims, but they would perhaps save Kant from the charge of inconsistency sometimes leveled against him for his support of capital punishment and of the killing of enemies during "just" wars.

33. Kant, *Metaphysics of Morals*, 47.

6

Post-Kantian British and Continental Philosophy
The Nineteenth Century

If Kant believed that his "critical philosophy" would spell the end of speculative metaphysics, he was sorely mistaken. Even during his lifetime, there was emerging a generation of metaphysicians, some of whom, ironically, were using Kantian principles to advance their speculations well beyond the limits that Kant lay down in his *Critique*. Kant was especially embarrassed by the use of his ideas and terminology by philosophers who were calling themselves Kantians while creating a kind of highly metaphysical idealism of the type Kant had repudiated. But it must be said that he himself was somewhat responsible for this turn of events. After all, he had defined nonhuman reality as a noumenal thing-in-itself and then announced that it was inaccessible to human thought, with the consequence that human thought had access only to itself. As that earlier idealist George Berkeley would have pointed out, an inaccessible noumenal world is hardly better than no noumenal world at all. Indeed, this new generation of German philosophers derived their idealism from their dissatisfaction with Kant's claim that there existed a nonmental world that was unknowable.

Hegel

Primary among the ranks of the German idealists were Johann Gottlieb Fichte (1762–1814), Friedrich Wilhelm Joseph von Schelling

G. W. F. Hegel

(1775–1854), and Georg Wilhelm Friedrich Hegel (1770–1831). Of these, it was Hegel who achieved the greatest prominence, and it will be he who will represent German idealism for us.

Kant had argued that the appearances of ultimate reality are processed by the human mind, which thereby creates a world for us humans to inhabit. Hegel went further and claimed that the mind did not merely *structure* and *regulate* reality but actually *generated* it and *constituted* it. That is to say, reality is simply mind or spirit (*Geist* in German). This claim left Hegel with a philosophy that he himself called "absolute idealism." It is *absolute* idealism not only in the sense that absolutely nothing but ideas exists, but also because ultimately Hegel equated "mind" with "divine mind," or "absolute mind." This meant that if mind = reality, then reality = God. This view, in some ways similar to Spinoza's, brought Hegel close to pantheism. Furthermore, besides equating *Geist* with reality and God, Hegel also equated it with history. Kant had seen the mind as structurally identical from individual to individual, culture to culture, and historical period to historical period. Hegel criticized Kant's view as static and ahistorical. According to Hegel, even though the

The Evolution of the Mind

mind does have a universal, abstract structure, its content changes evolutionarily from period to period. There exists a mode of philosophical introspection that reveals the general structure of Mind and even allows us to reconstruct history in an a priori manner. In our attempt as philosophers to investigate the nature of the mind, we can reconstruct the *logical* (not chronological) beginnings of creation. They go something like this:

In the beginning, God, pure Mind, and hence Pure Being, attempted to *think himself*. But the thought of pure Being is an impossible thought; therefore, when God attempted to think Being, he thought *nothing*. That is, he thought the opposite of Being.

But remember, in the unusual system being suggested here, God *is* God's thought; therefore, in his failure to think pure Being, God has distanced himself from his own essence. This is what Hegel calls God's *self-alienation*. The "truth" of Hegel's insight can be seen in biblical symbolism in the relation between God and Satan. Satan is a fallen angel. He has "fallen away" from divinity. He is, in Hegel's

Satan Falls Away from God—Divine Self-Alienation

way of thinking, divinity self-alienated. Another biblical indication of Hegel's "truth" can be seen in God's answer to Moses when God spoke to him through the burning bush. When the shrub burst into flame, Moses asked it, "Who art thou?" and God answered, "I am that which is" (or, in ungrammatical Hebrew, "I am that what am"). Here we see that God cannot say himself without dividing his essence into a subject-object relationship. ("I am . . ." [= subject] "that which is" [= object]. If the subject is the object, then it is not itself as subject.) Hegel's God, then, is in a kind of identity crisis. But if God experiences an identity crisis, so does the human because the human mind is nothing but a manifestation of the Divine Mind. The history of an individual's mind, like history itself, is the process of self-awareness and self-recovery.

Returning to the dichotomy Being ↔ Nothingness—can there be any reconciliation between the two? Well, these two impossible thoughts (neither Pure Being nor Pure Nothingness can truly be thought)

God's Identity Crisis

represent the absolute limitation of all thinking and all reality. That is, all thought and all reality must fall somewhere between these two extremes. Hegel's term for anything occurring between these polar opposites is "Becoming." So we can call Being a *thesis* (positive, +), Nothingness an *antithesis* (negative, –), and Becoming a *synthesis* (combination of positive and negative +/–). Hegel calls this universal structure of all thought and reality the dialectic.

Therefore, anything in the world—a table, for instance—is in fact a *process* synthesizing a positivity and a negativity. It *is* the

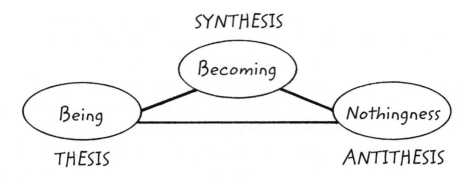

SYNTHESIS

Becoming

Being

Nothingness

THESIS

ANTITHESIS

table by *not* being the chair or the floor. This process is the nature of thought, language, and reality, which are systems of positivities created by negativities, and vice versa. Every thought, word, and thing exists only as a part of a system of exclusions. Again, a thing is what it is by *not* being its other, yet that "otherness" is what defines it as a being. This fact now explains why the thoughts of Pure Being and Pure Nothingness are impossible. Thought and language only function in a system of contrasts, yet Pure Being encompasses all; hence, there is nothing to contrast with it, *except* Nothingness, which is nothing. (Are you following this dizzying "logic"?) Furthermore, it can be deduced from this system that every synthesis must become a new thesis, and defined as it is by its opposite, this new thesis must spawn its own antithesis. So history is an eternal process of the dialectic, with each historical moment being a concatenation of contradictions— the tension between

BECOMING

HISTORY

BEING

NOTHINGNESS

the positive and the negative. These forces are opposed to each other, yet mutually dependent on each other. Eventually, the tension between the thesis and the antithesis destroys the historical moment, but out of its ashes a new historical moment is born, one that *brings forward the best of the old moment*. Here is Hegel's optimism: progress is built into history. And if we individuals think we see regression and backsliding at specific times in history, this is because we are blind to "the cunning of Reason," which uses *apparent* retrograde movements to make hidden progress. Such is the nature of Reason's (i.e., God's) process of self-recovery. Consider, for example, the period of Graeco-Roman democracy. On the one hand, there existed among the Greek and Roman democrats the commitment to self-determination, freedom, and human dignity (as seen, e.g., in Pericles's "funeral speech"). On the other hand, during their democratic periods, both Greece and Rome were imperialistic, slave-holding states. These two essential features of the society in question were contradictory but, ironically, were mutually dependent on each other. The slaves existed for the pleasure of the new democratic class, but without slavery and the booty from plundering, there never would have been a class of men liberated from toil who could dedicate their time, skills, and intellect to the creation of a democratic state. Yet eventually the *conceptual* contradiction between freedom and unfreedom, the two pillars of Graeco-Roman democracy, tore the society apart and prepared the way for a new kind of society, medieval feudalism.

Now, feudalism might not seem to you and me like a progression over earlier democratic societies, and in fact, it might seem like a retrogression. But from Hegel's point of view, medieval society represents an advance in freedom over Greece and Rome because in feudalism there were no slaves. Even the most humble serf had legal rights.

What happened in history also happens individually. Each of us passes through various stages in our conceptions of our self and our freedom. There is the stage at which we believe we can be free only by escaping the domination of others and by dominating them. Then we come to realize that in dominating them we ourselves are dominated because we become dependent on those we dominate, both materially and in terms of self-identity. (Who am I? I am the lord. But only as long as I am recognized as such by the bondsman. Without his recognition, I am nobody. Hence, in effect, *he* is the lord, and I am the bondsman.) Only by acknowledging that neither we nor others around us are free can we transcend the unfreedom of relationships of domination and discover higher forms of freedom— which is to say, discover the path of Reason and Divinity.

This sample of Hegelian thinking gives us an inkling of the psychological, sociological, historical, and theological dimensions of Hegel's thought. Hegel saw his dialectical system as moving from fragmented individualities to ever larger, more integrated communities, but always through oppositional conflict. For example, he saw the State as the highest synthesis of all individual, familial, and social interests, which often conflicted with one another, and called it the culmination of Objective Spirit (the antithesis of Subjective Spirit (mind as self-conscious and introverted).

Many of Hegel's critics point this out when they call attention to his eventual worship of the authoritarian, repressive Prussian state. Some even claim his whole system was contrived to be in the political service of the newly restored Prussian monarch, Hegel's paymaster.[1]

A more positive interpretation of Hegel's objective spirit concentrates on his designation of Napoleon as a sign of the end of history.[2] On this account, *history* is the history of the opposition between masters and slaves, or lords and bondsmen. The labor of the bondsmen had created a world of culture that transcended nature. Before the French Revolution the fruit of their labor was enjoyed only by the lords, who had finally proven themselves to be useless. The rise of Napoleon marked the end of the reign of the lords and the advent of a new universal and homogeneous state in which lords no longer looked down contemptuously on bondsmen; rather, this new state was one in which "one consciousness recognizes itself in another, and in which each knows that reciprocal recognition";[3] that is, each person will recognize all other people's individuality in their universality and their universality in their individuality. Napoleon's cannons at the Battle of Jena, which Hegel could hear as he hurried through the last pages of his *The Phenomenology of Mind*, were finishing off the old world of masters and slaves. Napoleon himself was the harbinger of the posthistorical world. Yet to Hegel it was no surprise that people caught up in the turbulent events of the moment did not grasp their significance at the time. The end of history cannot be understood by those *in* history. This is the meaning of

Hegel's aphorism "The owl of Minerva spreads its wings only with the falling of dusk."[4] But perhaps in Hegel's mind his own philosophy represented the posthistorical world even more than did Napoleon. It also must be noted that it is not Objective Spirit that is the apogee of Hegel's system; rather, it is absolute spirit, and the highest pinnacle of Absolute Spirit—the synthesis, of course, of what Hegel calls Subjective Spirit (introverted self-consciousness) and Objective Spirit—is not the state but *philosophy* (and, one assumes, particularly *Hegel's* philosophy).

The Owl of Minerva

Schopenhauer

Arthur Schopenhauer (1788–1860) was one of Hegel's sharpest critics. He was a younger contemporary who refused to be intimidated by Hegel's immense fame. As a beginning philosophy teacher at the University of Berlin, Schopenhauer had scheduled classes at the same time as Hegel's, knowing full well that thereby he was guaranteeing for himself few, if any, students. This arrogant young philosopher's opinion of Hegel was one of undisguised contempt, as can be seen in the following un-flattering portrait he drew.

> Hegel, installed from above by the powers that be as the certified Great Phi-losopher, was a flat-headed, insipid, nauseating, illiterate charlatan, who reached the pinnacle of audacity in scrib-bling together and dishing up the craziest mystifying nonsense.[5]

Arthur Schopenhauer

Schopenhauer, in fact, showed deep respect for only two Western philosophers: Plato and Kant. He also admired the philosophical traditions of India. To Schopenhauer, the rest of the philosophers throughout history had been merely "windbags." Schopenhauer began his work demanding a return to Kant, and indeed, the first part of Schopenhauer's main work, *The World as Will and Idea*, was fundamentally a repetition of Kantian ideas. He agreed with Kant that the human mind is incapable of

The History of Philosophy as the History of Windbags

knowing ultimate reality, that the only reality we are capable of grasping intellectually is that which has passed through the grid work of space and time and through the categories of the understanding. Schopenhauer wrote:

> "The world is my idea":—this is a truth which holds good for everything that lives and knows, though man alone can bring it into reflective and abstract consciousness. If he really does this, he has attained to philosophical wisdom. It then becomes clear and certain to him that what he knows is not a sun and an earth, but only an eye that sees a sun, a hand that feels an earth; that the world which surrounds him is there only as idea.[6]

Recall that when Kant alluded to the noumenal world, he claimed that we could not know it, though we had the right to hold various beliefs about it based on certain of our practical needs. We saw that for Kant, these beliefs were extremely optimistic ones: faith in God, freedom, immortality, and eternal justice. Furthermore, Kant had pointed out certain human experiences, certain positive intuitions of ours, that he hoped might be extrarational hints about the nature of that unknowable noumenal world. For example, there were those feelings of the sublime that we experience when we look deeply into the sky on a clear summer night, and equally inspiring to Kant were the feelings of moral duty that we experience in certain moments of crisis. As Kant put it, "Two things fill the mind with ever new and increasing admiration and awe . . . the starry heavens above and the moral law within."[7]

Well, Schopenhauer too believed that there were certain intuitive experiences that should be heeded because they might well give us an extrarational insight into ultimate reality. But Schopenhauer's examples of such insights were very different indeed from those of Kant.

For example, Schopenhauer wondered why it is that when someone is told of the death of an acquaintance, the first impulse that person experiences is the urge to grin—an urge that, of course, must be suppressed. And Schopenhauer wondered why it

It's Not Nice to Giggle at Funerals

is that a respectable businessman or government official, who may have worked tirelessly for years to achieve the success and power that he has finally obtained, is willing to risk all of it for a moment's sexual pleasure with a forbidden partner. These and similar human experiences left Schopenhauer with a much more pessimistic hunch about the nature of ultimate reality than that held by Kant. Schopenhauer's dark suspicions quickly became "truths" in his system. (The curious status of these nonepistemological truths has not escaped the eyes of Schopenhauer's critics.) Said Schopenhauer: "This truth, which must be very serious and impressive if not awful to everyone, is that a man can also say and must say, 'The world is my will.'"[8]

Schopenhauer's awful truth amounts to this: Behind appearances, behind the phenomenal veil, there does lie a noumenal reality; but far from being the benign sphere where Kant hoped to find God, immortality, and justice, Schopenhauer found there a

**Schopenhauer Peers beyond the Curtain
of the Phenomenal World**

wild, seething, inexorable, meaningless force that he called "will."
This force creates all and destroys all in its insatiable demand
for "More!" (More of *what* it does not know—it only knows that it
wants more.)

The best phenomenal images for understanding Schopenhauer's
will are images of sex and violence. Not only in nature but even in
the human sphere, every event is an act of procreation or destruction. Our actions, whether intentional or unintentional, motivated
consciously or unconsciously, are, in fact, actions that in one
way or another are in the service of procreation and destruction.
(If you are familiar with Freud's theories, you know now where he
got his idea of the id. Even the name "id" [Latin for "it"] indicates
the same noumenal indeterminacy as Schopenhauer's will. Freud

himself said in 1920, "We have unwittingly steered our course into the harbour of Schopenhauer's philosophy.")[9]

According to Schopenhauer, everything in the phenomenal world is merely the manifestation of this perverse will, or as he called it, an "objectification of the will" (that is to say, the will passed through the categories and the grid work of space and time).

Even though Schopenhauer's images of the will are ones of dumb brutality, he also conceived of the will as immensely cunning. The will is capable of disguising its heartless purposes from any of its own "experiments" that might be capable of taking offense or even taking reprisals against the will. In other words, the human mind is constructed in such a way as to be self-deceiving, even concerning its view on the world. The will is denatured as it passes through the grid work and the categories. Nevertheless, if we could strip away our natural optimism, itself a product of the cunning of the will, we could look into nature and see that it cares not a whit for the happiness or well-being of any of its creatures beyond the bare needs of reproduction. Schopenhauer illustrated his point with descriptions of the giant turtles of the South Pacific that were known to have been smashed to death by the hundreds against the rocky coast in storms during mating season as they tried to get to shore to lay their eggs in the sand. Schopenhauer also called attention to that strange species of moth that emerges from its cocoon with full reproductive and digestive systems; yet nature forgot to give it one little detail—a mouth!

So the moth reproduces and then seeks food but quickly starves to death. Yet nature does not care; the moth has laid its little eggs. And, according to Schopenhauer, what's true of the turtle and the moth is true of the human being. If you are over eighteen years of age, your body is deteriorating. Your body, which is just the scaffolding for the reproductive system, begins to die once it has held its eggs in place and given them a chance to duplicate themselves.

This news is terrible indeed. Why do people not realize that we are all in a state of bondage to the irrational, meaningless will? Precisely because of the cunning of the will. Human culture itself is nothing but one more experiment of the will, and human optimism and hope are simply the will's gift to us to guarantee that we continue to deceive ourselves about the true state of affairs. The whole of human culture is nothing more than a grand deception. Art, religion, law, morality, science, and even philosophy are only **sublimations** of the will, sublimations that are still acting in its service. Hegel's glorification of higher culture is simply proof of the absolute triumph of the will.

All our hopes and aspirations will be dashed. Happiness is an impossible dream. It is absurd that anyone can remain an optimist after even a glance at the newspaper on any given day. A mudslide swallows up whole villages. A mad assassin's bullet strikes down the hope of a people. A single parent, mother of three, is killed by a painful disease. The drums of war never cease beating, and an inglorious

What Seems to Be
the Case

What Is the Case

death awaits all. Verily, only a fool can remain optimistic in the face of the truth.

Surely philosophy was never so disheartened and disheartening as in the case of Schopenhauer. But, according to him, his pessimism was a *rational* pessimism, and he sought a *rational* solution to it. There had, of course, been others who understood the truth and sought rational responses to it. Both Jesus and the Buddha had been pessimists, according to Schopenhauer, but their solutions were chimerical and still in the service of the will (besides, their doctrines were perverted by the cunning of the will manifested in the optimism of their disciples who presented their masters' pessimistic messages as "good news"). Plato too had offered a *nearly* successful solution, but his eternal Forms were still part of the world of ideas, hence of the will.

It might seem that suicide should be the only recommendation that Schopenhauer's philosophy could make. But in fact, Schopenhauer recommended against suicide on the grounds that self-murder would

Plato's Solution

be a last, desperate act of will, hence still a manifestation of the will (that is to say, no act requires as much concentration of will as does suicide; hence, suicide cannot possibly be the negation of the will).

Do not despair! There is a Schopenhauerian solution. Even though all culture is nothing but a sublimation of sex and violence, hence an experiment of the will, there is a point at which the cultural world can achieve such a degree of subtlety that it can break off from its own unconscious origins and set up an independent sphere that is, in fact,

Elvis's Solution

counternature and therefore antiwill. This autonomy from the will occurs in a specific corner of the art world—that of music. But not just any music. Certainly, popular music won't do, evoking as it does the imagery and emotions of the phenomenal world. Nor will most classical music serve. For example, in Beethoven's works, the imagery is still too strong; hence its link to the will is too obvious. (When listening to the "Pastoral," we see the cows in the meadow, the bright green grass and the wildflowers, and the puffy little white clouds in the blue sky.) No, an escape from the will can be achieved only in the contemplation of purely *formal* music, a music without words and without imagery. There is a kind of baroque music that fits the bill—a music of pure mathematical formalism: point, counterpoint, point. It is possible to dedicate one's life to the disinterested contemplation of such music, and Schopenhauer recommended precisely this contemplation as his version of Nirvana—an escape from the world into pure form and hence a triumph over the will. It was this goal toward

Schopenhauer's Solution

which Plato and the Buddha were clumsily struggling.

Schopenhauer's philosophy was deeply influential among intellectuals in the German-speaking world. The work of Friedrich Nietzsche, Sigmund Freud, and Thomas Mann is hardly conceivable without Schopenhauer. Yet nobody seems to have taken Schopenhauer's solution very seriously. It was perhaps too obvious, as Nietzsche was to point out, that baroque music is the most sensual of all music and that the desire to immerse oneself in it is after all a *desire*, hence still the work of the will.

Kierkegaard

Schopenhauer's method of dealing with Hegel was first to call him names and then to ignore him. But the generation of Continental philosophers who followed Schopenhauer had to deal more directly

Søren Kierkegaard

with Hegel, whose influence by the 1830s had become immense. One of the most curious members of this generation was the Dane Søren Kierkegaard (1813–1855). Kierkegaard, who is generally recognized today as the father of **existentialism,** thought of himself primarily as a religious author and an antiphilosopher. In truth, he was not opposed to philosophy as such but to *Hegel's* philosophy. Nevertheless, like the rest of his generation, Kierkegaard fell more under Hegel's spell than he would have liked to admit.

Kierkegaard blamed Hegel for much of what he took to be the dehumanization of the intellectual life of a whole generation. This dehumanization was the result of a "correction" that Hegel made to Aristotelian logic. We saw that Aristotle laid down the three basic principles of logic as

1. The principle of identity (A = A)
2. The principle of noncontradiction [not (A and not-A)]
3. The principle of the excluded middle [either (A) or (not-A)]

Hegel believed these principles to be erroneous. His new dialectical logic overturned them. In the dialectic, everything is in some sense its opposite; therefore, it is not the case that A = A because A = not-A. (Greek democracy was in some sense equivalent to Greek slavery; hence, it was its own opposite.) If the principle of identity falls, then the principles of noncontradiction and of the excluded middle collapse too. Kierkegaard took offense at the pompousness of Hegel's suggestion. He mocked it with vignettes like the following:

> If you marry, you will regret it; if you do not marry, you will also regret it; . . . whether you marry or do not marry, you will regret both. Laugh at the world's follies, you will regret it; weep over them, you will regret that; laugh at the world's follies or weep over them, you will regret both. . . . Believe a woman, you will regret it, believe her not, you will also regret that; believe a woman or believe her not, you will regret both. . . . Hang yourself, you will regret it, do not hang yourself, and you will also regret that; hang yourself or do not hang yourself, you will regret both. . . . This, gentlemen, is the sum and substance of all philosophy.[10]

What Kierkegaard writes is not really the sum and substance of all philosophy. It is the sum and substance of *Hegel's* philosophy, a philosophy in which all oppositions are swallowed up, creating absolute apathy and demoralization, and which, by abrogating the principle of the excluded middle, thereby annuls the "either/or" of decision making—and therewith denies freedom, which, for Kierkegaard and his existentialist followers, is the essence of human existence. Therefore,

Kierkegaard published the foregoing "ecstatic lecture" in a book that he called *Either/Or*, whose very title was an attack on Hegel.

Not only had Hegel collapsed the distinction between the "either" and the "or," but he had also abolished the difference between epistemology and ontology by asserting "the Rational is the Real and the Real is the Rational,"[11] which is another way of saying that existence and thought are identical. Kierkegaard inverted Hegel's assertion, claiming that existence is the one thing that cannot be thought. This claim is a double entendre, meaning (1) Thought and existence are *not* identical, and (2) it is impossible to think "existence."

Recall that Hegel's god had found himself incapable of thinking pure existence (Pure Being). Kierkegaard pushed this limitation to the fore, claiming not just that *pure* existence is impossible to think but that *any* existence is unthinkable, because, in Kierkegaard's Platonic theory of meaning, thought is always a form of abstraction. Words are signifiers that denote concepts, and concepts are general categories. Every word in the sentence "The brown dog obeys its master" denotes for Kierkegaard an abstraction. Language abstracts from experience and suppresses differences in order to allow the possibility of thought and communication; hence, thought (which is language-bound) distances us from real existence, which is never abstract but always *concrete*.

Language Alienates One from Lived Experience

Kierkegaard's philosophy, as opposed to the abstractions of Hegelian philosophy, would return us to the concreteness of existence. But he was not so much interested in the concreteness of existence of things in the world as he was in the concreteness of individual human existence. René Descartes had been right to begin philosophy with the self ("I think, there-

When All the Roles Have Been Stripped Away, What's Left Is My Existence

fore I am"), but he had been wrong, as was Hegel after him, to equate the self with thought. "To think is one thing, to exist is another," said Kierkegaard. I can think and say many things about myself—"I am a teacher, I am a man, I am an American, I am in love, I prefer chocolate to vanilla." Yet, when I am done talking and thinking about myself, there is one thing remaining that cannot be thought—*my existence*, which is a "surd" (an irrational residue). I cannot *think* it; rather, I must *live* it.

My lived existence, according to Kierkegaard, is equated with passion, decision, and action. None of these categories can be exhausted by thought. But Kierkegaard is not saying that there is no connection between existence and thought. In fact, existence must be interpenetrated with thought. What kind of thought? An "existential probing" that "dedicates itself more and more profoundly to the task of existing, and with the consciousness of what existence is, penetrates all illusions, becoming more and more concrete through reconstructing existence in action."[12]

To explain this notion I must clarify a distinction that Kierkegaard drew in his *Concluding Unscientific Postscript to the Philosophical Fragments* between "objective thought" and "subjective thought." The first category is a kind of thinking for which there exist objective criteria of truth, such as in the case of math, science, and history. If you wonder whether "3 + 2 = 5," "f = ma," or "Caesar crossed the Rubicon in 49 B.C.E.," recognized standards can be used to determine the truth of these assertions. Objective truths exist, then, but they are existentially indifferent. That is, they have no essential relationship to my existence. If I found out that one of them was false, I might be surprised, but I would not thereby become a different person. Therefore, Kierkegaard's philosophy is uninterested in objective truths.

Subjective thought, however, is thought for which there exist no objective criteria of truth. Subjective thought exists, for example, in the case of values, for instance, ethical and religious claims. If I tell you that it is immoral to cause unnecessary misery to others and if you challenge my assertion, ultimately there are no objective standards for me to appeal to and I cannot prove my claim. (Kantianism won't work, according to Kierkegaard, because it presupposes a valuing of notions of consistency and noncontradictoriness. But what if you refuse to accept that value?) Similarly, if I claim that "God is love" and you challenge me, I cannot appeal to any objective criterion of truth to justify my assertion.

Nevertheless, these subjective truths are essential to my existence in the way that objective truths are indifferent. We pretty much *are* what we do, and what we do—the actions we perform—is the result of *decisions*, which are embodiments of *values* chosen. Yet those values cannot be grounded in certainty but are always accepted on faith—a faith in the uncertain.

This need for values and decisiveness in the face of the uncertainty of all things provokes, according to Kierkegaard, a kind of dizziness and loss of footing that reveals the true human condition as one of anguish and despair. Hegel was wrong. The real is not the rational. Rather, the lived experience of true human reality lies underneath rationality as a kind of despairing nothingness longing to be a something. (Yet, had Hegel not said this too?)

Vertigo in the Face of the Uncertainty of Reality

There are other subjective truths besides those of moral and religious valuation. But these truths can only be communicated indirectly, Kierkegaard told us. They can be hinted at, alluded to, overstated, understated, misstated, joked about, poeticized, or ignored. But they cannot be *said*—or at least, if they are said, they can't be directly understood. Such a truth would be the truth of "my death." Now, I know that all humans die and that, being a human, someday I too will die. I know much about death from the studies I have made in my history and biology classes. But that knowledge does not mean that I have grasped my death as a subjective truth. In the *Postscript*, Kierkegaard relates the story of a man who meets a friend on a street corner of Copenhagen and is invited to dinner by him. The invitee enthusiastically promises to attend, but at that very moment the prospective guest is struck and killed by a tile that happens to fall from the roof. Kierkegaard mocks the dead man, saying that one could laugh oneself to death over this case. Here is a person who makes an absolute commitment into the future, yet whose existence is whisked away by a gust of wind. After chuckling for a while over the irony of this story, Kierkegaard then asks himself if he is not being too harsh on the chap. Surely we don't expect the guest to respond to his invitation saying, "You can count on me, I shall certainly come; but I must make an exception for the contingency that a tile happens to blow down from a roof, and kills me; for in that case I cannot come."[13] Yet the reader of the *Post-script* comes to the realization that that is exactly what Kierkegaard wanted. When we reach the understanding that after every utterance we make about the future, we can correctly add the rider: "However, I may be dead in the next moment, in which case I shall not attend," then we will have grasped the subjective truth of *our* death.

The point of Kierkegaard's story is not to provoke a sense of morbidity. According to him, the discovery of one's death as a subjective truth becomes the pretext for another discovery—that of "one's existence" as a subjective truth. Only against a backdrop of the yawning abyss of eternity can the immediacy and fragility of

The Individual before the Yawning Abyss of Eternity

existence be understood. Most people are oblivious to the proximity of nothingness, and they spend their lives engaged in petty thoughts and pointless projects. ("Do my socks have holes? What will people think of me if I wear a soiled tie?") But the discovery of our subjective truths concretizes and intensifies our existence. It helps us to order our priorities and clarify our values and to recover the self from its alienation into social roles, material possessions, and linguistic abstractions. It reveals (and at the same time creates) the self that had been invisible to the self.

For Kierkegaard, the self is essentially subjectivity, and subjectivity is constituted by the individual's commitment to his or her subjective truths. The authentic self, for Kierkegaard, is one that "chooses itself" by a form of self-reflective activity that both clarifies and creates values while assuming total responsibility for those values. It was this process that Hegel had left out of his system, according to Kierkegaard; or, more correctly, it was this process that any system would necessarily swallow up. Therefore, Kierkegaard was antisystematic and titled one of his books *Philosophical Fragments*, yet another slap in Hegel's face.

Kierkegaard saw as his task not the development of a new epistemology nor the creation of a new system of metaphysics, but the creation of a whole new kind of human being—people who could grasp their own freedom and create their own destiny. (In this task he was joined by two other wayward nineteenth-century thinkers at whom we have yet to look: Karl Marx and Friedrich Nietzsche.) Kierkegaard called his version of the new human being "a Knight of Faith." This person, for Kierkegaard, has an almost superhuman kind of strength and greatness. Kierkegaard wrote of the archetypal Knight of Faith,

> Not one shall be forgotten who was great in the world. But each was great in his own way . . . each became great in proportion to his expectation. One became great by expecting the possible, another by expecting the eternal, but he who expected the impossible became greater than all. Everyone shall be remembered but each was great in proportion to the greatness of that with which he strove. For he who

strove with the world became great by overcoming the world, and he who strove with himself became great by overcoming himself, but he who strove with God became greater than all.[14]

These knights have grasped the absurdity and contingency of all existence. David Hume had meditated on the disconnectedness of all things. But Hume had *only* meditated on it, whereas the Knights of Faith feel it in their bones. Yet they find the strength within themselves to unify their world, to hold it together with an act of will, which Kierkegaard called "faith." These knights are individuals who have looked profoundly into the world of humans and seen that at the deepest level we are alone. We are in "absolute isolation"—an aloneness that constitutes a kind of madness, or "divine madness," for

That Other "Knight of Faith"

Kierkegaard's heroes are alone with their god. In fact, Kierkegaard's Knights of Faith, his "new humans," are not new at all. Rather, they are based on Kierkegaard's tortured interpretation of the biblical patriarch Abraham, who heard a voice in the night telling him to sacrifice his son. Abraham took full responsibility for the meaning of the message—it was *his* meaning, his subjective truth—and for his actions, thereby becoming a Kierkegaardian hero. Kierkegaard wrote of him, "Abraham was greater than all, great by reason of his power whose strength is impotence, great by reason of his wisdom whose secret is foolishness, great by reason of his hope whose form is madness."[15] Hegel had transformed human existence into pure thought. Kierkegaard counteracted Hegel's rationalization by introducing into philosophy a new category, "the category of the absurd," and putting it in the heart of his ideal human being.

Marx

Of course, Søren Kierkegaard was not
the only philosopher of his generation to be deeply influenced by Hegel.
When Karl Marx (1818–1883) arrived
as a young philosophy student at the
University of Berlin in the mid-1830s,
Hegel had been dead of cholera for
five years, but his spirit still reigned
supreme. To do philosophy in the Germany of the 1830s was to do Hegelian
philosophy. Nevertheless, the Hegelians
were by no means in agreement as to
what "doing philosophy" truly consisted

Hegel's Spirit Reigns Supreme

of. In fact, they had broken into two warring camps, the "Hegelian Left"
and the "Hegelian Right." The Right gave the more orthodox reading of
Hegel and was composed mostly of older, more conservative members
of their generation. They were primarily interested in what Hegel had
to say about religion and morality. The Left was composed of younger,
more radical philosophers. They sometimes called themselves the
"Young Hegelians." They were mostly interested in developing what they
took to be still inchoate Hegelian notions about social and political issues. They believed that Hegel's ideas as he himself understood them
were false but that there was a hidden truth in them that needed revealing. Their attitude toward Hegel's writing was very much like Freud's
attitude toward dreams. There is a "manifest content" (the dream images) and a "latent content" (the true meaning of the dream, which can
be discovered only by interpreting the manifest content).

Sometimes the analysis of the imagery, like Freud's dream
analysis, demonstrates that the meaning is the opposite of what it
appears to be.

Needless to say, Marx fell under the influence of the Hegelian
Left, not the Right. The foremost practitioner of the art of Hegelian

The Manifest Content

The Latent Content

Leftism was Ludwig Feuerbach (1804–1872), whose *Essence of Christianity* became holy scripture to a whole generation of progressive German youth.

Feuerbach's book, which was meant to be a kind of anthropological analysis of religion, contained an inversion of a key Hegelian idea. Hegel had asserted, "Man is God self-alienated." Feuerbach reversed this proposition, saying, "God is man self-alienated." That is, the idea of God is the perversion of the idea of man. Feuerbach believed that there were certain (Platonic) universal values to which all humans aspired. Every culture throughout history has longed for truth, beauty, justice, strength, and purity. It is part of the human essence to have these longings. But as historical peoples were frustrated in their attempts to achieve these ideals, the ideals themselves became alienated from the human and were projected onto an Ideal Being, a God who demanded that all be sacrificed to his glory. Feuerbach believed that as long as we humans continued to alienate our ideals into some nonhuman extraneous being, we would never be able to achieve the fullness of our own being. Hegel had caught only a glimpse of the truth. Man *is* God, but we can only become the god that we are by an act of self-recovery that can be brought about exclusively by annulling our traditional concept of religion. For example, consider the Feuerbachian concept of the Holy Family.

According to Feuerbach, only by abolishing the image of the heavenly family can we bring peace, happiness, and love into the earthly family, because as long as we hold the image of the former before us, we will consider the earth merely a place of trial and punishment. Workers will attend church on Sunday, confess their sins, become resigned to misery as the human lot, and on the next payday return to the tavern to drink away their meager salaries.

Marx fell directly under Feuerbach's influence. As a young philosophy student, Marx wrote, "One cannot do philosophy without passing through the fiery brook." (In German, *Feuerbach* means "fiery brook.") But Marx soon became disenchanted with Feuerbach, and his own philosophy began with a critique of his old mentor. Feuerbach had prided himself on having escaped from Hegel's idealism, proclaiming himself a materialist. But Marx criticized Feuerbach as a crypto-idealist, that is, an idealist who believed himself to be a materialist. Marx pointed out the idealistic implications of Feuerbach's account of the heavenly family. According to it, we could bring about changes in the *material* configurations of the earthly family by changing the

This is the heavenly family. It is the idealization of the earthly family. Here peace, happiness, and love reign.

This is the earthly family. The frustrated father comes home drunk from the tavern where he has spent much of the pittance that is his weekly wage. He expends his rage terrorizing his wife and children.

idea of the heavenly family. Marx, to the contrary, argued that all change must begin at the level of material configurations. In his "Theses on Feuerbach" he wrote, "Once the earthly family is discovered to be the secret of the holy family, the former must then itself be theoretically criticized and radically changed in practice."[16] Consistent with this attitude, Marx ended his tract against Feuerbach with the following famous line: "The philosophers have only *interpreted* the world in various ways: the point however is to *change* it."[17] Marx believed that once the family was revolutionized (i.e., once its hierarchy of power was restructured, along with the hierarchy of power in the society of which the family was the mirror image), then the idea of the holy family would simply disappear. Religion would not need to be abolished; it would simply dissolve. This disappearance would occur because, contrary to what Feuerbach believed, religion is not the *cause* of alienation; it is, rather, a *symptom* of alienation and sometimes even a remonstration against it. Marx's statement that religion is the opiate of the masses is often taken out of context and misunderstood. What he actually said is this: "*Religious* distress is at the same time the *expression* of real distress and the *protest* against real distress. Religion is the sigh of the oppressed creature, the heart of a heartless world, just as it is the spirit of an unspiritual situation. It is the *opium of the people*."[18] Here the word "opium" refers to the drug's power to dull pain.

The Disappearance of the Heavenly Family

Like Feuerbach and Hegel before him, Marx was interested in analyzing **alienation** (the process of the subject being split from its natural object). Although Marx discussed alienation in a number of its manifestations (alienation from nature, social alienation, and self-alienation), he was most philosophically original perhaps in his account of "the alienation of labor." Marx believed that it was the nature of human beings to be producers. We create of necessity, Marx thought. He preferred the designation *homo faber* (man the maker) to *homo sapiens* (man the knower) because our *knowing* is dependent on our *doing*. According to Marx, to a great extent we are what we make. We create our products, and our products re-create us. Our minds begin to take on the features of the objects we create. If we create in piecemeal, fragmented ways, we become piecemeal and fragmented ourselves. If we create useless objects, we ourselves become useless human beings.[19] Unfortunately, the processes of production are influenced by historical forces that are not always in our control. When these forces, usually socio-politico-economic ones, drive a wedge between individual humans and their products, the result is "alienated labor." This alienation happens if the work a person performs is not the expression of a natural creative need but is motivated by the necessity of fulfilling other needs, such as economic or avaricious ones. Further alienation occurs if the product that a worker creates is for the profit of another person and if the product enters into an economic system meant to fulfill desires of greed rather than true human needs. And above all, alienated labor comes about if the worker's product returns to the worker as a disabling

You Are What You Make

The Worker Confronts Himself as an Alien

alien force. (Extreme case: The worker produces cigarettes, which give that worker lung cancer.) It will come as no surprise to you to hear that, according to Marx, of all the historical socioeconomic systems, with the exception of slavery, capitalism is the one that promotes the most intense forms of alienated labor. Alienated labor, in turn, produces self-alienation—workers confront themselves as strangers and as strangers to the human race. (This is Marx's version of Hegel's divine identity crisis.) The goal of the young Karl Marx's communism was to create a society in which all alienation would be overcome and in which humans would recover their lost essence as *homo faber*.

In converting Hegel's idealism into a form of materialism (thereby "standing Hegel on his head"), Marx created a philosophy unique in history. We have run across material-ists before, of course; Democritus and Hobbes were such. But each of them, in claiming that ultimately everything resolves into matter, chose to define the key category in terms of physics. Their material

Marx Stands Hegel on His Head

reality was simply mass in motion. But Marx chose his key category not from physics but from economics. He did not try to explain the whole of reality but only human reality. Marx used an analytic model involving a *foundation* and a *superstructure*. According to him, the foundations of the social world are material ones: natural resources, means of production, and means of distribution as well as the human work relations involved at this level. Built on this foundation is a level composed of certain other social relations, such as legal and political arrangements, and above this is yet another level, comprising "higher culture," such social features as art, religion, morality, poetry, and philosophy. According to Marx,

> In the social production of their life, men enter into definite relations that are indispensable and independent of their will, relations of production which correspond to a definite stage of development of their material productive forces. The sum total of these relations of production constitutes the economic structure of society, the real foundation, on which rises a legal and political superstructure and to which correspond definite forms of social consciousness. The mode of production of material life conditions the social, political, and intellectual life process in general. It is not the consciousness of men that determines their social being, but, on the contrary, their social being that determines their consciousness.[20]

In this and similar passages, Marx made the relationship between the foundation and the superstructure seem simple. Higher culture, or what he called the "ideological" sphere, was merely a "reflex" or a "sublimate" of the socioeconomic foundation. Later he modified this, admitting that the ideational superstructure and the material foundation mutually influenced each other, though ultimately the foundation dominated. The ideational features of society never ceased to be **ideology,** that is, a system of unconscious propaganda for the foundational economic structure in which the contradictions in that structure are disguised or denied. Therefore, to find out the true status of the symbols in a society, you simply ask, "Who owns the foundation?" Find out who controls the natural resources, the means of production, and the means of distribution (the raw materials, the factories, the trucking lines, and the distribution outlets), and you will discover the secret behind the laws, the politics, the science, the art, the morality, and the religion of any society. As the old saw has it, "He who pays the piper calls the tune." Marx's version is, "The ruling ideas of each age have ever been the ideas of its ruling class."[21]

Portrait of Louis XIV
(after Hyacinthe Rigaud)

Laws Establishing
Aristocratic Privilege
(e.g., antipoaching laws)

Property Ownership
by the Nobility

Art as Ideology

Add to Marx's materialistic model of foundation and superstructure his dialectical interpretation of the foundation. The possession of a society's material wealth by a specific group of people automatically creates a class system—basically, the owning class (the "haves") and the class controlled by the owning class (the "have nots"). Because the interests of these two classes are always in opposition, these classes must be in perpetual conflict. In the first line of *The Communist Manifesto*, Marx announced, "The history of all hitherto existing society is the history of class struggle."[22] This conflict, which began in prehistoric times with the creation of tools, had, in Marx's time, reached what he took to be its most clearly delineated stage, and indeed, according to him, it had reached its final stage, a struggle between the owning class of capitalism (the bourgeoisie) and the

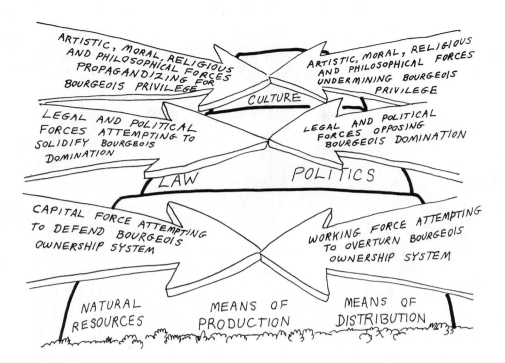

working class that capitalism exploited (the proletariat). Marx spent the bulk of his mature years describing the structure of capitalism in all its internal contradictions (memories of the Hegelian dialectic!). Here are some examples: capitalism's emphasis on competition leads to its own opposite, monopoly—and the consequent expulsion of some former members of the economic elite into the ranks of the paupers; capitalism's constant need for new sources of raw materials, cheap labor, and dumping grounds for its products leads to imperialistic wars among capitalist states; capitalism's need to solve the problem of unemployment, achieved by pumping more money into the system, thereby creates inflation, and its need to solve the problem of inflation is achieved by increasing unemployment. Marx thought that these internal contradictions of capitalism, along with the massive unrest that would be caused by the ever-growing misery of its dispossessed, would necessarily bring on a simultaneous internal collapse of capitalism and a revolt of the working class that would produce Marx's notorious "dictatorship of the proletariat," whose function it would be to ensure that the victorious proletariat did not reconstitute the

As per Karl Marx's Prediction, Capitalism Collapses in the Middle Because of Its Own Excesses

institutions of classism. (After all, these conquering street fighters themselves grew up in conditions of alienation and hence in **"false consciousness."**)[23] According to Marx, once this dictatorship has performed its essential service, it will simply step down from power—"wither," as Marx worded it. Marx's critics are quick to point out that he did not deal with the question of the abuse of power in his socialistic utopia. Perhaps this neglect was due to the philosophical optimism he inherited from Hegel. (Unfortunately, as the Stalinist period in the Soviet Union proved, Lord Acton's pessimism was more realistic than Marx's optimism. It was Acton who said, "Power corrupts, and absolute power corrupts absolutely.") This relinquishing of control by the dictatorship, predicted

Marx, will usher in a classless society, which will end the dialectic of conflict and therefore end history as we know it. (Marx defined history, after all, as "the history of class conflict.") Humans will live under optimum conditions for the first time since aboriginal times. Private ownership will be abolished, as well as the division of labor (i.e., the type of specialization in which a person is defined throughout life by the practice of one speciality). We will all be artists and philosophers, and we will "hunt in the morning, fish in the afternoon, rear cattle in the evening, criticize [poetry] after dinner, just as [we] have in mind, without ever becoming hunter, fisherman, shepherd or critic."[24] Elsewhere Marx's picture of the ideal world includes socializing in the pub, going to dances, going to the theater, buying books, loving, theorizing, painting, singing, and even fencing. (Fencing?) Sometimes Marx's

The New Golden Age?

true communist society seems more like a bourgeois pastoral than a working-class paradise; and sometimes, as was the case with Kierkegaard's "new human being," Marx's "new human being" seems to be a very "old human being," though one not from the historical past but from the mythical Golden Age.

Nietzsche

Friedrich Nietzsche (1844–1900) was the third post-Kantian who responded to the crisis of his time not by demanding a new "critique of reason" but by calling for a new kind of human existence. (The other two post-Kantians, as we have seen, were Kierkegaard and Marx.) Nietzsche was a solitary thinker who liked Alpine trails more than the halls of academia (which he abandoned in his mid-thirties). He spent most of his life using his authorship in an attempt to triumph over

Friedrich Nietzsche

the powerful influences on his childhood: Lutheranism, German nationalism, and the domination of his forceful mother, granny, aunts, and sister. (His attempts were more successful in some of these endeavors than in others.) The material result of his efforts was an unprecedented stream of the most eccentric books ever to have been introduced into the history of philosophy, including such titles as *The Birth of Tragedy, Beyond Good and Evil, The Genealogy of Morals, Thus Spake Zarathustra,* and his outrageous intellectual autobiography, pretentiously titled *Ecce Homo* ("behold the man"—the phrase with which Pilate introduced Jesus to the masses), with such chapter headings as "Why I Am So Wise," "Why I Am So Clever," and "Why I Write Such Good Books." Nietzsche's short, prolific authorship ended in 1888 with the onset of insanity (probably syphilis-induced).

Nietzsche's epistemological theory constituted a radical return to the sophistic period. His theory is usually called perspectivism, and it derived from Nietzsche's early training in **philology.** Philologists, those students of ancient languages, knew that what were called the Bible, the Vedas, the Upanishads, and the *Iliad* were not direct translations of single existing documents; rather, they were compilations of fragments of conflicting evidence derived from a dizzying number of sources. The dream of the philologists was to find *the original texts of each of the great scriptures in history.* Nietzsche's conclusion as a philologist was that *there is no original text.* Each of these books is simply the result

There is no original text.

of a *decision* to let a particular interpretation represent an end product, even though, in fact, that "end product" is merely an emblem of a relationship that exists among a number of fragmentary documents, reports, historical studies, and items of gossip. This theory is now called **"differential repetition."**[25]

Nietzsche translated his philological insight into an ontological and epistemological doctrine. Just as in philology there is no original text, so in reality and knowledge there is no "pure being" nor "original datum." There are no gods, no Platonic Forms, no substances, no "things-in-themselves," or even any "things." There exist only flux and chaos, upon which we must impose our will. Therefore, said Nietzsche, there can be no such thing as *knowing* in the Platonic sense. All "knowing" is inventing, and all inventing is lying. But then, there are lies, and there are *lies*. Inauthentic lying is *self-deception*. According to Nietzsche, self-deceivers are people who "lie traditionally," that is, who lie in terms of established traditions, not realizing that they are merely perpetuating lies that were forced upon them early in their lives.

Nietzsche's recommendation in the face of what appears to be a condemnation to a life of lying is to "lie creatively," which is to say to invent, or "know," creatively. To lie creatively is to express what Nietzsche, borrowing and subverting a Schopenhauerian idea, calls "will to power." To express will to power is to force reality to submit to one's own creative might. Nietzsche also calls will to power "the urge to freedom." All our biological instincts expend themselves as manifestations of

Forcing Reality to Bend to One's Will

this desire for freedom, even though in most cases these instincts have been constrained by the forces of normalization (themselves other manifestations of will to power, or manifestations of the will to power of others).

Not only our biology but also our thought and language are manifestations of will to power. But at the same time, language and thought are the main vehicles of self-deception. According to Nietzsche's radical *nominalism* (reminiscent of William of Ockham's nominalism), language functions precisely by lying, that is, by denying real dissimilarities and inventing fictitious similarities. For example, the only way we can classify as "leaves" all the forms of foliage that sprout from trees and shrubs is by ignoring and, indeed, *suppressing* the fact that no two of these entities are alike and by asserting an identity among them that does not, in fact, exist. So language can be and usually is a medium of **reification** and petrification of being. It produces errors that "tyrannize over us as a condition of life."[26] But the fact that language *must* lie is also the source of the creative possibilities inherent in language. Nietzsche rejected the traditional view of language, namely, that its poetic function is peripheral to its literal function. He felt that the so-called literal function was merely a subclass of its poetic nature. Language, according to Nietzsche, is "a mobile army of metaphors, metonyms and anthropomorphisms."[27] (Reminder: A metaphor is a form of speech in which one image replaces another, importing the new meaning into the old context, such as "Achilles is a lion in battle." A metonym is a form of speech in which meaning is displaced from one image onto an adjacent image that now bears the weight of both images, such as "He likes the bottle too much." Anthropomorphisms—the projections of human traits onto the nonhuman world, such as "The rose is striving to reach the light"— are themselves usually unconscious metaphors or metonyms.) Whole chains of metaphors and metonyms can create a poetic rendition of reality. Nietzsche recognized these chains of reasoning as felicitous expressions of will to power.

In fact, as Nietzsche understood full well, his own term "will to power" was the product of such a metaphorical/metonymical chain of reasoning, as were his other key terms, such as "the overman," "eternal recurrence," and "the death of God." It follows, then, that a claim of Nietzsche's—such as "life simply *is* will to power"[28]— constitutes not a philosophical insight into the ultimate nature

**Language: A Mobile Army of Metaphors,
Metonyms, and Anthropomorphisms**

of life but simply another poetic interpretation of life. (When confronted with this charge, Nietzsche responded, "Well, so much the better!")[29]

If it is true that there are only interpretations, are all interpretations equally valid? Despite his relativism, Nietzsche did not think so. Only those lies that affirm life are truly *noble* lies for him. All other lies are nihilistic and on the side of death. This belief is why Nietzsche says will to power must be full of laughter, dancing, and affirmation and why we must condemn Platonism ("that fear of time") and Christianity ("Platonism for the people"),[30] which in

Der Übermensch?

longing for another world deny reality as it is (i.e., they refuse to recognize reality as chaos and flux that must be molded in the image of each will), and thereby long not for being but for nothingness and death. (One detects Hegel in all this, somehow.) Nietzsche embodied his doctrine in a *goal* that he called "the overman" (*der Übermensch*). The overman represents the triumph of the will to power. Besides teaching laughter and dance, the overman teaches the death of God and eternal recurrence. Of course, there can be no single correct answer to the question, What did Nietzsche mean by "the death of God"? (any more than there can be to the question concerning what Prufrock meant when he said, "I should have been a pair of ragged claws scuttling across the floors of silent seas"),[31] but surely Nietzsche at least meant to announce the end of traditional forms of authority: historical, political, religious, moral, and textual. (For an interesting reading of Nietzsche's phrase "God is dead," try replacing the term "God" with the term "Santa Claus." Why is the claim "Santa Claus does not exist" less tragic than the claim "Santa Claus is dead"?)

What is true of the death of God is true of eternal recurrence. There has been a great river of literature trying to interpret this enigmatic doctrine. But whatever else it means, it was certainly

The Death of Santa Claus

meant to assert Nietzsche's allegiance to reality as it is. Nietzsche advocated what he took to be the opposite of the Schopenhauerian ideal of pessimism, namely,

> the ideal of the most high-spirited, alive and world-affirming human being who has not only come to terms and learned to get along with whatever was and is, but who wants to have *what was and is* repeated into all eternity.[32]

> Let us think this thought in its most terrible form: existence as it is, without meaning or aim, yet recurring inevitably without any finale of nothingness: the eternal recurrence.[33]

It is easy enough to criticize Nietzsche for his inconsistency and faulty logic. (How can we will life as it really is if there is no such thing as life or will—only interpretations of interpretations? If everything is a lie, then isn't the claim that everything is a lie also a lie?) But this criticism misses Nietzsche's point. He meant to teach neither consistency nor logic but a radically new kind of subversive subjectivity that would undermine all previous forms of thought and being. However, there is a price to pay for such subversiveness. One will have disciples that one might not have hoped for. And, indeed, many diverse groups have claimed the Nietzschean heritage, including Nazis, psychoanalysts, existentialists, and more recently, a group called **"deconstructionists,"** whom some

The Thought in Its Most Terrible Form:
The Eternal Recurrence

people see as the new liberators and others as the new nihilists.

Utilitarianism

Let us leave the extravagant frenzy of Nietzsche's (ultimately) deranged mind and turn to the orderly and complacent minds of his contemporaries in the British Isles (whom Nietzsche dismissed as "blockheads"). Despite Hume's facetious suggestion that philosophy be abandoned altogether, a philosophical empiricism was alive and thriving in mid-nineteenth-century Britain. It derived from a

**Nietzsche's View of a Meeting
of the Utilitarian Society**

side of Hume's thought that was not explored in this book and that is difficult to square with his radical skepticism. Despite his denial of the possibility of true knowledge concerning causality, self, and the external world, Hume held that what is commonly taken as "knowledge" in these areas is really a set of reasonable beliefs that are well founded because they are based on experience. The tradition deriving from this more practical side of Hume was inherited by a group of philosophers known as the utilitarians, headed by Jeremy Bentham (1748–1832) and his wayward follower John Stuart Mill (1808–1873), who were interested in applying the principles of empiricism to moral and social issues.

Bentham

The eccentric Jeremy Bentham (whose fully dressed, mummified body still presides over the trustees' meetings at University College in London because his fortune was left to them with the provision that he be able to attend all their meetings) concluded that all theory, including moral and political theory, must be grounded in

John Stuart Mill with the Mummified Head of Jeremy Bentham

empirical fact. He claimed that in the case of the human sciences this fact would have to be the primacy of the pleasure principle. That is to say, all analyses of human behavior and all recommendations for change in behavior would have to begin with the fact that humans are motivated by the desire for pleasure and by the aversion to pain. In this way of thinking, of course, he was not unlike Hobbes, though Bentham's conclusions were much more liberal.

The doctrine that only pleasure can (or should) have value is known as hedonism, and we have seen this philosophy before, not just with Hobbes but also with Epicurus and Callicles. Bentham's innovation was the claim that hedonism doesn't have to be egoistic; it can be social. That is, one can (and should) be motivated to act in the name of the pleasure of others as well as for one's own pleasure. His social hedonism is reflected in his most famous maxim, "It is the greatest happiness of the greatest number that is the measure of right and wrong"[34] (where "happiness" is defined in terms of pleasure). This principle, in association with the "one person, one vote" principle (i.e., each person gets to define his or her version of happiness), gave Bentham's utilitarianism a distinctly democratic cast. Furthermore, it meant that the moral worth of an act depended exclusively on the amount of happiness or unhappiness that the act promoted. This view is sometimes called consequentialism (because it is the consequence of the act that determines the act's value), and it is the opposite extreme from Kant's moral perspective, according to which the moral worth of an action depended on the *intention* of the agent, on whether the act was motivated by a desire to do one's duty, and on whether the act was consistent with the laws of rationality.

Kant and Bentham between them have provided us with the two key moral models used in Western ethics. Unfortunately, the conclusions drawn from these two models sometimes contradict each other, and when applied to specific cases, sometimes the utilitarian view seems much more reasonable than the Kantian one; yet in other cases, the Kantian view seems better than the utilitarian one. For instance, the Kantian ethic tells us we are duty-bound never to lie. But what if an armed man, frothing at the mouth, asks us where Bill Jones is? Do we have a duty to tell the truth, knowing full well that doing so may lead to Jones's death? Here Bentham's principle seems better: The act of lying is not immoral if by lying we can prevent grievous harm. But consider another famous example: What if you pay a visit to a friend in the hospital, and a utilitarian physician decides to sacrifice you and distribute your vital organs to five patients who will die if they do not receive immediate organ implants? The doctor is acting on the "greatest amount of happiness for the greatest number of people" principle and maybe even on the "one person, one vote" principle. But most of us probably feel that Kant would be right to call this sacrifice immoral. Many critics believe that the principle of utility ("greatest amount of happiness for the greatest number of people") is bound to conflict with what they take to be individual rights that protect the individual from the tyranny of the majority.

As we saw, Bentham believed that happiness could be defined in terms of pleasure, and he held that the study of pleasure could be refined to a science. Pleasures could be experienced in terms of seven categories. These categories could be articulated in terms of a set of seven questions:

1. Intensity (How intense is the pleasure?)
2. Duration (How long does the pleasure last?)
3. Certainty (How sure is the pleasure?)
4. Proximity (How soon will the pleasure be experienced?)

On a scale of one to ten, this is about a ten in all categories.

5. Fecundity (How many more pleasures will follow in the train of this pleasure?)
6. Purity (How free from pain is the pleasure?)
7. Extent (How many people will experience the pleasure? [It is this category that makes Bentham's hedonism a social one.])

When considering any act whatsoever, one should analyze it in terms of the pleasure it will produce in these seven categories, which Bentham called "the calculus of felicity."

He thought that after some practice one could learn to apply this calculus rather intuitively, but until that point, one should actually work out the figures as often as possible. (Indeed, the story goes that Bentham himself used the calculus of felicity in choosing between remaining a bachelor or marrying. [He married!]) Try out the calculus on a decision such as that between studying for a chemistry midterm exam and going to the beach with some friends. Obviously,

Beach Guilt

the beach party will be strong in some categories (1, 3, 4, 6), and weaker in others (2, 5). Studying will be weak in most categories but strong in a few (2 and 5, and 7 also, if other persons have an interest in your succeeding in college). Are the assets of studying strong enough to overcome its deficits in the face of the fun enticing you to the beach? (Of course, the guilt you would experience at the beach has to be taken into consideration too.) According to the "one person, one vote" principle, each person must decide for himself or herself.

Mill

John Stuart Mill, who was raised in strict adherence to Benthamite tenets, developed certain qualms about those views after suffering a nervous breakdown at twenty-one years of age. Among other concerns, he was worried about the beach/chemistry—type decision, or perhaps more about the six-pack of beer/Shakespearean sonnet—type decision. If the average person were given the choice between reading a Renaissance poem and guzzling beer while watching the 49ers on the tube . . . well, you can't force people to read poetry or watch football if they don't think it's fun. But in a democracy, under the "one person, one vote" principle, what if you gave people a choice of making public expenditures for the teaching of Shakespeare in universities or receiving a tax rebate? Mill feared the worst and thought it bode ill for the advancement of civilization. If we let ourselves be guided by the calculus of felicity, perhaps the pig

Go Niners!

would prove to be right; wallowing in the mud might rank higher than studying philosophy.

Mill solved the problem by saying that only those who are competent judges of both of two competing experiences can "vote" for one or the other of them. (You get a vote only if you know beer *and* Shakespeare or have wallowed *and* read Plato.) Mill's conclusion was that "some kinds of pleasure are more desirable and more valuable than others."[35] We assume that he had in mind the reading of Shakespeare and Plato.

Mill claimed that in abandoning the calculus of felicity, he was simply defining pleasure in qualitative and not merely quantitative terms. His critics charge, however, that in asserting that some pleasures are better than others, Mill had abandoned the "principle of utility" (i.e., the pleasure principle) altogether. They have also charged him with elitism and with undermining the democratic foundation that Bentham had given utilitarianism. For what it's worth, Mill's doctrine did leave us some questions to ponder: In a democracy, must the "one person, one vote" principle apply at all levels of decision making? And if so, are democracy and higher culture compatible?

In his most famous book, *On Liberty,* Mill outlined his doctrine of *laissez-faire* (hands off!). There are certain spheres in which the government has no business interfering in the lives of its citizens. Mill's principle of liberty states, "the only purpose for which power can be rightfully exercised over any member of a civilized community, against his will, is to prevent harm to others."[36] In other words, Mill was against state paternalism, the condition in which the state tells a citizen what to do for his or her own good. For Mill, there could be no such thing as a victimless crime. If a man decides to ride his Harley without a helmet, get bombed on cheap wine or drugs in the privacy of his own house, visit a prostitute, or even *become* a prostitute, that's his own business and not the state's. (This is Mill's attempt to provide the individual rights that many critics claim are missing in utilitarianism.)

For moral reasons, we should perhaps try to persuade this man of the error of his ways, but we have no business passing laws to

**A Drunken Male Prostitute without a Helmet
Riding His Motorcycle in the Privacy of His Own Home**

protect him from himself as long as he is doing no harm to others. (Contemporary commentators point out that it was probably easier to draw this distinction in Mill's day than in our own. In today's world, very few acts are purely private. If you go to a hospital because of a motorcycle injury, my tax dollars may well have to nurse you back to health.)

Mill also believed in the hands-off doctrine in the marketplace. He said, "Laissez-faire . . . should be the general practice: every departure from it, unless required by some great good, is a certain evil."[37] He thought that under most conditions, the government should not interfere in the exchange of commodities, that the law of supply and demand should determine the nature and quality of production.

Even though Mill was considered a liberal in his own day, in many ways his views sound to us more like those that today we associate with political conservatism. But the proof that he was not a pure supply-side theorist can be seen in the restrictions he placed on the laissez-faire doctrine. He excluded from the application of his hands-off policy any products that the buyer is not competent to judge and any product "in the quality of which society has much at stake." Mill said,

> There are . . . things of the worth of which the demand of the market is by no means a test, things . . . the want of which is least felt where the need is greatest. This is peculiarly true of those things which are chiefly useful as tending to raise the character of human beings. The uncultivated cannot be competent judges of cultivation.[38]

"The Uncultivated Cannot Be Competent Judges of Cultivation"

Key Philosophical Ideas in Chapter 6

G.W.F. Hegel:

- Hegel's <u>goal</u>: To <u>equate Reason with divinity</u>, and establish <u>the history of human civilization as the advance of Reason through time as a dialectical process</u> of confrontations of opposing ideas that are resolved in compromises in which <u>the best is always brought forward</u>. (Optimism about the human condition.)

- Overview: Hegel's grandiose systematic metaphysical speculation exactly what Kant's *Critique of Pure Reason* was meant to prevent.
- <u>Key Hegelian concepts</u>:
  - <u>Absolute Idealism</u>: The history of the world as the history of ideas.
  - <u>The Dialectic</u>: thesis—antithesis—synthesis
    - Applications of the Dialectic:
      - metaphysical example: the history of the world begins with God's dialectical thought of <u>Being and Nothingness synthesizes into</u> <u>Becoming</u>
      - historical example: <u>masters vs. slaves</u>; lords and serfs; <u>Napoleon as the end of history in a new, homogeneous Universal State</u>, where each recognizes him—or herself—in the other
      - <u>The "cunning" of Reason</u>.
      - Why <u>the "owl of Minerva" flies only at dusk</u>.
- Schopenhauer's criticism of Hegel: A "windbag" who glorifies his paymaster the oppressive Prussian state.

Arthur Schopenhauer:

- Schopenhauer's <u>goals</u>: <u>a return to Kant</u> (or a perversion of Kant; a refutation of Hegel's optimism).
- Key Schopenhauerian concepts:
  - "<u>The world as idea</u>": <u>We do not directly know ultimate reality</u>; we only know the world as presented to the senses passing through the categories of time, space, and causality (Kant).
  - "<u>The world as will</u>": hints found in the world as idea that <u>ultimate reality</u> (the noumenal world) is an <u>uncaring, seething, irrational force of reproductive and destructive powers that end only in death</u>.
- Human **civilization** (laws, customs, morals, religions, science, art, traditional philosophy) is <u>only sublimations of the Will</u>.
- Schopenhauer's philosophy is <u>an escape from the Will</u>.

Søren Kierkegaard:

  - Kierkegaard's <u>goal</u>: To attack the shallow, complacent, convenient, wishy-washy Christendom of his day by presenting <u>a harsh, demanding, imposing picture of what a true commitment to a religious life</u> would require

- Key Kierkegaardian ideas:
  - "Existence" is not a concept; it cannot be the object of thought—it can only be lived.
  - One's existence must be determined by choice and decision.
  - Thought and language are based on abstraction; existence is never abstract, always concrete.
  - Distinction between objective truths (science, math, history, etc.) and subjective truths (truths that matter to one's subjectivity).
  - Kierkegaard's philosophy of religion: "the category of the absurd," the "Knight of Faith."
- Kierkegaard seen today as the father of existentialism by virtue of his emphasis on decisiveness, freedom, responsibility, and self-creation

Karl Marx:

- Marx's goal: Not to philosophize about the world but to change it.
- Key Marxian ideas:
  - The "Young Hegelians" (aka "the Hegelian Left") stand Hegel on his head, using Hegelian methods to change "dialectical idealism" to "dialectical materialism."
  - Ludwig Feuerbach's "materialism" shown to be crypto-idealism.
  - Young Marx sees the human as homo faber (man the maker), who under industrialism and capitalism, is alienated from his essence, made an object rather than a subject.
  - Marx's analysis of society into foundation and superstructure.
  - Whoever controls the foundation controls society (the ruling class).
  - The superstructure as "ideologically" motivated.
  - Dialectical materialism: bourgeoisie (thesis) vs. proletariat (synthesis).
  - The history of . . . society is the history of class struggle; the classless society as the end of history.
  - The Marxian utopia at the end of history.

Friedrich Nietzsche:

- Nietzsche's goal: to teach a radically new form of subversive subjectivity that would undermine all previous forms of thought and language.
- Key Nietzschean ideas:
  - Nietzsche's "differential repetition" (no original texts) as philologist converted into an epistemological view (no foundation of knowledge)

and an ontological view (no ultimate reality—only appearances of appearances exist).

- The "Will to Power": all activity is Will to Power, whether physical action or linguistic action (language as lying: a "mobile army of metaphors, metonyms and anthropomorphisms: radical nominalism).
- The overman: the triumph of the Will to Power.
- The death of God: the new human being is unmoored from all traditional forms of authority, therefore from all forms of mental and emotional tyranny.
- The eternal return: joyfully choosing one's fate; loving everything that is just as it is; living one's life in such a way that one could will to live every minute of it again.

Utilitarianism: Bentham and Mill:

- Goal: to place ethics on a firm, objective, empirical foundation.

Jeremy Bentham:

- Key Benthamite ideas:
  - Human happiness will be the goal of ethics: "the greatest amount of happiness for the greatest number of people (where "happiness" is defined in terms of pleasure": Hedonism).
  - The "one person, one vote" principle: each individual has the right to determine what happiness is for him- or herself.
  - The "calculus of felicity" and its seven categories.

John Stuart Mill:

- Key Millian ideas:
  - The attempt to make Bentham's utilitarianism more sophisticated by replacing the calculus of felicity with qualitative analyses of pleasure (some pleasure is better than other pleasure)
  - Qualifying the "one person, one vote" principle by allowing only those to judge between two pleasures who have competence with both forms of pleasure (e.g., drinking beer and reading poetry)
  - Laissez-faire:
    - Laissez-faire in private lives: Government intervention in private life allowed only to prevent harm to others
    - Laissez-faire in the market place: should be the general practice; government may intervene only in certain exceptional cases, when the good of the general public is at stake

Topics for Consideration

1. Hegel's philosophy is teleological. History is revealed as progressive, directed toward a goal. Explain how progress takes place in his system, and why, according to Hegel, that advancement may appear to us to be backsliding.

2. Use Hegel's master/slave dynamics to explain relations in traditional society between husband and wife, parent and child, teacher and student, and employer and employee.

3. Discuss those features of Schopenhauer's philosophy that are in agreement with Kant, and those that are in disagreement.

4. Discuss Kierkegaard's notion of subjective truths, and say why they can be communicated only indirectly.

5. Compare and contrast Hegel, Feuerbach, and Marx on the idea of alienation.

6. Pick an example of a work of art that you think would support Marx's claim that most art is ideological.

7. Explain what you think Nietzsche means when he recommends that we lie creatively.

8. It has been said that Kierkegaard, Marx, and Nietzsche did not demand a new critique of reason; rather, they demanded a whole new kind of human. Explain what it means to say this.

9. After reviewing Kant's discussion of the categorical imperative (pp. 223–28), contrast Kant's moral idea with Bentham's greatest happiness principle. What, would you say, is the strongest and weakest point of each moral system?

10. Do you think Mill contradicts himself when he says both that pleasure is the ultimate criterion of value and that some pleasures are more valuable than others? Defend or attack his view.

Notes

1. See, for example, Karl Popper, *The Open Society and Its Enemies*, vol. 2, *Hegel and Marx* (Princeton, N.J.: Princeton University Press, 1966).

2. See, for example, Alexandre Kojève, *Introduction to the Reading of Hegel: Lectures on the "Phenomenology of Spirit,"* trans. James H. Nichols Jr. (Ithaca, N.Y., and London: Cornell University Press, 1993).

3. G. W. F. Hegel, *The Phenomenology of Mind*, trans. J. B. Baillie (New York and Evanston, Ill.: Harper Torchbooks, 1967), 457. The newer translation is

Phenomenology of Spirit, trans. A. V. Miller (Oxford and New York: Oxford University Press, 1977). But I "grew up" on Baillie's translation and prefer it.

4. G. W. F. Hegel, *The Philosophy of Right*, in *Hegel: The Essential Writings*, ed. Frederick G. Weiss (New York: Harper Torchbooks, 1974), 256. In Roman mythology Minerva is the goddess of wisdom, and the owl symbolizes her.

5. Quoted by Popper, 32–33.

6. Arthur Schopenhauer, *The World as Will and Idea*, vol. 1, trans. R. B. Haldane and J. Kemp (London: Routledge and Kegan Paul, 1964), 3.

7. Immanuel Kant, *Critique of Practical Reason*, trans. Lewis White Beck (Chicago: University of Chicago Press, 1949), 258.

8. Schopenhauer, 4–5.

9. Sigmund Freud, *Beyond the Pleasure Principle*, trans. James Stachey (New York: Bantam Books, 1963), 88.

10. Søren Kierkegaard, *Either/Or*, vol. 1, trans. David F. Swenson and Lillian Marvin Swenson (Garden City, N.Y.: Doubleday Anchor, 1969), 37.

11. The original German reads "*Was vernünftig ist, das ist wirklich; und was wirklich ist, das ist vernünftig*" (*Grundlinien der Philosophie des Rechts*, in *Sämtliche Werke*, vol. 7, ed. Hermann Glockner [Stuttgart: Fr. Frommanns Verlag, 1952], 33). My translation is the traditional one, but I should add that Hegelian scholars now tend to prefer: "What is rational is actual and what is actual is rational," because Hegel used *Wirklichkeit* as a technical term meaning a synthesis of essence and existence. This scholarly translation avoids the mistaken impression that Hegel's view is that whatever is, is right—which would be a tacit approval of all sorts of vicious political regimes. See, for example, G. W. F. Hegel, *Philosophy of Right*, trans. T. M. Knox (Oxford: Clarendon Press, 1949), 10.

12. Søren Kierkegaard, *Concluding Unscientific Postscript*, trans. Walter Lowrie and David F. Swenson (Princeton, N.J.: Princeton University Press, 1960), 315, 387.

13. Ibid., 81.

14. Søren Kierkegaard, *Fear and Trembling*, in *Fear and Trembling and The Sickness unto Death*, trans. Walter Lowrie (Garden City, N.Y.: Doubleday Anchor, 1954), 31.

15. Ibid.

16. Karl Marx, "Theses on Feuerbach," in *Marx and Engels: Basic Writings on Politics and Philosophy*, ed. Lewis S. Feuer (Garden City, N.Y.: Doubleday Anchor, 1989), 244.

17. Ibid.

18. Karl Marx, *Toward the Critique of Hegel's "Philosophy of Right,"* in Feuer, 263.

19. Marx writes: "the production of too many useful things results in too many useless people" (Karl Marx, *Economic and Philosophical Manuscripts*, in *Marx's Concept of Man*, ed. Erich Fromm [New York: Ungar, 1969], 145).

20. Karl Marx, *A Contribution to the Critique of Political Economy*, in Feuer, 43.

21. Karl Marx and Friedrich Engels, "Manifesto of the Communist Party," in Feuer, 26.

22. Ibid., 7.

23. Friedrich Engels, "Letters on Historical Materialism: Engels to Franz Mehring," in Feuer, 408.

24. Karl Marx and Friedrich Engels, *The German Ideology*, in Feuer, 254.

25. See Stephen G. Nichols, "Writing the New Middle Ages," *PMLA* 120.2 (March 2005): 422–441.

26.	Friedrich Nietzsche, *The Will to Power*, trans. Walter Kaufmann and R. J. Hollingdale (New York: Vintage Books, 1968), 535.

27.	Friedrich Nietzsche, "On Truth and Lie in an Extra-Moral Sense," in *The Portable Nietzsche*, ed. and trans. Walter Kaufmann (New York: Viking Press, 1954), 46–47.

28.	Friedrich Nietzsche, *Beyond Good and Evil*, trans. Walter Kaufmann (New York: Vintage Books, 1966), 203.

29.	Ibid., 30–31.

30.	Ibid., 3.

31.	From the poem, "The Love Song of J. Alfred Prufrock," by T. S. Eliot (1917), whose narrator is a Nietzschean anti-hero, an elderly man filled with regret over acts he did not perform. In *The Waste Land and Other Poems* (New York and London: Harcourt, Brace, Jovanovich, 1962), 6.

32.	Ibid., 68.

33.	Nietzsche, *The Will to Power*, 35.

34.	Jeremy Bentham, "A Fragment on Government," in *A Bentham Reader*, ed. Mary Peter Mack (New York: Pegasus, 1969), 45.

35.	John Stuart Mill, *Utilitarianism* (New York: E. P. Dutton, 1951), 10.

36.	John Stuart Mill, *On Liberty*, in *Utilitarianism, Liberty, and Representative Government* (New York: E. P. Dutton, 1950), 95–96.

37.	John Stuart Mill, *Principles of Political Economy*, ed. J. M. Robson, in *Collected Works: John Stuart Mill*, vol. 3 (Toronto: University of Toronto Press/Routledge and Kegan Paul, 1965), 945.

38.	Ibid., 947.

7

The Phenomenological Tradition and Its Aftermath

The Late Nineteenth and Twentieth Centuries, into the Twenty-First

Husserl

In the nineteenth century, a number of European thinkers had continued to work well within the Continental philosophical tradition inaugurated by Descartes. Primary among them was Edmund Husserl (1859–1938), the founder of a philosophy that he called "phenomenology" (from the Greek *phainómenon*, meaning "appearance"—hence, the study of appearances). Like Descartes, Husserl placed consciousness at the center of all philosophizing, but Husserl had learned from Kant that a theory of consciousness must be as concerned with the *form* of consciousness as with its *content* (Descartes had failed to realize this), so he developed a method that would demonstrate both the structure and the content of the mind. This method would be purely *descriptive* and not *theoretical*. That is, it would describe the way the world actually reveals itself to consciousness without the aid of any theoretical constructs from either philosophy, science, or social tradition. This method laid bare the world of what Husserl called "the natural standpoint," which is pretty much the everyday world as experienced unencumbered by the claims of theoretical and historical overlays. Writing about the natural standpoint in *Ideas: General Introduction to Pure Phenomenology*, Husserl said,

> I am aware of a world, spread out in space endlessly, and in time becoming and become, without end. I am aware of it, that means, first

301

of all, I discover it immediately, intuitively, I experience it. Through sight, touch, hearing, etc., . . . corporeal things . . . are for me simply there, . . . "present," whether or not I pay them special attention.[1]

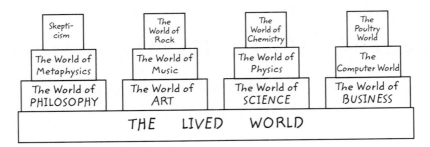

Skepti-cism		The World of Rock		The World of Chemistry		The Poultry World	
The World of Metaphysics		The World of Music		The World of Physics		The Computer World	
The World of PHILOSOPHY		The World of ART		The World of SCIENCE		The World of BUSINESS	
THE LIVED WORLD							

Worlds upon Worlds

This world of the natural standpoint is the absolute beginning of all philosophy and science. It is the world as actually *lived*. Other worlds can be built upon the *lived world* but can never replace it or undermine it. For human beings ultimately there is only the lived world of the natural standpoint. But Husserl wanted to "get behind" the content of the natural standpoint to reveal its structure. To do so, he employed a method like Descartes's radical doubt, a method that Husserl called "phenomenological reduction" (or *epochê*, a Greek word meaning "suspension of belief," as we saw in our study of ancient Skepticism in chapter 3.). This method brackets any experience whatsoever and describes it while suspending all presuppositions and assumptions normally made about that experience. Bracketing the experience of looking at a coffee cup, for instance, requires suspending the belief that the cup is for holding coffee and that its handle is for grasping. Bracketing reveals the way the cup presents itself to consciousness as a number of possible structures. (I can't see the front

Prof. Edmund Husserl Performs an *Epochê* on a Coffee Cup

and the back at the same time, nor the top and the bottom, nor see more than one of its possible presentations at any given moment.)

If we apply the *epoché* to the more philosophically significant example of the experience of time, we must suspend all belief in clocks, train schedules, and calendars. Then we will discover that *lived time* is always experienced as an eternal *now*, which is tempered by a memory of earlier nows (the thenness of the past) and is always rushing into the semi-experienceable but ultimately nonexperienceable thenness of the future. Phenomenologically speaking, the time is always "now." To do anything is to do something now. You can never act *then*.

Similarly, a phenomenological reduction of the experience of space reveals the difference between *lived space* and *mapped space*. Lived space is always experienced in terms of a here-there dichotomy, in which I am always here and everything else is always at different intensities of thereness. (Jean-Paul Sartre, Husserl's errant disciple, would later draw very pessimistic conclusions from this discovery.) So the here-now experience is the ground zero of the experience of space and time. It is somehow the locus of the self.

One of Husserl's main insights (actually derived from the work of his teacher Franz von Brentano), and one that was to be incorporated into both the later phenomenological tradition and, in some cases, the analytic tradition,[2] was his treatment of the *intentionality of* all consciousness (i.e., its referentiality). The Husserlian motto here

From the Natural
Standpoint

From the Standpoint
of the *Epoché*

is "All consciousness is consciousness of . . ." (This motto means
there is no such thing as self-enclosed thought; one thinks *about*
something. You can't be just *aware*—you have to be aware of something, and afraid *of* something, and concerned *about* something.
There are no intransitive mental states, not even Kierkegaard's
"dread"—the fear of absolutely nothing. It is still the fear of nothing.) It is this intentionality (or referentiality) that distinguishes
consciousness from everything else in the universe.

Husserl claimed that the phenomenological suspension could
be performed on the *object* of intentionality (e.g., the coffee cup)
or on the act of consciousness itself. Therefore, he believed it was
possible to step back from normal consciousness into a kind of pure
consciousness, a transcendental ego, a self-behind-the-self, which,
like Descartes's "I am" (but more deeply real), would be the starting
point of all knowledge. Husserl's ideas get very complex here, and
few of his disciples have chosen to follow him into these ethereal
regions.

Today, Husserl is most admired for his *method.* This method has had a number of outstanding adherents, including Martin Heidegger, Maurice Merleau-Ponty, and Sartre. Shortly, we will review the philosophies of Heidegger and Sartre, Husserl's best-known, if most wayward, disciples, and we will let them represent the outcome of the evolution of phenomenology into existentialism.

The Self behind the Self (But Is There a Self behind the Self behind the Self?)

Heidegger

Martin Heidegger (1889–1976) was an early colleague of Husserl and a student of his phenomenology, but it soon became clear that his philosophical concerns were quite different from Husserl's. The latter's phenomenological reduction claimed to discover certain essential features of objects like coffee cups and matchboxes and to provide an account of our knowledge of these kinds of beings. Heidegger, however, was interested in applying the method to a deeper question—that of Being itself. He was not concerned with questions about the nature of individual "beings" (questions that he called "ontic" questions); rather, he was interested in the Being of beings—the fact that individual beings are at all (what he called "ontological" concerns). We saw that Gottfried Leibniz in the seventeenth century had asked the primary ontological question, "Why is there something rather than nothing?" but he had asked it only as a theological query in order to prove the existence of God. Furthermore, by Leibniz's time it was already too late to ask the question correctly, according to Heidegger, for Being had already been concealed in the Western tradition by 1,000 philosophical and scientific misconceptions. But it had not always been so. The pre-Socratics had been astounded in the presence of Being and had asked truly ontological questions.

But these true thinkers (thinkers

Martin Heidegger

are better than mere philosophers, for Heidegger) were followed by Plato, who distracted thought away from Being and into an artificial idealistic world of Forms, and by Aristotle, who concentrated on "beings" and provoked a technological tradition in which Being itself would be forgotten. Heidegger wanted to "call us back to a remembrance of Being"—to return us to our primordial astonishment in its presence. We must come home to Being—stand in its presence and establish a harmonic concordance with it rather than merely intellectualize it.

A Pre-Socratic Philosopher Finds the Being of His Own Thumb (And Is Duly Impressed!)

One thing that prevents us from returning home to Being is the

Being Speaks

language we employ to do it. It has become encrusted with the fragments and dust of a ruined past, and it must be cleansed and purged if it is to become a viable path to Being. Luckily (and quite conveniently, if you are German, as was Heidegger), of the modern languages, German is the closest to the truth, because it's less bespattered with lies and because it's more powerful and more spiritual than other languages—though ancient Greek, the language of the pre-Socratics themselves, remains the most powerful. The Greek of those first thinkers comes to us from a time when its speakers were direct witnesses to Being.

Heidegger mined this language, going into its deepest **etymologies.** For instance, he discovered that the Greek word for "being," *Parousia,* designates something that "stands firmly by itself and thus manifests and declares itself"[3] and that the Greek word for "truth," *aletheia,* means "uncoveredness."[4] But simply studying Greek

Heidegger Mining Language

or being able to speak German is not enough. A new beginning must be found that will be radically innovative and return us to origins at the same time. To this end, Heidegger generated a flood of technical vocabulary, to the delight of some and the annoyance of others.

Take a look, for example, at one of his characterizations of the meaning of the word "care": "ahead-of-itself-Being-already-in-(the-world) as Being-alongside (entities encountered within-the-world)."[5] (ten dashes already!) It is not easy to see that these clumsy **neologisms** restore lost meanings—that Heidegger's artificial language is closer to the Truth of Being than is the language of everyday life.

Humans have certain attitudes toward beings. In this respect, we are like other animals. But unlike other animals, humans also have an attitude toward Being itself. We "comport" ourselves toward it. We are unique not simply because only we can question Being, but also in that, in questioning Being, we put our own Being in question. We are the only being whose own Being is a question for itself. Therefore, our being is different. Heidegger designated that difference by saying that other beings *are;* we exist, or "ek-sist."[6] He named human existence *Dasein* (being there). Unlike other beings, which are merely *in* the world, Dasein *has* a world. Heidegger rejected the intellectualism of most philosophers who have seen the world as primarily the object of human knowledge. For him, knowing was just one way of being-in-the-world. Furthermore, knowing is itself not just an intellectual act.

To "understand" something is to understand it in the context of usage, to understand it as something serviceable or dangerous. Things are not just "present-at-hand"; they are not just objects for disinterested scientific investigation; they are "ready-to-hand." The there of our being-there (Dasein) is filled with objects that are there for us, ready-to-hand. We have *care* or *concern* for them. This "care" (*Sorge*) is one of the main characteristics of human existence; we care for the world around us, both the natural and the human world. And when we express care not just for beings but for Being itself, we are our most authentic selves as humans.

Being-within-the-world entails being-with-others. The there of Dasein is populated not only with objects for our use but also with the Dasein of others. Our relationship to others is neither that of presence-at-hand nor readiness-to-hand, for we must acknowledge that others make the same demands on us that we make on them. There is a danger, however, of giving in too much to their demands. We can "come not to be ourselves." We can be sucked into the third-person theyness of others. This form of inauthentic existence in which we live in the opinions and desires of the anonymous "they" is a form of fear that produces a hollowness. "Fallenness" is Heidegger's term for succumbing to this fear. Unfortunately, fallenness is not just a side effect of bad choices. It is of the essence of human existence. We have "fallen" into a world of others. But it is possible to come out of inauthenticity through *Sorge*: care for Being and care for beings, care for the future, for the past, and for the community.

We Have Fallen into a World of Others

We are also rescued from inauthenticity through *Angst*, anxiety. We experience anxiety in the recognition of death. This anxiety is not the same as the simple fear of death. Anxiety is cognitive. It produces knowledge that we are going to die. It reveals to us that Dasein is being-toward-death.

We discover the meaning of our being as Dasein in the possibility of not-being Dasein, that is, in death. It is also this discovery that reveals to us our own freedom, for in the face of our imminent annihilation we must choose a life that justifies its own worth despite its necessary termination.

Human Existence Is Being-toward-Death

Most of these ideas were developed in Heidegger's major work *Being and Time*, published in 1927. It contained two parts and ended with a series of questions that Heidegger promised to answer in a third part. But Part 3 was never written. One critic says that Heidegger himself felt that the path to Being had "come to a dead end."[7]

A Dead End?

After 1927, rather than returning to the unfinished section of *Being and Time*, Heidegger wrote a number of shorter works, some of which still have not been released in an English translation. These writings have provoked a great debate among both Heideggerians and his critics as to whether Heidegger changed his mind after 1927 concerning the key philosophical questions. There seems to be at least a change of emphasis, in which *language* (the new path to Being) almost eclipses Being, including the human being, as language swallows up the individual. "Language is the house of Being in which man ek-sists by dwelling."[8] It is not that humans speak language but that language speaks itself through humans. It follows therefore that poets rather than philosophers are the true custodians of Being—and particularly the German poet Friedrich Hölderlin, who conveniently happened to be from Heidegger's neck of the woods but who inconveniently ended up in an asylum. The key feature of poetry is a kind of naming, nomination, an act that "realizes" in the sense of making real. As in Nietzsche, the Platonic hierarchy has been inverted. It is the artists and not the scientists who speak Truth. Eventually, in Heidegger's final works, poetic language itself seems to give way to the poetic silence between words. Truth would have to be "silence about silence."

Despite the enormous influence of Heidegger's philosophy, a shadow has been cast over his life and his work. In 1933, as rector of the University of Freiburg, Heidegger had joined the Nazi party and had given speeches praising Adolf Hitler. Within a year, he resigned his post and issued no more praise of the Führer. In fact, Heidegger himself came under the scrutiny of the Nazis. Yet he never publicly apologized for his support of a party that was soon to commit unimaginable atrocities, and he remained silent about the Holocaust. What is the connection between his silence and the Silence that speaks Truth? Apparently none. His critics say that his silence conceals a sinister truth. They also claim to find a concordance between his bombastic pseudointellectual German diction and his obsession with death and land, on the one hand, and the ghoulish and vacuous ideas of Nazism on the other.

His defenders say that Heidegger was a politically naive philosophical genius who made a political mistake and, when he realized it was a mistake, made another by not publicly denouncing his first mistake. They say this major personal flaw does not detract from the value of his work.

Sartre

Another of Edmund Husserl's erstwhile disciples was Jean-Paul Sartre (1905–1980). Besides being one of the most important philosophers of the twentieth century, Sartre was also an essayist, novelist, and playwright. His early philosophical ideas are developed in his novel *Nausea* (1938); in his treatises, *Transcendence of the Ego* (1936) and *Being and Nothingness* (1943); and in his essay "Existentialism Is a Humanism" (1946). In these works, we see the influence not only of Husserl but also of Heidegger and Kierkegaard.

First, let us look at Sartre's theory of consciousness. From Husserl, Sartre had learned that consciousness is always referential, in that it always refers beyond itself to an *object*. "Unreflected consciousness" is consciousness before it is reflected upon or philosophized about. When I read a novel, the object of the unreflected consciousness is the hero of the novel. When I run to catch a trolley, the object of the unreflected consciousness is "streetcar-to-be-caught." In unreflected consciousness, there is no self, no "I" to be found; only its objects exist—Don Quixote or the streetcar.

Jean-Paul Sartre (1905–1980)

Consciousness always refers

Unreflected consciousness

Reflective consciousness is consciousness that reflects on itself. According to Sartre (and contrary to Descartes), the ego, or the I, is to be discovered only in reflected consciousness. Not only is it *discovered* there, but it also is actually partially created there.

Reflective consciousness — consciousness reflecting on consciousness

Once we study consciousness phenomenologically (perform an epochê on it, bracket it, make it the object of reflective consciousness), we discover that it is "a monstrous . . . impersonal spontaneity"[9] in which thoughts come and go at *their* will, not ours. This spontaneity is a form of dizzying freedom, according to Sartre, and contemplation of it leads to anguish. We actively struggle to impose order on this free spontaneity, and when we fail, neurosis and psychosis ensue.

Sartre mentioned the case of a woman who dreaded her husband's leaving for work because she feared that upon his departure she would sit nude in the window like a prostitute. Because she knew she was *free* to do so, she feared she *would* do so. (This theme was inspired by Kierkegaard's account of dread. When God told Adam not to eat the apple, Adam then knew that he *could* eat it—that he was *free* to do so—and he knew that if he could, he *might*. That is, he experienced his freedom as dread.)

In our own case, as in the case of that woman, sometimes the order we impose upon consciousness breaks down, and consciousness is revealed to us as the monstrous spontaneity that it is. As a philosophical exercise, Husserl had suspended all beliefs and all "normality" in the epoché, but Sartre discovered that an epoché can break in on us when we least expect it, not as a philosophical exercise but as a crisis of consciousness, as when we look into a chasm and suddenly feel the urge to throw ourselves in.

This crisis of consciousness is what happens to Roquentin, the "hero" of Sartre's novel Nausea, as he sits on a park bench looking at the knotted roots of a chestnut tree, and experiences a spontaneous epoché—showing that Husserl was wrong to assume that an epoché could be brought about only artificially by a philosophical intention.

Suddenly, all the old assumptions break down, and he sees the tree not as a tree but as a "black, knotty, raw, doughy, melted, soft, monstrous, naked, obscene, frightening lump of existence."[10] Suddenly, the tree's Being has presented itself to him. Roquentin discovers that that Being, as it reveals itself in the crisis of consciousness, is pure superfluity, pure excess.

The rationalists Spinoza and Leibniz were badly mistaken. Not only is Being not necessary, but it also is *absurd*. Far from there existing a "sufficient reason" for the being of Being, there is no reason for it to exist at all. So the Sartrean existentialist finds his or her own existence as a superfluity in an absurd world. Yet human beings *do* exist. They have been thrown into a meaningless world without their permission. What is the relation between human beings and the world?

The most significant form of this relationship is that of "the question." By questioning the world, I reveal a *nothingness* in Being. When I seek Pierre in a café and discover that Pierre is *not* there, I reveal a nothingness in reality. (Pierre's absence is *real*.)

In the same way, I discover that a nothingness separates me from myself. There is a nothingness between me and my past (I am *not* who I was) and between me and my future (the person I will be is *not* who I am).

This realization again makes me aware that "I await myself in the future. Anguish is the fear of not finding myself there, of no longer even wishing to be there."[11] This anguish stems from my discovery that my self is not a stable, solid entity that lasts through time; rather, it is a *creation* that I must make and remake from moment to moment.

Not only must I create myself, but I must also create my world. I do so by bestowing values on the world. Accord-

I Await Myself in the Future

ing to the pre-Sartrean view of freedom, values preexist my free-dom. I am placed between these values, and my freedom consists in my ability to choose between these preexisting values. According to the Sartrean view, through freedom, I bestow value on the world by choosing aspects of it. Freedom preexists values. Life has no

The Old View of Freedom

meaning or value except that which I give to it. Ultimately, my choice of values cannot be justified because there are no eternal (Platonic) values, no stone tablets, no Scriptures to which I can appeal to justify my choices. In the final analysis, no set of values is objectively any more valuable than any other set. This discovery leads to more anguish (of course!).

Certainly my freedom is not absolute. Consciousness runs up against "facticity" in existence (i.e., that which cannot be changed). If a boulder falls in my path, I cannot change the fact that it is there

The Sartrean View of Freedom

"My freedom is anguished at being the foundation of values while being itself without foundation."[12]

or that it is impenetrable. But I am free to interpret the meaning of its "thereness" for me. It may mean an obstacle to be conquered, or it may mean that my goal of reaching the mountain top is defeated, or I may interpret it as an object of aesthetic contemplation or as a scientific specimen. "Situation" is what Sartre called the interpretation of facticity. To interpret facticity is to create a world for me to inhabit. I am always "in situation" and am always freely creating worlds. In fact, in this respect . . .

Most people create worlds in "bad faith." That is, rather than facing up to their responsibility and freedom, people flee from them by denying them or by blaming them on others, on fate, or on "the Establishment."

But there can be no blaming in good faith. We cannot blame our upbringing, our parents, our poverty (or our wealth), or the "hard times" because we alone

". . . I am condemned to be free."[13]

determine the *meaning* that these things have for us.

We are always free because there are always alternative choices—the ultimate alternative is death. If I do not shoot myself, then I have chosen whatever is the alternative to death.

A major complication in the experience of our freedom is that we must encounter other free beings. The unity that I have imposed on my consciousness is momentarily shattered when the Other *looks* at me

and transforms me into the *object* of his gaze. I can recover my own selfhood only by looking at him and transforming him into my object. (This is like Hegel's master-slave relation, except that no synthesis is possible.) "Hell," said Sartre, "is other people."[14]

THE LOOK

Sartre's philosophy ends with what many philosophers take to be a pessimism that reflects the plight of the human in the modern world. Sartre denied that he was a pessimist. Instead, he made heroes of us all. The authentic human being knows that all her acts are ultimately futile in the face of death and the absurdity of existence, yet she chooses to persevere. In God-like fashion, she creates worlds upon worlds. Like Sisyphus, she pushes her boulder daily up the steep incline of existence, without excuse and without complaint. It is, after all, *her* boulder. She created it.

Structuralism and Poststructuralism

Beginning in the 1960s, Europe's fascination with phenomenology and existentialism gave way to an interest in a new movement called structuralism. This movement was in its inception a reaction against phenomenology and existentialism; nevertheless, its members kept returning to the themes raised by existential phenomenology.

Saussure

Although structuralism had a major influence on philosophy, it actually began in the social sciences and found its inspiration in the turn-of-the-century work of the Swiss linguist Ferdinand de Saussure (1857–1913). In his posthumously published *Course of General Linguistics*, agreeing with his contemporaries the pragmatists and anticipating the view of the later Wittgenstein, Saussure argued that

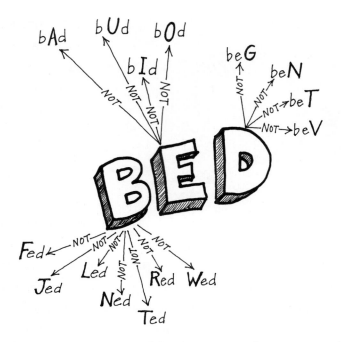

"meanings" are neither names of fixed essences (as in rationalism) nor names of sensorial experiences (as in empiricism). Rather, the meaning of a linguistic phenomenon is a function of its location in an underlying linguistic structure. This linguistic object is defined not by some positive feature inherent to it, but rather in terms of the negative relations in which it stands to other objects in the system. (Both in terms of its sound [phonic value] and its meaning [semantic value], the word "bed" is what it is by *not* being "bad," "bid," "bod," or "bud.")

According to Saussure, a language is a system of *signs*. A sign is a combination of a sound (or an audio-image) and an idea (or concept). The former is called a "signifier," the latter a "signified." (This terminological

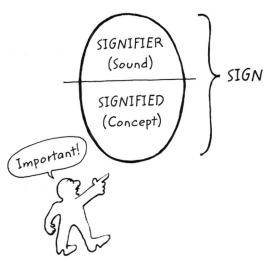

distinction is germinal for all structuralist thinkers.) A sound can only be a sign if it is related to a concept. Therefore, there must be a system of conventions that relates sounds to concepts. Saussure's linguistics studies this system.

A major emphasis of Saussurean theory is on the *arbitrary* nature of the sign. That is to say, the relation between the signifier and the signified is a purely conventional one, not one based in nature. The sound "cat" could have denoted the idea "dog," but it just didn't turn out that way. There is no natural connection

Wau-Wau!

And I say, Ouâ-Ouâ!

between the sound "cat" and the ideas we have of that particular feline.

There *are* exceptions—so-called onomatopoeia. But even these are usually more arbitrary than they seem. Dogs in California say, "Bow-Wow"; but in France they say, "Ouâ-Ouâ"; and in Germany, "Wau-Wau"; and in Italy, "Bau-Bau."

There is an anti-Platonic philosophical implication in this aspect of Saussurean theory. The sign is arbitrary at both ends. That is, there are no absolutes at either end. Both the signifier and the signified evolve in relation to other entities within their

WHAT? No Absolutes?

audio-conceptual system and in relation to other such systems, which means that there are no fixed universal concepts. In that case, the Platonic ideal of absolute knowledge is a myth.

So the signifier and the signified are both purely *relational* entities. They exist only insofar as they relate to other entities, and the relationship is mainly a *negative* one. Saussure said of signs, "Their most precise characteristic is being what the others are not."[15]

As Wittgenstein was to do later, Saussure drew an analogy between language and chess. The shape of the chess piece is arbitrary. Any shape will do as long as the piece can be distinguished from other pieces with different functions. The identity of a chess piece (or of a signifier, or of a signified, or of a sign) is not dependent on some inherent essence that it has but is totally a function of differences within the system to which it belongs. As Saussure said, "there are only differences, without positive terms."[16]

Lévi-Strauss

At the end of his work, Saussure called for a new science, *the general science of signs,* which he named **semiology,** with linguistics as its model, even though linguistics would be only *part* of this science. In semiology, human conventions, rituals, and acts would be studied as *signs* (combinations of signifiers and signifieds). These behavioral signs would be demonstrated to be as arbitrary as linguistic signs and would be shown to stand in the same relationship to other parts of the behavioral system that linguistic signs do to language.

It is only a slight exaggeration to say that **structuralism** is the science that Saussure called for, a science whose specific

Claude Lévi-Strauss

formulation is the creation of the French anthropologist Claude Lévi-Strauss (1908–2009).

Most contemporary anthropology is concerned with the organization of specific societies. It tends to correspond to a form of anthropological **functionalism** in that it often explains social institutions and phenomena in terms of their utilitarian value within the culture. (E.g., any nomadic desert tribes that became dependent on swine herding would not survive. Therefore, the prohibition against eating the flesh of pigs will become institutionalized in such societies. Hence "Jehovah's" and "Allah's" prohibition against pork.)

Lévi-Strauss rejects the functionalist interpretation of social phenomena. Many social institutions have no utility at all in and of themselves but take on meaning when related to all the other institutions within the society. Furthermore, rather than concerning himself exclusively with the organization of particular societies, Lévi-Strauss looks for *universal* characteristics of all societies. All cultures, despite their many differences, are products of the human brain. Therefore, "there must be somewhere beneath the surface features common to all."[17]

Thou shalt not pig out!

The search for universals distinguishes Lévi-Strauss from the mainstream functionalist movement in anthropology and puts him in a philosophical tradition that originated with Socrates and Plato (so Plato isn't completely dead after all!) and that is most clearly expressed in the modern period by Kant's search for synthetic a priori truths. What is new in Lévi-Strauss is the claim that the human universals exist only latently at the level of *structure* and not at the level of manifest fact. (Though, of course, Marx and Freud said something similar. And, indeed, Marx and Freud, as well as Saussure, have influenced structuralism deeply.) When we look at Lévi-Strauss's statement of his method, we see the impact of Saussurean linguistics on his thought because he treats cultural phenomena the way Saussure treated signifiers.

1. "Define the phenomenon under study as a relation between two or more terms, real or supposed."
2. "Construct a table of possible permutations between these terms."
3. Treat the table as the structure of necessary logical connections ("a sort of periodic chart of chemical elements"), which will demonstrate that the empirical phenomenon under study "is only one possible combination among others."[18]

Notice two things here. First, Lévi-Strauss's method is a *rationalistic* method (rationalistic because its goal is the discovery of necessary logical relations, which are in fact a priori) in which empirical phenomena themselves are "demoted" and empiricism goes by the board. Second, there is offered here a kind of halfway house between freedom and determinism. There are choices, but they are severely restricted for both individuals and cultures. These choices are at the same time created and limited by the structural system of which they are a part. Lévi-Strauss says, "human societies, like individual human beings . . . never create absolutely; all they do is choose certain combinations from a repertory of ideas."[19]

In *The Savage Mind* (*La pensée sauvage*, 1962), Lévi-Strauss tries to demonstrate the essentially *logical* nature of all human thought,

Periodic Chart of Possible Social Relations

Chart #72—Mother

Mother to Son	Mother to Daughter	Mother to Husband	Mother to Her Father
Mother to Her Mother	Mother to Nephew	Mother to Niece	Mother to Sister
Mother to Brother	Mother to Uncle	Mother to Aunt	Mother to Grand-mother
Mother to Grand-father	Mother to Female Cousin	Mother to Male Cousin	Mother to God-mother

including that of so-called primitives. The logical foundation of all mental activity is the recognition of opposites, contrasts, and similarities. In this sense, the "savage mind" (perhaps better translated as "thinking in the raw") is as rational as any other mind. Furthermore, it demonstrates an exceptional awareness of the crude sensory data of nature and an intuitive ability to detect analogous systems within the sensual vocabulary of colors, sounds, smells, and tastes.

Lévi-Strauss, in *The Savage Mind*, tries to destroy once and for all the myth ingrained in popular prejudice and supported by Lévi-Strauss's anthropological predecessors that primitives are like children and think in some pre-adult manner. He accomplishes this goal with a two-edged argument. First, he demonstrates areas of typical primitive thinking that are far more sophisticated than our own.

Second, he demonstrates examples of cultured thought that are in fact quite primitive.

As an example of sophisticated thought among the primitives, Lévi-Strauss tells us, concerning a tribe in the Philippines, that

> Ninety-three percent of the total number of native plants are recognized by the Hanunóo as culturally significant. . . . The Hanunóo classify all forms of the local avifauna into seventy-five categories. . . . They distinguish about a dozen kinds of snakes . . . sixty-odd types of fish . . . insect forms are grouped by the Hanunóo into a hundred and eight name categories, including thirteen for ants and termites.[20]

As an example of primitive thought among the "sophisticated," we need only consider our attitude toward such cultural icons as "the bed in which George Washington slept," or perhaps toward Dorothy's shoes from *The Wizard of Oz*, or Lady Gaga's costumes, or the parchment that claims to be the U.S. Constitution. (It is *not*. We would still have a constitution even if the parchment were destroyed.) Many people treat these articles like primitive fetishes.

In summary, according to Lévi-Strauss, universally valid principles of human thought hold for all peoples at all times. Historical and cultural contingencies can overlay these principles with levels of abstractions and technical obfuscations, but these contingencies never replace that which they disguise. To observe this universal logic in its purest form, we should study the "unpolluted" mind of pretechnical peoples. In such a way, we will discover the unity of the human race.

Lacan

By the end of the 1970s, structuralism itself began to give way to a series of splinter groups that, opposed as they often were to one another, can all be designated by the term "poststructuralism."

This "movement" is not really an outright rejection of structuralism. It is, rather, a radicalization and intensification of some of its themes. Like structuralism, it found its home not only in philosophy but also in the social sciences, in **psychoanalysis,** and in literary criticism. The bridge between structuralism and poststructuralism was constructed by the French psychoanalyst Jacques Lacan (1901–1981), as seen in his

**Jacques Lacan
Reads Sigmund Freud**

dense and often perversely obscure book *Écrits*. Yet Lacan claimed not to be inventing a new theory or even reinterpreting the theories of Sigmund Freud, the founder of psychoanalysis, but simply to be reading Freud's text carefully (something he apparently thought others had failed to do). Undaunted by the fact that neurology had failed to produce the empirical evidence for psychoanalysis that Freud had anticipated, Lacan claimed to find its justification in linguistics. Psychoanalysis is, after all, "the talking cure." It is essentially about language. According to Lacan, "the unconscious is structured like a language."[21] This epigram is an invitation to apply the insights of linguistics to the study of the human mind.

There is, of course, such a thing as prelinguistic experience. It gives the infant access to the Real, in all its Nietzschean disorder. The Real is experienced as pain and joy, but the child's access to language alienates it from the Real. Organic need (what Freud called "instinct," or *Trieb*) is experienced as an aboriginal *lack*. As organic need is translated into language, it becomes *desire*, and the original experience of lack is cast into the unconscious. Human existence is so hopelessly insatiable because underneath desire is *a radical lack of being*. But desire cannot address it directly because desire is language-bound.

Desire takes a metonymical course ("metonymy" refers to the displacement of meaning from one signifier to another signifier that is contiguous to the first, in terms of either meaning or sound; e.g., "He takes too much to the bottle," or any rhyme: "cat, fat, mat"); it moves from sign to tangential sign without ever being able to grasp

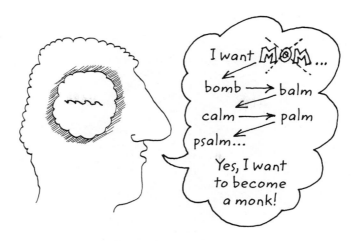

Metonymical Reasoning

the absolute lack that it conceals. Lacan's "desire is a metonymy"[22] refers to this process. Desire is translated into *demand,* but demand is not really concerned with any particular object because no particular object can replace the forever-lost object.

If we retrace the metonymical wanderings of true need (which has been caught in the nets of the signifier), we find that desire, in its labyrinthine course, ends up with itself as its own object. Desire desires desire. This is one meaning of Lacan's infamous phrase, "Desire is the desire of the Other."[23] Every desire is, finally, the desire to be desired by the Other, a desire to impose oneself upon the Other. Ultimately, then, every demand is a demand for love.

What have been repressed into the unconscious are not biological instincts because these have already been translated into words. It is *words*—signifiers—that have been consigned to the unconscious. "The unconscious [is] a chain of signifiers."[24] In conscious language and thought, the emphasis is on the objectivity of the signified (i.e., the objectivity of meaning). This emphasis disguises the creativity of the signifier (the word). It obscures and even denies the fact that the signifier can slide easily past its normal frontiers to reveal amazing new relations between itself and its possible signifieds. Unconscious language and thought know this truth, but the institutional strictures of conscious thought and language ("the discourse of reason," or Logos) ignore this scandalous wisdom. Conscious language uses conventional signs associated with fixed meanings. It *must* do so; otherwise we wouldn't understand each other. But the unconscious is freed from the necessity of public understanding. It can *play* with the signifier without regard for its real meaning. It can produce its own private "meanings." However, there is a bridge between consciousness and the unconscious. That bridge is *poetry*. Poetic language is close to a form of unconscious language. It constitutes a kind of intermediary level between conscious and unconscious discourse. (". . . the silken, sad, uncertain rustling of each purple curtain thrilled me—filled me with terrors never felt before.")[25]

The poet hovers somewhere between the expressly public and the intensely private. According to Lacan, the difference between the patient and the poet is that the former's poetic play with the relationships among signifiers is strictly private. The psychotic who feared birds because he knew that, in French slang, police officers on bicycles are referred to as "swallows," lives in a purely private poetic world. He does so because of an incommunicable personal experience that he has suffered, an experience that can be traced in the unconscious by following the network of signifiers in which his mind is enmeshed.

What Lacan called the Imaginary designates the world of the infant (and the world of some psychotics), a world in which the subject is lost in its own imagery, in its own fantasy. The "images" of the Imaginary are representations of lived experience before that experience is alienated into language. We deliver ourselves from the entrapment of the Imaginary by entering into the fullness of

Silence: Poet at Work   Silence: Lunatic at Work

language, which is to say, by entering into the Symbolic. By naming a thing, the subject distances herself from it. When she names it, she denies that she *is* it. Access to the Symbolic fixates the mind and rescues it from the undifferentiated flux of the Imaginary. It mediates between self and self, between self and thing. If there were no possibility of "registering oneself in the Symbolic," there would be no possibility of individuality because individuality requires differentiation.

However, when the subject gains access to the Symbolic, that individual enters into a preestablished system with its own rules and structures. The self is assimilated into a network of relations in which the self is always an effect and never a cause. The subject becomes fashioned by the structure of language. The logic of the relations between signs replaces the lived experience of the Real. The individual becomes a prisoner of the autonomous order of signs. As in the later Heidegger, it is not the subject but the language that speaks.

Derrida

Another important theorist in the Continental poststructuralist movement (and one who came to teach philosophy in southern California) is the French philosopher Jacques Derrida (1930–2004). Well, at least he was *trained* in philosophy, but one of the hallmarks of his view is the demotion of philosophy from the privileged status it has always claimed for itself as arbiter of Reason. Traditional philosophy, which Derrida derides as **logocentrism,** has devalued other forms of writing, especially poetic, metaphorical, and literary writing, as being further from the Truth than is philosophical discourse. Philosophy only grudgingly uses language to express its insights into meaning and reality. Yet, according to Derrida, philosophical discourse suffers from the same vicissitudes as every other form of speech and writing, and every attempt even to say what one means by "meaning" and "reality" must necessarily self-destruct.

The Parisian Philosopher at Disneyland

So Derrida willingly plays twentieth-century Sophist to would-be twentieth-century Platos. His version of relativism derives from a radicalization of Saussure's linguistics. If, as Saussure had argued, every sign is what it is by not being the others, then every sign involves every other sign. Therefore, there is never any "meaning" fully present; rather, all meaning is infinitely deferred. (Derrida recognizes that this conclusion is true of his own meaning as well—that *his* discourse is parasitical on the discourse that he criticizes—but he accepts this paradox playfully, albeit a little *too* playfully for some of his critics.)

An Excess of Meaning

Every presence of meaning or of being (because "being" can only present itself in the context of "meaning") is an absence, and every absence is a presence. Derrida designates this fact of "surplus meaning" as "*différance*," wittingly misspelling the French word *différence*, punning on the fact that the French verb *différer* means both "to differ" and "to defer."[26]

In fact, punning is very much to the point here. Derrida's idea can be partially understood by thinking of how almost all words have multiple meanings. "Dog," for instance, according to the *Random House Dictionary*, can be correctly used to distinguish between domestic canines, on the one hand, and wolves, jackals, and foxes on the other, *or* it can include all these animals. It can designate the *male* canine, as opposed to the bitch, or can include both. It can also refer to "any of various animals resembling a dog." It can designate "a despicable man or youth," an "ugly, boring, or crude girl or woman," or *anybody* in general, as in "a gay dog," can refer to feet, or to "something worthless or of extremely poor quality." It's also the name of "any of various mechanical devices for gripping or holding something," or it is a sausage (hot dog), or the object of ruin (to go to the dogs), or of unhappiness (a dog's life), or as a verb, it can mean to track with hostile intent, or to put on airs, and so on and so on.

If Derrida is right, the word "dog" cannot help but carry with it some, or most, of these meanings in any of its uses. Every meaning is, to use Freud's language, "over-determined" (overloaded with significance). If we say, "but the context determines the meaning," we forget that the meaning also determines the context. (The English literary critic Terry Eagleton reminds us of the sign in the London subway: "Dogs must be carried on the escalator." And if I don't own a dog, may I not use the escalator?)

Getting Caught on the Escalator without a Dog

Because of this constant excess and slippage of meaning, every text, philosophical or otherwise, ends up defeating the first principles of its own logic, as Derrida tries to demonstrate: The key philosophical dichotomies collapse in upon themselves, for example, reality-appearance, being-nothingness, knowledge-ignorance, certainty-doubt, theism-atheism, noumenon-phenomenon, fact-value, reason-unreason, waking-dreaming. Or, to use Derrida's language, they "deconstruct" themselves. (His form of analysis is known as deconstruction.) According to Derrida, the fact that all texts self-destruct is really a fact about language, hence about human thought. Yet every attempt to escape from "the prison-house of language" is an avenue leading back to it. And because, as Heidegger and Lacan pointed out, language creates the self (and not the other way around, as was traditionally supposed), the self itself is decentered and demoted under Derrida's deconstructive gaze.

There are other important figures in the poststructuralist philosophical movement, such as Michel Foucault, Gilles Deleuze, and Félix Guattari in France and Richard Rorty in America, but perhaps the interest in the relation between language and selfhood has been most doggedly pursued by certain women philosophers in France, notably Hélène Cixous, Julia Kristeva, and Luce Irigaray. These philosophers play an important role in poststructuralism.

Poststructuralism, associated with the larger cultural movement, postmodernism, has lost some of its impetus in the last twenty years. Even in its heyday in Continental Europe, the movement seemed to be undergoing constant evolution and sea changes. In philosophy departments in the United States and Britain—dominated as they were by analytic philosophers—poststructuralism was always only a minority voice; it appeared to have gained more of a foothold among professors of literary criticism and film studies than among philosophers. I believe it is correct to say, at the time of this writing, that there is no cohesive, systematic philosophical worldview that has taken over from poststructuralism in Europe today, though most European philosophers seem to remain deeply influenced in one way or another by the individual "stars" of poststructuralism.

Key Philosophical Ideas in Chapter 7

Phenomenology

Edmund Husserl:

- Key Husserlian ideas:
  - Cartesian foundation ("I think, therefore I am").
  - Assumption: all knowledge of the world based on consciousness.
  - Requirement: a study of consciousness and the world it encounters.

- Study consciousness by <u>eliminating all presuppositions</u>.
- The <u>*epochê*</u> (phenomenological suspension, bracketing).
- Conclusion as applied to <u>time and space</u>: it is always <u>"Now"</u> on the phenomenological clock; I am always <u>"Here"</u> on the phenomenological map.
- Conclusion as applied to consciousness: <u>consciousness is always intentional</u>, referential ("all consciousness is consciousness of . . .").
- Husserl's quest for the "<u>transcendental ego</u>."

Existential Phenomenology

Martin Heidegger:

- <u>Key Heideggerian ideas</u>:
  - <u>Being has been hidden</u> by linguists and metaphysical misconceptions beginning with Plato.
  - Heidegger calls for <u>a return to the pre-Socratic mentality</u>.
  - Ancient <u>Greek is the language truest to being; German comes in second; Heideggerian neologisms will reapproach Being</u>: e.g., "Dasein," "present-at-hand," "ready-to-hand," "ek-sistence," "Sorge," "being-within-the-world," "being-with-others," "being-toward death."
  - Part 3 of *Being and Time* was never written.
  - <u>Has "the path to Being" come to an end, or is language the new path?</u> Or is "poetic silence" that path?
  - <u>Heidegger and Hitler</u>: is Heidegger a dupe or a naïf?

Jean-Paul Sartre:

- Key Sartrean ideas:
  - <u>Theory of consciousness</u> (in *Transcendence of the Ego* and *Nausea*):
    - There is <u>no "I"</u> (no ego) <u>in "unreflected consciousness."</u>
    - The "<u>I</u>" comes into existence <u>in "reflected consciousness."</u> (Descartes was wrong.)
    - In "reflective consciousness" (consciousness as studied <u>in the epochê</u>), <u>consciousness proves to be "a monstrous spontaneity," a "monstrous freedom" that the ego tries to contain</u>.
  - The spontaneous *epochê* of <u>the roots of a giant chestnut tree</u>.
  - <u>Being reveals itself</u> not in marvel (as in Heidegger) but <u>in horror, as pure superfluity, pure excess, as absurd</u>.
  - The human relation to the world is exemplified in <u>"the question," which reveals the "nothingness" in being ("Pierre is not here"), and freedom is possible because of this nothingness</u>.

- This <u>freedom produces anguish</u> (as in Kierkegaard).
- <u>In freedom I create myself, values, and the world itself</u>.
- "<u>Facticity</u>" preexists consciousness and choice, but <u>my choice determines its meaning</u> (and the meaning of the world).
- "<u>I am condemned to be free</u>."
- Other free beings challenge my being and my freedom: <u>the "look."</u>
- Does Sartre consign human existence to <u>pessimism or</u> to <u>heroism?</u>

Structuralism and Poststructuralism

- As enthusiasm for <u>existentialism</u> waned in Europe in the 1950s and early '60s, it was <u>replaced by structuralism</u>, which soon <u>evolved into poststructuralism</u>.

- Structuralism <u>rejects the assumption of phenomenology that philosophy must begin with subjectivity</u>, replacing "consciousness" with objective "structures" as the starting point.

Ferdinand de Saussure: structural linguistics

- <u>Key Saussurean ideas</u>:
  - Word recognition (<u>phonic value</u>) <u>and</u> meaning (<u>semantic value</u>) <u>determined</u> not by naming essences (Plato) nor by naming collections of sense-data (Hume) but <u>by the location that a word occupies in a specific linguistic system</u>, which gives the word relationships with all other components of the system.
  - <u>Language is a system of</u> <u>signs</u>.
  - A sign is a combination of a <u>signifier</u> (sound or image) and a <u>signified</u> (concept).
  - The <u>relation</u> between signs and between signifier and signified is <u>conventional and arbitrary</u>.
  - <u>Signs are</u> negative: they are "<u>what the others are not.</u>"

Claude Lévi-Strauss: structural anthropology

- Replaces anthropological functionalism with structuralism.
  - <u>The meaning of social institutions is determined by their relations to other social institutions</u>.
  - <u>The universality of the human mind is made manifest</u> in the overall structure of social institutions (like in rationalism: a priori logical relations exhibited in social structures).
  - All human thought—even <u>the "savage mind"</u>—<u>is logical</u>.

- Though <u>different societies recognize similarities and dissimilari-</u><u>ties in</u> <u>different ways</u>, comparative structural analysis shows that <u>universally</u> <u>valid principles of human thought hold for all peoples at</u> <u>all times</u>.

Jacques Lacan: poststructural psychoanalysis

- <u>Poststructuralism: a radicalization and intensification of</u> certain structuralist themes (e.g., <u>relativity and arbitrariness</u>).
- Lacan gives <u>Freud</u>'s text a close reading <u>through Saussurean eyes</u>:
  - <u>Justifies psychoanalysis through linguistics, not biology</u>
- "<u>The unconscious is structured like a language</u>."
- <u>Desire is metonymy</u>: "*organic need*" (Freud's "*instinct*"), experienced as <u>*lack*</u>, becomes *demand*, which travels metonymically from sign to sign.
- Ultimately, *every desire is the desire to be desired* ("<u>Desire is the desire</u> <u>of the other</u>").
- Words (signifiers) become attached to the unconscious.
- <u>The unconscious speaks its own language</u>, which, like poetry, can be read and interpreted.
- <u>Three registers of the mind</u>:
  - <u>The Real</u>: pre-linguistic experience (pain and joy)
  - <u>The Imaginary</u>: the world of the young child (and of some psychotics), lost in fantasy
  - <u>The Symbolic</u>: full access to language, allowing individuation and sociality, but at the cost of self-alienation and incarceration in the prison of language

Jacques Derrida: deconstruction

- <u>Key Derridean ideas</u>:
  - Traditional philosophy decried as <u>*logocentrism*</u>.
  - Further radicalization of Saussure's linguistics:
    - Every sign involves every other sign, and <u>"meaning" is never fully</u> <u>present</u>.
    - Every <u>presence is an absence, and vice versa</u>.
  - Incomplete or surplus meaning designated as <u>"*différance*"</u> (a difference and a deferral).

- Because of "*différance*" <u>every philosophical text (indeed, any form of discourse) defeats itself, or "deconstructs."</u>
- The word "deconstruction" denotes both the act of linguistic self-defeat and the philosophical analysis of such defeat.
- Derrida <u>demotes all forms of textual authority</u> including that of philosophy.

Topics for Consideration

1. Choose an object, event, or experience on which you can perform a phenomenological reduction (i.e., an *epoché*). First, write a description of that object, event, or experience from the perspective of everyday life. Then, after performing the *epoché*, write a report describing the same object, event, or experience from the perspective of the phenomenological reduction.

2. What do you suppose Heidegger means when he "calls us back to a remembrance of Being"? What obstacles stand in the way of our responding to this call, according to him?

3. Compare Heidegger and Sartre on the topic of our relations to other people.

4. Kierkegaard has been called "the father of existentialism." Write an essay explaining how Kierkegaard, who is a radical Christian, and Sartre, who is a radical atheist, can both be called existentialists.

5. Compare and contrast Lévi-Strauss's theory of how the human mind functions with the theory of mind developed by any other philosopher who appeared in this book (e.g., Descartes, Locke, Kant).

6. Show the extent to which Saussure's linguistic theory has influenced Lacan's version of psychoanalysis and Derrida's deconstruction.

Notes

1. Edmund Husserl, *Ideas: General Introduction to Pure Phenomenology*, trans. W. R. Boyce Gibson (London: Collier-Macmillan, 1969), 91.
2. For a good example of treatment of intentionality by an analytic philosopher, see John Searle, *Intentionality: An Essay in the Philosophy of Mind* (New York: Cambridge University Press, 1983).
3. Martin Heidegger, quoted in George Steiner, *Martin Heidegger* (New York: Viking, 1979), 46.

4. Martin Heidegger, *Being and Time*, trans. John Macquarrie and Edward Robinson (New York: Harper and Brothers, 1962), 265.

5. Ibid., 237.

6. The word "ek-sistence" is Heidegger's revision of the word "existence" in which he stresses the Greek etymology of standing out and relating existence to ecstasy ("ek-stasy," stepping out of oneself).

7. Steiner, 114.

8. Martin Heidegger, "Letter on Humanism," trans. Frank A. Capuzzi and J. Glenn Gray, in *Martin Heidegger: Basic Writings*, ed. David Farrell Krell (New York: Harper and Row, 1977), 213.

9. Jean-Paul Sartre, *The Transcendence of the Ego*, trans. Forrest Williams and Robert Kirkpatrick (New York: Noonday Press, 1957), 98–99.

10. Jean-Paul Sartre, *Nausea*, trans. Lloyd Alexander (New York: New Directions, 1964), 127.

11. Jean-Paul Sartre, *Being and Nothingness*, trans. Hazel Barnes (New York: Washington Square Press, 1992), 73.

12. Ibid., 76.

13. Jean-Paul Sartre, "Existentialism Is a Humanism," trans. Bernard Frechtman, in *Existentialism and Human Emotions* (New York: Citadel Press, 1990), 23.

14. Jean-Paul Sartre, *No Exit*, trans. Stuart Gilbert (New York: Alfred A. Knopf, 1948), 61.

15. Ferdinand de Saussure, *Course in General Linguistics*, trans. Wade Baskin (New York: Philosophical Library, 1959), 117.

16. Ibid., 120.

17. Edmund Leach, *Lévi-Strauss* (London: Fontana, 1970), 26.

18. Claude Lévi-Strauss, *Totemism*, trans. Rodney Neeham (Boston: Beacon Press, 1963), 16.

19. Claude Lévi-Strauss, *Tristes Tropiques*, trans. John Russell (New York: Atheneum, 1964), 160.

20. Claude Lévi-Strauss, *The Savage Mind*, trans. George Weidenfeld and Nicolson, Ltd. (Chicago: University of Chicago Press, 1966), 4. In this passage Lévi-Strauss is quoting with approval a Yale University doctoral dissertation by H. C. Conklin.

21. Jacques Lacan, *The Four Fundamental Concepts of Psycho-Analysis*, trans. Alan Sheridan (New York: W. W. Norton, 1978), 20.

22. Jacques Lacan, *Écrits: A Selection*, trans. Alan Sheridan (New York: W. W. Norton, 1982), 175.

23. Ibid., 264.

24. Ibid., 297.

25. From Edgar Allan Poe's poem, "The Raven." Poe was one of Lucan's favorite writers.

26. See Gayatri Chakravorty Spivak's explanation of the term "différance" in the Translator's Preface to Jacques Derrida, *Of Grammatology*, trans. G. C. Spivak (Baltimore and London: Johns Hopkins University Press, 1976), xliii–xliv.

8

Pragmatism and the Analytic Tradition
The Late Nineteenth and Twentieth Centuries, into the Twenty-First

Pragmatism

Let us back up a bit historically and cross at last from Europe to the New World and visit the pragmatists—a school that makes the first truly American contribution to the history of philosophy and one that also provides a bridge between the nineteenth and twentieth centuries. The logician and semiologist Charles Peirce (1839–1914) invented the term **pragmatism** and meant it to be the name of a method whose primary goal was the clarification of thought. Perhaps pragmatism was conceived in Peirce's mind when he read the definition of "belief" offered by the psychologist Alexander Bain. Belief is "that upon which a man is prepared to act," said Bain. Peirce agreed and decided that it followed from this definition that beliefs produce habits and that the way to distinguish between beliefs is to compare the habits they produce. *Beliefs, then, are rules for action, and they get their meaning from the action for which they are rules.* With this definition, Peirce had bypassed the privacy and secrecy of the Cartesian mind and had provided a direct access to mental processes (because a person's belief could be established by observing that person's actions).

In its inventor's hands, pragmatism was a form of radical empiricism, and some of Peirce's claims are reminiscent of Berkeley's.

Providing Direct Access to the Cartesian Mind

For example, what Berkeley said about ideas ("our idea of anything is our idea of its sensible effects") is not unlike what Peirce said about belief.

James

Peirce's essay "How to Make Our Ideas Clear," published in 1878, was generally ignored until interpreted by William James (1842–1910) some twenty-five years later. James swore allegiance to what he took to be Peircean principles and set out to promote the doctrine of pragmatism. But Peirce was so chagrined at what James was doing to pragmatism that he changed its name to "pragmaticism," which he said was "ugly enough to be safe enough from kidnappers."[1]

William James was born into a wealthy New England family. (His Irish grandfather, after whom he was named, had wisely invested in the Erie Canal and established his family's fortune.) His father was a theologian with somewhat eccentric religious ideas, but he encouraged the development of his son's independent thought. William and his eventually equally famous brother, Henry—who became one of America's most revered novelists— were schooled in France, Germany, Switzerland, and England before

Ugly Enough to Be Safe from Kidnappers

William finally attached himself to Harvard University, first as a student of science and medicine and then as a professor of medicine, psychology, and ultimately, philosophy. The philosophy that James taught was influenced by his study of psychology and evolutionary theory, but his philosophy was also in many ways a response to personal psychological, moral, and religious crises that he experienced throughout his life. Peirce's pragmatism, as James interpreted it, provided an objective way to address these crises.

Where Peirce had meant for pragmatism merely to provide a formula for making ordinary thought more scientific, James saw it as a philosophy capable of resolving metaphysical and religious dilemmas. Furthermore, he saw it as both a theory of meaning and a theory of truth. Let us first look at James's pragmatic theory of meaning. In *Pragmatism*, he wrote:

> Is the world one or many?—fated or free?—material or spiritual?—here are notions either of which may or may not hold good of the world; and disputes over such notions are unending. The pragmatic method in such cases is to try to interpret each notion by tracing its respective practical consequences. What difference would it practically make to anyone if this notion rather than that notion were true? If no practical difference whatever can be traced, then the alternatives mean practically the same thing, and all dispute is idle.[2]

James concluded from this thought process the following principle: "There can *be* no difference anywhere that doesn't *make* a difference elsewhere."[3]

To clarify James's point, we will take three sentences, each quite different from the others, and test them for pragmatic meaning:

A. Steel is harder than flesh.
B. There is a Bengal tiger loose outside.
C. God exists.

From a pragmatic point of view, the meanings of sentences A and B are unproblematic. We know exactly what it would be like to believe them, as opposed to believing their opposites. If we believed an alternative to A, it is clear that in many cases we would behave very differently than we do behave now. And what we believe about B will also have an immediate impact on our behavior. What about sentence C? Here we see what James himself would admit to be the subjective feature of his theory of meaning. If certain people believed that God existed, they would conceive of the world very differently than they would conceive of it if they believed God did not exist. However, there are other people whose conceptions of the world would be *practically* identical (i.e., identical in practice) whether they believed that God did or did not exist. For these people, the propositions "God exists" and "God does not exist" would *mean* (practically) the same thing. For certain other people who find themselves somewhere between these two extremes, the proposition "God exists" *means* something like, "On Sunday, I put on nice clothes and go to church," because, for them, engaging in this activity is the only practical outcome of their belief (and a belief is just a rule for action, as Peirce had said).

> I now believe that steel is harder than flesh.

So much for the pragmatic theory of meaning. Now for the pragmatic theory of truth. James had this to say about truth: "ideas (which themselves are but parts of our experience) become true just insofar as they help us to get into satisfactory relation with other parts of our experience, . . . Truth

> I am dressed up, therefore God exists.

A Pragmatic Proof of God's Existence

in our ideas means their power to 'work.'"[4] James also said (perhaps less felicitously) that the issue was that of the "cash value" of ideas.[5]

It is interesting to compare the pragmatic theory of truth with the other two theories of truth that have competed with each other throughout the history of Western philosophy: the *correspondence* theory and the *coherence* theory. The correspondence theory has been the dominant one and has been especially favored by empiricists. It says simply that a proposition is true if it corresponds with the facts. The sentence "The cat is on the mat" is true if and only if the cat is in fact on the mat. The main attractions of this theory are its simplicity and its appeal to common sense. The main weaknesses are (1) the difficulties in explaining how linguistic entities (words, sentences) can *correspond* to things that are nothing like language, (2) the difficulty in stating exactly what it is that sentences are supposed to correspond to (facts? What is a "fact" if not that which a true sentence asserts?), and (3) a particular awkwardness in its application to mathematics (what is it to which the proposition "$5 + 2 = 7$" corresponds?). The coherence theory of truth asserts that a proposition is true if it coheres with all the other propositions taken to be true. This theory has been preferred by rationalists. Its greatest strength is that it makes sense out of the idea of mathematical truth ("$5 + 2 = 7$" is true because it is entailed by "$7 = 7$," and by "$1 + 6 = 7$," and by "$21 \div 3 = 2 \times 3 + 1$," etc., etc.). Its greatest weakness is its vicious circularity. Proposition A is true by virtue of its coherence with propositions B, C, and D. Proposition B is true by virtue of its coherence with propositions A, C, and D. Proposition C is true by virtue of its coherence with A, B, and D, and so forth. (Think of the belief system of a paranoid. All his beliefs cohere perfectly with one another. Everything that happens to him is evidence that everybody is out to get him.)

Now, the pragmatist says that the test of correspondence and the test of coherence are not competing theories, but simply different tools to be applied to beliefs to see if those beliefs "work."

The Paranoid Theory of Truth

Sometimes one test is a satisfactory tool, sometimes the other, but neither is the sole criterion of truth. James's most extended account of truth is this:

> True ideas are those that we can assimilate, validate, corroborate and verify. False ideas are those that we cannot. . . . The truth of an idea is not a stagnant property inherent in it. Truth *happens* to an idea. It *becomes* true, is *made* true by events.[6]

If we return to our three model sentences, we see that A certainly *works*. Believing that steel is harder than flesh definitely puts us in a much more satisfactory relation to the rest of our experience than does believing the opposite. For most of us, B usually *does not* work. Under typical conditions, believing that there is a Bengal tiger loose outside the room we now occupy would put us in a paranoid relation with the rest of our experience. Of course, sometimes believing it to be true *would* work. (Namely, we are tempted to say, when there really is a tiger outside.)

What about the third example? Obviously, the truth or falsity of the claim that God exists cannot even come up for those people for whom there is no practical difference whether they believe it or not. But for those people for whom the distinction is meaningful, the pragmatic test of truth is available. Unlike for the propositions in sentences A and B, there is no *direct* pragmatic test of the proposition "God exists." In fact, the empirical evidence, according to James, is equally indecisive for or against God's existence. About this and similar cases, James said, "Our passional nature not only lawfully may, but must, decide an option between propositions, whenever it is a genuine option that cannot by its nature be decided on intellectual grounds."[7] (In asserting this, James sounded very much like Kant.) James went on to say that for many people, the belief in God *does* work, though he was prepared to admit that for a few it does *not* work. Rather, a belief in God puts some people in a state of paranoic fear vis-à-vis the rest of their experiences. So, for the first group, the proposition "God exists" is true, and for the second group, it is false.

It was this subjective side of James's theory of truth that displeased many philosophers, including Peirce. This feature of pragmatism was somewhat ameliorated by the work of John Dewey. First, one last point about James: The allusion earlier to the similarity between him and Kant was not gratuitous. Both Kant and James tried to justify on practical grounds our right to hold certain

For Some, a Belief in God Definitely Has Cash Value

moral and religious values that cannot be justified on purely intellectual grounds. Furthermore, just as Kant had seen himself as trying to mediate between the rationalists and the empiricists, so did James see himself as mediating between what he called the "tender-minded" and the "tough-minded" philosophers:

The Tender-Minded	The Tough-Minded
Rationalistic (going by "principles")	Empiricist (going by "facts")
Intellectualistic	Sensationalistic
Idealistic	Materialistic
Optimistic	Pessimistic
Religious	Irreligious
Free-willist	Fatalistic
Monistic	Pluralistic
Dogmatical	Skeptical

The trouble with these alternatives, said James, was that "you find an empirical philosophy that is not religious enough, and a religious philosophy that is not empirical enough."[8] Obviously, James thought that his pragmatism offered a third, more satisfying, alternative.

Dewey

John Dewey (1859–1952) was perhaps the most influential of the pragmatists—if for no other reason than that he outlived them by so many years.

He was actually schooled in Hegelian idealism (which in the second half of the nineteenth century had a great impact on American and British philosophy, as we will see), and it left a permanent dent in Dewey's way of thinking, contextualizing as it did all philosophy in terms of history, society, and culture.

As I was saying . . .

WILLIAM JAMES 1842–1910

CHARLES PEIRCE 1839–1914

Hegel Putting a Permanent Dent in Dewey's Thought

But under the influence of James as well as Charles Darwin's theory of evolution, Dewey drifted away from Hegelianism. Whereas Hegel found humanity progressing by resolving certain logical contradictions in the ideational sphere, Dewey found progress in the resolution of certain organic conflicts between individuals and their social and natural environments. From Darwin, Dewey learned that consciousness, mind, and intellect were not something different from nature, opposed to it and standing in splendid aloofness above it; rather, they were adaptations to nature, continuous with it, and like other appendages of plants, insects, and animals, they functioned best when used to solve problems posed to them by the natural world.

Such an idea fit easily into the schema of the pragmatism of Peirce and James. For James, however, pragmatism had been a therapeutic tool for dealing primarily with certain religious and metaphysical conflicts, and with individual psychology. Dewey was more concerned with social psychology. His basic philosophical interests were in politics, education, and morality.

According to Dewey, higher organisms develop as problem-solving mechanisms by learning routines that transcend purely instinctual

Jamesian Therapy

responses. We call these routines "habits." As the organism's environment becomes more ambiguous and the organism itself becomes more complex, its responses become more "mental." Intelligence evolves when habit fails to perform efficiently. Intelligence interrupts and delays a response to the environment when a problematic situation is recognized as problematic. Thought is, in fact, a "response to the doubtful as such." The function of reflective thought is to turn obscurity into clarity. Such a transformation is called "knowledge." The move from ignorance to knowledge is the transition from "a perplexed, troubled, or confused situation at the beginning [to] a cleared-up, unified, resolved situation at the close."[9] Ideas are plans

Ideas Are Deferred Actions

for action. They are "designations of operations to be performed"; they are hypotheses. Thinking is simply "deferred action." Thoughts that do not pass into actions that rearrange experience are useless thoughts. (The same is true of philosophies.)

> There is [a] first-rate test of the value of any philosophy which is offered us: Does it end in conclusions which, when they are referred back to ordinary life-experiences and their predicaments, render them more significant, more luminous to us, and make our dealing with them more fruitful? Or does it terminate in rendering the things of ordinary experience more opaque than they were before and depriving them of having in "reality" even the significance that they seemed to have?[10]

Traditional epistemologists, whether rationalist or empiricist, have erred. They believed that what was to be known was some reality pre-existing the act of knowing. For them, the mind is the mirror of reality, or what Dewey called "the spectator theory of knowledge." It sought to find certainty, either in universals (rationalism) or in sense data (empiricism). But universals and sense data are not the *objects* of knowledge; rather, they are the instruments of knowledge. One of the consequences of Dewey's revision is that philosophy must abandon what hitherto had been considered as "ultimate questions" about Being and Knowledge. Knowledge must be instrumental. Its function is to solve problems.

Strictly speaking, then, the object of knowledge is constructed by the inquiring mind. Knowledge changes the world that existed prior to its being known, but not in the Kantian sense in which it *distorts* reality (the noumenal world); rather, knowledge changes the world in the sense that it imposes new traits on the world, for example, by clarifying that which was inherently unclear.

> The function of reflective thought is to transform a situation in which there is experienced obscurity, doubt, conflict, disturbances of some sort, into a situation that is clear, coherent, settled, harmonious.[11]

According to Dewey, the definition of the world as the totality of substances (things) was abandoned with the advent of modern science, which revealed not "objects" but relationships. In abandoning that definition, science also dissolved the distinction between *knowing* and *doing*. Galileo is credited by Dewey for initiating this revolution, a revolution that all but philosophers have accepted. Science allows us to escape from the tyranny of the past and allows us to exert some control over our natural and social environment. And yet, it is not only scientists who know. Poets, farmers, teachers, statespeople, and dramatists *know*. Nevertheless, ultimately all must look to the scientists for a methodology. In fact, science is just a sophisticated form of common sense. Science, or its strategies, should play the role in the contemporary world that the Church played in the medieval world. Scientific techniques must be applied to the development of both values and social reform.

For Dewey, there is no dichotomy between scientific facts and values. Values are a certain kind of facts found in experience, facts such as beauty, splendor, and humor. But like the products of every other intervention into reality, they reveal themselves relative to the interests of the inquirer. But Dewey's "pragmatic instrumentalism" is *not* just a form of utilitarianism. The error of utilitarianism is to define value in terms of objects antecedently enjoyed; but for Dewey, just because something *has been* enjoyed does not make that thing *worthy* of enjoyment. Without the intervention of thought, enjoyments are not values. To call something valuable is to say that

**Science Must Take Over the Role
Played by the Medieval Church**

it fulfills certain conditions—namely, that it directs conduct well. There is a difference between the loved and the lovable, the blamed and the blamable, the admired and the admirable. What is needed is an active and cultivated appreciation of value. Its development is a supreme goal, whether the problem confronted is intellectual, aesthetic, or moral.

In fact, the ultimate goal of action should be the full development of individuals as human beings. Therefore, democracy and education have the same goal. Each individual has something to contribute to the construction of social institutions, and the test of value of all institutions will be the contributions they make back to the individual in terms of creating the conditions for the all-around growth of every member of society. Such growth involves achieving certain kinds of experiences that are *final*, in that they do not provoke the search for some other experience. These are aesthetic experiences. Sometimes, according to Dewey, these experiences are so intense that they are designated as "religious."

The Analytic Tradition

Analytic philosophy has been the dominant philosophical tradition in Britain and in North America for sixty years, and has made significant inroads into the European Continent (just as Continental philosophy has a minority representation in British, American, and Canadian universities). Though there are many variations of analytic philosophy, let us say for the moment that this school of thought tends to scoff at the great metaphysical systems of the most prominent historical philosophers that have been studied in earlier chapters, and tends to restrict itself to the analysis of meaning and truth in the language of scientific, ethical, aesthetic, and everyday discourse.

One reason these practitioners tend to avoid the speculation of traditional philosophy is that they reject earlier conceptions of philosophy's function. Plato, Descartes, Schopenhauer, and many other philosophers we've studied saw philosophy's goal as that of giving a complete picture of reality and explaining reality's many facets. But by the end of the nineteenth century most intellectuals had ceded that job to the sciences, and restricted philosophy's role to the analysis of different forms of discourse about reality. For a number of philosophers the main tool of analysis is logic. Others stressed linguistic analysis; in most cases a combination of these two methods were adopted. Some analytic philosophers have held that the key task is the conceptual analysis of philosophically puzzling features of natural languages, that is, the analysis of the meaning of concepts employed in everyday discourse—concepts like "mind," "body," "perception," "duty," "art," and "justice." Others have seen the main task as the analysis of an artificial logical language that can be detected as a hidden structure behind natural languages, that is, the analysis of categories like "number," "equivalence," "inference," "disjunction," "necessity," and "contingency." A group of philosophers related to the previous one sees the philosopher's job as the logical analysis of the key concepts of science, ideas like "causality," "probability," and "natural law."

Above, I implied that analytic philosophy was primarily an intellectual development in the English-speaking world. Yet, the individual who is now seen as a true pioneer in analytic philosophy is Gottlob Frege (1848–1925), who was born in Europe—in fact, in the old city of Jena, in central Germany.

Frege

Jena had been the site of Napoleon's decisive defeat of the Prussian forces in 1806. It was then and there that G. W. F. Hegel hastily finished his metaphysical masterpiece, *The Phenomenology of Mind*, as Napoleon's cannon fire blasted the city walls. We began our overview of nineteenth-century philosophy in Jena, and we now return there, seventy years later, to complete it. In Jena we encounter Hegel's countryman Gottlob Frege (1848–1925), but Frege's work is in every way the opposite of Hegel's—and, indeed, is radically different from that of everyone presented in chapter 6, which treats a period that has been called "the wild

Gottlob Frege

years of philosophy."[12] Frege toiled in relative obscurity at his office in the mathematics department of the University of Jena attempting to solve problems concerning the foundations of arithmetic that seemed at the time to have very little to do with philosophy. But his efforts to support his mathematical hypotheses led him to develop a general theory of meaning that would eventually have a major impact on the history of philosophy. He died without realizing that his accomplishments would come to be seen as the initial steps in what is now called analytic philosophy and that he would be looked back on as a pioneer. Frege directed philosophy toward new themes and new techniques that would come to dominate British and American philosophy throughout the twentieth century and that would have some impact on the Continent as well.

For Frege, questions about meaning were ultimately related to questions about *logic*. Our best philosophical arguments about any topic whatsoever are only as good as the logic that structures them. We can say that modern logic began in 1879 with the publication of Frege's *Begriffschrift*.[13] This book lays out the first extensive discussion of the ideas of existence and generality in logic—the relation between propositions asserting, "There exists at least one X where X is Y," and those stating, "All X is Y." This apparently simple notion had been completely missing from Aristotle's logic, which had dominated philosophy from his time until the eighteenth century, when Leibniz had made significant contributions. (In fact, Leibniz had stuck most of his papers on logic in a desk drawer, and they saw the light of day only in the twentieth century. Much of the actual notation in contemporary symbolic logic derives from Leibniz's scribblings, but much of it also comes from Frege.)

Frege's next book, *The Foundations of Arithmetic* (1884), addresses the need for a theory proving that arithmetic is internally self-consistent (a "consistency proof"). Frege tries to show that an extension of the basic principles of logic generates all the fundamental notions of arithmetic and that therefore the consistency of arithmetic can be proved from purely logical considerations.

A successful definition of "number," for example, could be derived from the principle of identity, that is, A = A. This finding means, in fact, that arithmetic can be reduced to logic (yet another step in the history of reductionism that commenced with the pre-Socratics). If arithmetic derives from logic, then it has a purely analytic a priori status. This thesis, if true, eliminates Plato's and Descartes's claim that mathematics is grounded in innate ideas, and it gets rid of Kant's mathematical synthetic a priori category. (You may want to review all these terms in the Glossary.) But it also replaces the unconvincing thesis of empiricists like Mill, who asserted that mathematical truths are empirical generalizations. ("Well, whenever in the past we have put two things together with three things, we've ended up with a total of five things, so we will hazard that '2 + 3 = 5' is true, or at least highly probable. Still, it's not *certain*. Nobody knows for sure that we won't get six things next time!")

A significant feature of the theory of meaning that Frege developed shows up in many contemporary discussions of the topic of meaning. It is a distinction he drew between *Sinn* and *Bedeutung*, usually translated as "sense" and "reference." These terms are meant to be applied to the analysis of **proper names.** (If you are unfamiliar with this phrase, check it out in the Glossary.) The older view about these terms was that their meaning was exhausted in the function of **denotation**; that is, the function of naming, or

I don't get it! Every time I count them, I come up with a different number

John Stuart Mill Inspects His Rabbit Collection

referring to, or pointing at, the object that they named. For example, the meaning of the name "George Washington" would be the actual person named. The words simply stand for him and have no meaning other than the function of designation. But Frege points out a major difficulty with this commonsense account. Take three proper names: (A) the morning star; (B) the evening star; and (C) Venus. (A) refers to a heavenly body appearing in the east immediately before sunrise, used for centuries by sailors to navigate the morning seas. (B) refers to a heavenly body appearing in the west immediately after sunset, used for centuries by sailors to navigate the evening seas. (C) refers

**The Rime of the Ancient Mariner
(A Collaborative Work of Art by Praxiteles,
Coleridge, Palmer, and an Anonymous
Author of Annoying Kiddie-Jingles)**

to the most brilliant planet in the solar system, second in order to the sun. Now, it was an empirical discovery that (A) = (B) = (C), that is, that the so-called morning star and the so-called evening star are in fact the same body and, furthermore, that that body is the planet Venus. Now, suppose that the meaning of a proper name is simply the object named; call that object "X." In that case, the sentence "The morning star is the evening star, which in fact is the planet Venus" means "X = X, which in fact = X." In other words, the sentence is a tautology that conveys no information at all. Yet, clearly the sentence in question *does* convey information. Anyone who knows it to be true knows *more* than did the ancient mariners. Therefore, concluded Frege, there must be a third element to meaning in these cases in addition to the *name* and the *object named*, and he called that third element *Sinn* (pronounced "zinn" in German), or sense. The sense in each case "sheds a different light" on the object referred to. It is a "mode of presentation" of the object—a way of representing it.

Frege's theory has not satisfied all the analytic philosophers that descended from Frege, but it pointed out an important problem with which any serious theory of meaning must deal. Furthermore, it set the tone for the whole school of analytic philosophy that now reveres Frege as a founding father. Despite their differences, all analytic philosophers owe a debt to Frege, partly because two of the most famous analytic philosophers—Bertrand Russell and Ludwig Wittgenstein—read his work with great interest, discussed his ideas with him, and were influenced by his theories.

Shortly before the turn of the century—and before Frege's work impacted British philosophy—an amazing phenomenon occurred in Britain, and the ripple effect brought it to America. The British discovered Hegel! This discovery took place long after Hegelianism had been declared dead on the Continent. Neo-Hegelianism found some able defenders in men like F. H. Bradley at Oxford, J. E. McTaggart at Cambridge, and Josiah Royce at the University of California. But the Anglo-American national characters (if there are such things) could not have been very comfortable with Hegelian idealism, and it is not

The British Discover Hegel

surprising that a realist reaction was soon provoked. (Notice that "realism" is used here in the Lockean sense of naming a *real* external world and not in the medieval sense of naming the reality of Platonic Forms.) This revolt was led by G. E. Moore and Bertrand Russell.

Moore

George Edward Moore (1873–1958) had come to Cambridge to study classical literature ("the Greats," as it is known there), and part of his program involved taking philosophy classes, where, according to him, he heard the most astonishing things asserted—things to which he could attach no precise meaning. It seemed to him that the lectures were full of denials of things that every sane human knew to be true. Moore must have been an annoying undergraduate. If McTaggart asserted that space was unreal, Moore would ask if that meant that the wall next to him was *not* nearer than the library building; if McTaggart asserted that time was unreal, Moore wanted to know if that meant that the class would *not* end at noon. Russell found Moore's "naive" questions to be very exciting. Years later Russell wrote of Moore:

> He took the lead in rebellion, and I followed, with a sense of emancipation. Bradley argued that everything common sense believes in is mere appearance; we reverted to the opposite extreme, and thought that everything is real that common sense, uninfluenced by philosophy or theology,

Young George Moore and Bertie Russell Discover That the Grass Is Green

supposes real. With a sense of escaping from prison we allowed ourselves to think that grass is green, that the sun and stars would exist if no one was aware of them.[14]

Moore continued to defend common sense throughout his life, even though Russell would later find his own reasons for doubting it. (Russell: "Science itself has shown that none of these common-sense notions will quite serve for the explanation of the world.")[15] Indeed, Moore came to be known as the "philosopher of common sense." Common sense became for him what sense data had been for the empiricists and what reason had been for the rationalists—namely, the foundation of certainty. In one of his most famous essays, "A Defence of Common Sense," Moore listed a series of propositions that he claimed *to know with certainty* to be true, including these:

A. There exists at present a living human body, which is my body.
B. This body was much smaller when it was born than it is now.
C. Ever since it was born it has been in contact with, or not far from, the surface of the earth.

D. Ever since it was born it has been at various distances from a great number of physical objects.

E. The earth had existed many years before my body was born.

F. Many other human bodies had existed before my body was born, and many of them had already died before my birth.

This list goes on and on. It is a rather boring list, but Moore knew full well that his list was tedious. The point is that, according to him, *every one of these propositions has been denied by some philosopher, somewhere, sometime.* The truth usually *is* boring, and we should get suspicious when we hear dramatic metaphysical theses that deny commonplace beliefs, such as the Hegelian claims: Time and space have no objective reality; the individual is an abstraction; mathematics is only a stage in the dialectic; the Absolute is expressed, but not revealed, in the world. Moore did not necessarily want to claim that these assertions were untrue, only that they were *strange* and that no obvious meaning could be attached to them. As Moore's student and friend John Maynard Keynes said, the question most frequently on Moore's lips was, "What *exactly* do you mean?"

G. E. Moore Reads to His Students the List of Things He Knows for Certain

And, said Keynes, "If it appeared under cross-examination that you did not mean *exactly* anything, you lay under a strong suspicion of meaning nothing whatever."

The Hegelian philosophers at Cambridge and Oxford in the 1880s and 1890s had spent a lot of time inventing new philosophical terminology in order to devise novel ways of talking, because they all seemed to agree that there was something defective about our ordinary discourse concerning the world. Moore

What EXACTLY do you mean?

was not a bit convinced that these new ways of speaking were really necessary. He wanted to know *exactly* what was wrong with ordinary language. Moore's commitment to our normal way of thinking and talking about the world is seen very clearly in this passage from "A Defence of Common Sense":

> I [assume] that there is some meaning which is *the ordinary* . . . meaning of such expressions as "The earth has existed for many years past." And this, I am afraid is an assumption which some philosophers are capable of disputing. They seem to think that the question "Do you believe that the earth has existed for many years past?" is not a plain question, such as should be met either by a plain "Yes" or "No," or by a plain "I can't make up my mind," but is the sort of question which can be properly met by: "It all depends on what you mean by 'the earth' and 'exists' and 'years': If you mean so and so, and so and so, and so and so, then I do; but if you mean so and so, and so and so, and so and so, or so and so, and so and so, and so and so, or so and so, and so and so, and so and so, then I don't, or at least I think it is

extremely doubtful." It seems to me that such a view is as profoundly mistaken as any view can be.[16]

It is very clear that, with Moore, the aim of philosophy is not that of generating grandiose metaphysical schemes, nor is it even that of arriving at the truth (much less, the Truth); rather, its goal is the clarification of meaning. This goal puts Moore squarely in the camp of the ana- lytic philosophy that Frege had

> I'm conducting a survey. Do you believe that the earth has existed for many years past?

> It all depends. If you mean so and so, and so and so, then I do . . .

pioneered—a kind of philosophy that, for better or for worse, was to dominate a great part of the twentieth century. Moore was the initiator of what might almost be called a *movement:* one that was antimetaphysical, concerned with detailed analysis, obsessed with the problem of meaning, and far removed from the social, political, and personal problems that afflicted people of his day. Furthermore, with his concern with precise language, Moore took the first step in the direction that has since been called the "linguistic turn." We will see all these features again in Russell, in the logical positivists, and in Wittgenstein.

For all his virtues, Moore seems a bit too complacent to many philosophers today. His perhaps overly satisfied attitude toward the world can be easily detected in the following passage:

> I do not think that the world or the sciences would ever have suggested to me any philosophical problems. What has suggested philosophical

problems to me is things which other philosophers have said about the world and the sciences.[17]

Russell

Moore's friend at Cambridge, Bertrand Russell (1872–1970), was born into a prominent noble family. His grandfather, Lord John Russell, was a British prime minister. Bertrand himself inherited an earldom. He was privately educated, and he early demonstrated unusual mathematical skills. His temporary flirtation with Hegelianism must have gone against all his native instincts and abilities. The philosophy of McTaggart and Bradley had no use for the mathematical and scientific precision for which Russell had a natural affinity. As we saw, Moore

Hegelianism's Fatal Attraction

helped Russell break away from Hegelianism's fatal attraction, and for a brief period Moore and Russell thought alike. But Moore did not know mathematics and was uninterested in science; so even though Moore and Russell always agreed that the main job of the philosopher was that of analysis, they soon went their separate philosophical ways.

In 1900 Russell went to the International Congress of Philosophy in Paris and met the great mathematician and logician Guiseppe Peano. Conversations with him and other mathematical luminaries such as Gottlob Frege set Russell on a path that led to one of his major works, *Principia Mathematica*, written in collaboration with Alfred North Whitehead in 1910–1913. This work was a protracted defense of Frege's thesis that all of arithmetic is an extension of the basic principles of logic. Probably Russell's major contribution to the history of philosophy was his demonstration of the power of symbolic logic as a tool of philosophical analysis.

A key feature of Russell's overall view was his belief in philosophy's subordination to science. Russell thought that philosophy should be built on science rather than the other way around because there was less risk of error in science than in philosophy. He was one of many analytical philosophers who assumed that "science is innocent unless proved guilty, while philosophy is guilty unless proved innocent."[18] The fact that Russell saw philosophy as ancillary to science, along with the fact that science was changing so rapidly during the period in which Russell wrote,

Reading *Principia Mathematica*

partially explains why Russell's philosophy evolved so much over the many years that he developed it. His most uncharitable critics claimed that Russell made a philosophical career for himself by writing a book every year in which he refuted his book of the previous year. And indeed, it is difficult to state exactly what Russell's philosophy *is*, precisely because of its many transformations over the years. But there were certain common denominators that survived and unified his views despite all the changes. One constant in his thought was his view of philosophy as essentially analytical. In 1924 he wrote:

> Although . . . comprehensive construction is part of the business of philosophy, I do not believe it is the most important part. The most important part, to my mind, consists in criticizing and clarifying notions which are apt to be regarded as fundamental and accepted uncritically. As instances I might mention: mind, matter, consciousness, knowledge, experience, causality, will, time. I believe all these notions to be inexact and approximate, essentially infected with vagueness, incapable of forming part of any exact science.[19]

Lord Russell with Razor

Another constant in Russell's philosophy was his commitment to Ockham's razor, which, as we have seen, is a plea for theoretical simplicity, an injunction not to "multiply entities beyond necessity." Russell formulated it thus: "Wherever possible, substitute constructions out of known entities for inferences to unknown entities."[20] He thought we should try to account for the world in terms of those features of it with which we have direct acquaintance and we should avoid the temptation of positing the existence of anything with which we cannot be acquainted, unless we are forced to do so by undeniable facts or by a compelling logical argument.

I will let Russell's "Theory of Descriptions," which he took to be one of his major contributions to philosophy, represent his views: From Plato forward, philosophers had struggled with the logic of the concept of existence, and many of them, including Plato, were driven to create grandiose metaphysical schemes to accommodate the problems caused by that concept. Russell found most of these schemes to be *too* metaphysical (i.e., too much in violation of the strictures of Ockham's razor) or to be simply too paradoxical. Let us look at three such problems dealing with the question of existence.

1. I say, "The golden mountain does not exist." You ask, "What is it that does not exist?" I answer, "The golden mountain." By doing so, I seem to be attributing a kind of existence to the very thing whose existence I just denied. (And what *thing* is that?) Furthermore, if I say, "Unicorns do not exist" and "Round squares do not exist," I seem to be saying that golden mountains, unicorns, and round squares are three different things, and none of them exists! The Platonists' solution to this problem was to say that terms like "the golden

mountain" designate ideals that exist in a realm of pure being, but not in the physical world. Clearly, such a view would be too metaphysical for Russell and would cry out for the application of Ockham's razor.

2. Consider the sentence "Scott is the author of *Waverley*." Logicians have held that if two terms denote the same object, these terms could be interchanged without changing the meaning or truth of the proposition being expressed by the sentence. (If $A = B$, then $[A = B] = [B = A] = [A = A] = [B = B]$.) Now, the novel *Waverley* was published anonymously, and many people wanted to know who wrote it. King George IV was particularly interested to know because he wanted to find out who was maligning his ancestors. The king did *not* want to know whether the sentence "The author of *Waverley* is the author of *Waverley*" was true, nor if the sentence "Sir Walter Scott is Sir Walter Scott" was true.

The Golden Mountain—Which (Unfortunately) Does Not Exist

(Though a Platonic/Leibnizian solution to the problem would be that, indeed, *all* sentences are versions of the proposition "Everything is everything," or "A = A." But such a metaphysical "solution" could never satisfy a Bertrand Russell.)

3. Consider this sentence: "The present king of France is bald." This assertion seems false (because there is no such person), but according to the law of the excluded middle, the negation of any false proposition must be true, so it follows that there must be truth to the claim "The present king of France is not bald." Yet surely that sentence is false too. Must we once again accept some kind of metaphysical solution to the dilemma by consigning to an ideal realm of being the object designated by the term "the present king of France," along with the ideal characteristics "bald" and "hairy"? The Platonic logicians thought so. Russell thought not. (Russell said that the Hegelians would find the solution in a synthesis: "The present king of France wears a toupee.")

The Hegelian Solution

So here we have three different logical problems concerning the concept of being or existence. The goal of Russell's Theory of Descriptions was to unveil the true logical structure of propositions about existence in order to eliminate paradoxes and metaphysical obfuscations. Russell discovered a formula that he thought could perform this job:

> There is an entity $\underline{C}$, such that the sentence "$\underline{X}$ is $\underline{Y}$" is true if and only if $\underline{X} = \underline{C}$.

In this formula, C is an entity, Y is a characteristic written in the form of an adjective, and X is the subject to which the adjective is attributed. For example, the sentence "The golden mountain does not exist" is rendered by Russell as: "There's no entity C, such that the sentence 'X is golden and mountainous' is true if and only if X = C." In other words, the offending term, "the golden mountain" (offending because it seems to *denote* an entity, that is, name a thing) has been transformed into a *description* (golden and mountainous), and the real assertion of the proposition is that there is no existing object that could be correctly characterized using that description. Notice that the notion of "existence" has been analyzed out of the term "the golden mountain."

Concerning the second problem, the sentence "Scott is the author of *Waverley*" becomes "There is an entity C, such that 'X wrote *Waverley*' is true if and only if X = C; moreover, C is Scott." So the characteristic "authorly" properly describes an existing entity (Scott) and does so in a way that is not merely tautological. Notice once again that the notion of existence has been analyzed out of the description "the author of *Waverley*."

Finally, the sentence "The present king of France is bald" means "There is an entity C, such that 'X is kingly, French, and bald' is true if and only if X = C." But there *is no* entity to which such a description correctly applies, so the sentence is false; and so is its negation because there is also no entity that is correctly described as being "kingly, French, and hairy." So we can assert that both sentences are false without violating the law of the excluded middle.

In each of these three cases, Russell applied Ockham's razor and excised the concept of existence. Russell rather immodestly said of his solution, "This clears up two millennia of muddle-headedness about 'existence,' beginning with Plato's *Theaetetus*."[21]

The exposition of the Theory of Descriptions has probably been the most technical presentation in this book, and even then, it has been greatly simplified. Much of Russell's philosophy was highly specialized, but Russell the technical philosopher contrasted greatly with Russell the social critic and activist. He spent part of World War I in jail as a pacifist. (He was disappointed that Moore joined the war effort as a British officer, and he was even more disappointed that his student Ludwig Wittgenstein returned to the Continent to join the Austrian army as a private.) Russell was a harsh critic of the social policies of both the United States and the Soviet Union, and after World War II he became an active protester against nuclear weapons. (He was jailed when he was eighty-nine years old for inciting the public to civil disobedience after an illegal rally in Hyde Park to protest the presence of American atomic weapons in Britain;

True Being exists only in the realm of Being: *Plato*

Being truly exists as an actuality of a potentiality: *Aristotle*

True Being is Perfection, and Perfection is True Being: *Anselm*

There is no True Being. Being is a mere word, naming nothing: *William of Ockham*

Being is truly a characteristic of either of two substances: *Descartes*

True Being is monadic: *Leibniz*

Being? Beats me! Truly, *Hume*

Being is not a predicate: *Kant*

Being is the Rational, and the Rational is (*Bes?*): *Hegel*

Being is the manifestation of the Will: *Schopenhauer*

Being does not exist; only Will to Power is: *Nietzsche*

Being cannot be thought: *Kierkegaard*

There is an entity c, such that "x is y" is true if and only if x = c.

in his nineties, he was actively engaged in preaching against the American involvement in Vietnam.) In this respect, Russell was the very opposite of G. E. Moore, who, as we've seen, never found anything to engage his intellect and passions except things said by other philosophers. In 1960 when the journalist Ved Mehta went to Russell's home to interview him about his philosophy, Mehta was met by Russell at the door and was asked by Russell if he had not heard about The Bomb. Russell told Mehta that in the face of the implications of the nuclear crisis, there was no time to discuss philosophy.

Logical Positivism

The paradigmatic case of the view that philosophy's job is that of logical analysis came from a group of European philosophers who are known as the **logical positivists.** Their movement grew out of some seminars in the philosophy of science offered at the University of Vienna in the early 1920s by Professor Moritz Schlick. The original group, which called itself the "Vienna Circle," was composed mostly of scientists with a flair for philosophy and a desire to render philosophy respectable by making it scientific. Their technical inspiration came primarily from the work of Ernst Mach, Jules Poincaré, and Albert Einstein. The models for their idea of logical analysis came from *Principia Mathematica,* by Russell and Whitehead, and from *Tractatus Logico-Philosophicus,* recently published by Ludwig Wittgenstein. (Much to the great annoyance of its members, Wittgenstein stayed aloof from the Vienna Circle—you will read a lot more about Wittgenstein shortly.)

The Vienna Circle was positively antagonistic toward most of the history of philosophy, finding only Hume's empiricism and Kant's antimetaphysical stance worthy of respect.

Wittgenstein Aloof from the Vienna Circle

Besides Schlick (who was murdered in 1936 by an insane student on the steps of the University of Vienna), other people associated with the movement were Otto Neurath, Hans Reichenbach, A. J. Ayer, and Rudolf Carnap. By the early 1930s, their passion for scientific truth was well known, so they were not much liked by the Nazis (whose views did not fare well in the light of scientific scrutiny); nor did the members of the Circle like the Nazis much, and the advent of Hitler's regime scattered the group throughout British and American universities, where they exerted even more influence than perhaps they might have done had they remained in Austria and Germany.

At the risk of oversimplifying the platform of logical positivism (but only slightly), I can say that the main project of the Vienna Circle was the resurrection and updating of Hume's Fork. All putative propositions would be shown to be either *analytic* (tautologies whose negation leads to self-contradiction), *synthetic* (propositions whose confirmation depends on observation and experimentation), or *nonsense*. The positivists' conclusions were therefore like Hume's in many respects. For example, Carnap wrote, "In the domain of *metaphysics*, including all philosophy of value and normative theory, logical analysis yields the negative result *that the alleged statements in this domain are entirely meaningless.*" Take a look at Carnap's analysis of the function of language:[22]

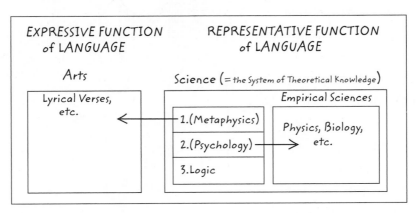

We see that language has only two duties: expression and representation. Once psychology has been correctly established as an empirical science and metaphysics correctly recognized as an art form, philosophy is seen to be nothing but logic. According to Carnap, there is nothing wrong with the poetic function of metaphysics as long as it is identified and treated as such. Carnap wrote,

> The non-theoretical character of metaphysics would not be in itself a defect; all arts have this non-theoretical character without thereby losing their high value for personal as well as social life. The danger lies in the *deceptive* character of metaphysics; it gives the illusion of knowledge without actually giving any knowledge.[23]

Even some of Hume's skeptical musings were too metaphysical for the positivists. Hume had claimed that there was no good reason to believe that any event ever caused another event because there was no sense datum representing any *cause*, only sense data representing series of events. But for Schlick, Hume's search for an entity to correspond to the name "cause" was itself suspect. Schlick said, "The word cause, as used in everyday life, implies *nothing* but regularity of sequence because *nothing else* is used to verify the propositions in which it occurs. . . . The criterion of causality is successful prediction. That is all we can say."[24]

Schlick's comments about causality reveal another feature of the positivistic view, namely, that (in the case of synthetic claims) *the meaning of a proposition is its method of verification.* Furthermore, the language of verification would have to be reduced to what were called **"protocol sentences."** Protocol sentences were to be assertions that expressed the raw verifiable facts with complete simplicity. These sentences would be "the absolutely indubitable starting points of all knowledge," according to Schlick. An example would be "Moritz Schlick perceived red on the 6th of May, 1934, at 3:03 P.M. in the room numbered 301 in the Philosophy Hall at the University of Vienna." The logical positivists, looking for **incorrigibility** as the foundation of science, decided that even protocol sentences were not certain enough because they did not designate the *simplest* facts, so they tried to reduce protocol sentences yet further to what they called **"confirmation sentences,"** an example of which would be "Red here now." These sentences were more certain because they were less complex than protocol sentences; but the trouble with them turned out to be that the act of writing down the phrase "here now" produced a meaning not identical to the actual pointing that took place when the confirmation sentence was uttered. Not only that, but to name the experience as "red"

"I saw a book."

The person whose acquaintances call him M.S., and whose passport No. 13456 is registered with the Austrian government, and who is myself, could correctly have said on May 6th, 1934, at 3:03 P.M. in room 301 of the University of Vienna, "I perceive red."

Red here now

GRUNT!

seemed to transcend the perceptual event by categorizing it as a member of the class of red experiences, thereby referring to more than what was actually present in the experience. Ultimately, it was suggested that certainty could be found only in an act of *pointing* and *grunting*.

By now it was beginning to become obvious that something had

GRUNT.

No! GRUNT, GRUNT.

No, No. GRUNT, GRUNT, GRUNT.

gone very wrong and that this part of the positivist program was hopeless. The logical positivists had tried to find the foundations of science, and instead they had reverted to the cave dweller mentality. They fell to squabbling over this problem, and it was never resolved to anyone's satisfaction, including their own.

Logical Positivists Arguing

We have seen Carnap's demonstration that metaphysics is only an expressive, not representative, form of language. The positivists performed a similar outrage on moral language, claiming that it was simply a disguised display of emotion, often coupled with "commands in a misleading grammatical form," according to Carnap.[25] So the sentence "Stealing is immoral" really means something like this:

STEALING!!! DON'T DO IT!!!

Therefore, the so-called sentence "Stealing is immoral" is really only the expression of emotion and can be neither true nor false. It expresses what Ayer called a "pseudo-concept."[26] Such were the moral consequences of the positivists' radical application of Hume's Fork.

Needless to say, most philosophers were not very satisfied with this account of ethics. Furthermore, as has been indicated, logical positivism began to come undone over its failure to find the much-heralded incorrigibility in protocol sentences and confirmation sentences. (As one commentator put it, the positivists set out to sea unfurling the sails of what they took to be a watertight "man-o'-war," only to find that it leaked badly. They began patching the leaks and discovered that the patches leaked. By the time the ship sank, they were patching patches on patches.) Logical positivism came to its final grief over another internal question: If all propositions are either analytic, synthetic, or nonsense, what is the status of the proposition "All propositions are either

Some Nonsense Is Better Than Other Nonsense (after Sir John Tenniel)

analytic, synthetic, or nonsense"? It too must be either analytic, synthetic, or nonsense. If it is analytic (Ayer's view), it is a mere tautology and tells us nothing about the world. Furthermore, in this case, we should be able to look up the word "proposition" in the dictionary and discover it to be defined in terms of analyticity and syntheticity. But it's not. If the proposition is synthetic (Carnap's view), then we should be able to verify it empirically. But verification isn't possible either. So it looks as though the key principle of positivism is neither analytic nor synthetic. Wittgenstein, whose *Tractatus Logico-Philosophicus* had been the main inspiration of positivism, took the heroic step of claiming that it was nonsense (though, as we will see, he thought *some* nonsense was better than other nonsense). This quandary pretty much spelled the end of logical positivism. Perhaps Professor Jon Wheatley was writing its obituary when he said, "Logical positivism is one of the very few philosophical positions which can be easily shown to be dead wrong, and that is its principal claim to fame."[27]

Wittgenstein

The author of the *Tractatus Logico-Philosophicus*, the book that so inspired the logical positivists, was Ludwig Wittgenstein (1889–1951). He has earned himself a longer discussion in this overview than have most philosophers because he has the unusual distinction of having inspired two philosophical movements: logical positivism and what came to be known as "ordinary language philosophy." Each of these movements dominated a portion of the analytic tradition in the twentieth century, and ironically, in many respects the later movement refutes the earlier movement.[28]

> Was sich überhaupt sagen lässt, lässt sich klar sagen; und wovon man nicht reden kann, darüber muss man schweigen.

Wittgenstein was born into a wealthy, refined Viennese family. Uninterested in material riches, he gave away his entire inheritance. In 1911 he went to Manchester, England, to study aeronautical engineering. His genius for mathematical thinking was soon recognized, and he was directed to Cambridge to study with Bertrand Russell. When Wittgenstein returned to Austria to enlist in the army during World War I, one story has it that he put a ream of paper in his backpack and went into the trenches with it. He was soon taken captive by the Italians and, as a prisoner of war, set about writing the *Tractatus* (which puts that work in the category of "great books written

Proposition 1: The World Is All That Is the Case

in jail," along with Boethius's *The Consolations of Philosophy* and part of Cervantes's *Don Quixote*).

The *Tractatus*, which is barely 100 pages long, is set up as a series of seven propositions. Each proposition is followed by a sequence of numbered observations about each proposition, or observations about the observations, or observations about the observations about the observations. For instance, the first page begins thus:

1. The world is all that is the case.
1.1 The world is the totality of facts, not of things.
1.11 The world is determined by the facts, and by their being *all* the facts.
1.12 For the totality of facts determines what is the case, and also whatever is not the case.
1.13 The facts in logical space are the world.
1.2 The world divides into facts.
1.21 Each item can be the case or not the case while everything else remains the same.
2. What is the case—a fact—is the existence of states of affairs.[29]

Wittgenstein held the view that, because we can say true things about the world, the structure of language must somehow reflect the structure of the world. That is part of what he means in paragraph 1.1, "The world is the totality of facts, not of things." Now, what are the facts of which the world consists? They are, to use Russell's term, **"atomic facts."** They are the simplest facts that can be asserted and are the simple truths into which all other more complex truths can be analyzed. In the *Tractatus*, Wittgenstein did not say exactly what these facts were, and it was these facts that the positivists were seeking with their attempts to construct protocol sentences and confirmation sentences.

The positivists liked other features of the *Tractatus* as well. They particularly approved of the conception of philosophy that Wittgenstein put forth:

Most of the propositions and questions to be found in philosophical works are not false but nonsensical. Consequently we cannot give any answer to questions of this kind, but can only establish that they are nonsensical. (4.003)

The correct method in philosophy would really be the following: to say nothing except what can be said, i.e., the propositions of natural science—i.e., something that has nothing to do with philosophy—and then, whenever someone else wanted to say something metaphysical, to demonstrate to him that he had failed to give a meaning to certain signs in his propositions . . . this method would be the only strictly correct one. (6.53)

It Cannot Be Said

These paragraphs seem to express perfectly the hard-liner position of logical positivists. No surprise that the latter thought of Wittgenstein as one of their own. However, certain puzzling statements in the *Tractatus* created quite a bit of discomfort for the members of the Vienna Circle. For example, in the preface Wittgenstein wrote, "The whole sense of this book might be summed up in the following words: what can be said at all can be said clearly and what we cannot talk about we must consign to silence." Now, the positivists wanted to interpret Wittgenstein as saying here, "Metaphysicians, shut up!" But Wittgenstein himself seemed curiously attracted to what he called "the silence" and made further enigmatic allusions to it. In paragraph 6.54 he wrote,

My propositions serve as elucidations in the following way: anyone who understands me eventually recognizes them as nonsensical, when he has used them—as steps—to climb up beyond them. (He must, so to speak, throw away the ladder after he has climbed up it.) He must transcend these propositions and then he will see the world aright.

It was here that Wittgenstein was admitting that his own propositions were nonsense, but apparently a special kind of higher nonsense. What would higher nonsense be like? Wittgenstein continued:

> How things are in the world is a matter of complete indifference for what is higher. God does not reveal himself *in* the world. (6.432)

> It is not *how* things are in the world that is mystical, but *that* it exists. (6.44)

> The solution to the enigma of life in space and time lies *outside* space and time. (6.4312)

Slowly and in horror the truth dawned on the Vienna Circle. Wittgenstein was a mystic! He was *worse* than the metaphysicians.

For a while, Wittgenstein seemed satisfied with the *Tractatus*. It had answered all the philosophy questions that could be sensibly asked. As he had written: "When the answer cannot be put into words, neither can the question be put into words. The *riddle* does not exist. If a question can be framed at all, it is possible to answer it" (6.5).

He's a mystic!

Wittgenstein dropped out of philosophy. He went off into the villages of the Austrian Alps as a primary schoolteacher. But he was not completely happy in his new work, and his mind was not at rest. Russell spearheaded a move to get Wittgenstein to return to Cambridge and to have the *Tractatus* accepted as Wittgenstein's doctoral dissertation. Wittgenstein was given the professional chair of the retiring G. E. Moore, and much excitement was generated over the fact that Wittgenstein had returned to philosophy.

However, word soon got around that what Wittgenstein was now saying about philosophy was not what had been expected of him. It was not easy to know exactly what *was* going on, however, because the eccentric Wittgenstein was very secretive about his new views and he insisted that his students be so too. Nevertheless, some mimeographed copies of notes from his lectures began to circulate. It was not until after his death that his work from this period was published as *Philosophical Investigations*. But long before the appearance of that book, it had become clear that a major shift had taken place in Wittgenstein's thinking. Both the positivism and the mysticism of the *Tractatus* were gone, for better or for worse. Yet there continued to be some common denominators between the two works. Philosophy was still seen as essentially the concern with meaning, and it was still very much language-oriented. In the *Tractatus*, Wittgenstein had written, "*The limits of my language are the limits of my world*" (5.6). That view continued to hold in the *Investigations*, but language itself now seemed much less limited than it had been in the earlier book.

Let us start our discussion of the *Investigations* with a look at the problem of meaning. Throughout the history of philosophy, from Plato to the *Tractatus*, the key model of meaning was that of *denotation*, that is, of *naming*. Even where philosophers like Frege, Russell, and the author of the *Tractatus* had distinguished between "reference" (denotation) and "sense," the former was given priority. According to Wittgenstein, the historical prioritizing of naming as the key feature of meaning had generated a certain kind of metaphysical picture that was pervasive in Western thought and that was in error. Plato thought that words had to be names of things that existed unchanging and eternally, and because there was no such thing in the observable world, he developed his theory of the other-worldly Forms. Aristotle thought words named something unchanging *in* the world, namely, substances. In the medieval period, the nominalists also thought of words as names but thought that they named *nothing*. Their conclusion therefore was like that of the last sentence of Eco's novel *The Name of the Rose*, namely, "we have only names." The empiricists held that words named sense data and that any word not doing so was suspect. The pragmatists thought that words named actions, and the positivists, Russell, and the early Wittgenstein thought they named atomic facts.

The later Wittgenstein broke completely with this tradition, claiming that "the meaning of a word is its use in the language."[30] He wrote,

> Think of the tools in a tool box: there is a hammer, pliers, a saw, a screwdriver, a rule, a glue pot, glue, nails and screws.—The functions

of words are as diverse as the functions of these objects. (And in both cases there are similarities.) ... It is like looking into the cabin of a locomotive. We see handles all looking more or less alike. (Naturally, since they are supposed to be handled.) But one is the handle of a crank which can be moved continuously (it regulates the opening of a valve); another is the handle of a switch, which

Wittgensteinians Arguing

has only two effective positions, it is either off or on; a third is the handle of a brake-lever, the harder one pulls on it, the harder it brakes; a fourth, the handle of a pump: it has an effect only so long as it is moved to and fro. (11, 12)

Well, the sun's going down. Or the earth's coming up, as the fashionable theory has it.

From *Rosencrantz and Guildenstern Are Dead*, a Play by Tom Stoppard

So language, like tools or like the gadgets in the cabin of a locomotive, can get jobs done, and its meaning is found in the work it accomplishes. Suppose two people are driving rapidly toward a certain destination, trying to arrive before sunset because the headlights are broken, and suppose the driver says, "Well, bad luck!

The sun just went down." Now, what if the passenger says, with a look of superiority, "We now know that the sun does not 'go down,' and that the illusion that it does is the result of the earth turning on its axis." Does what he said *mean* anything? No, because in that context, it gets no job done (even though in another context that same sentence *would* get a job done). In fact, there is something *mad* about inserting this scientific fact into the context described. There would also be something mad if the passenger, having found a hammer in the glove compartment, began hitting the driver with it and explained the action by saying "Hammers are for hitting." Yes, but not for hitting just any thing, any time, any place. And the same is the case with language.

Still, a tool can serve a number of functions. In some contexts, a hammer can serve as a weapon or as a paperweight. How about language? Does it have only two uses, as the logical positivists suggested (an expressive function and a representative function)? Wittgenstein asked:

> But how many kinds of sentence are there? Say assertion, question, and command?—There are *countless* kinds: countless different kinds of use of what we call "symbols," "words," "sentences." And this multiplicity is not something fixed, given once for all; but new types of language, new language-games, as we may say, come into existence, and others become obsolete and get forgotten. (23)

This comment brings up another feature of Wittgenstein's theory of meaning related to his claim that "the meaning is the use." He wrote, "The question 'What is a word really?' is analogous to 'what is a piece in chess?' . . . Let us say that the meaning of a piece is its role in the game" (108). Wittgenstein generalized his claim when he called any language a "language-game"; he also designated as "language-games" different *functions* of various features of language. Let's consider this point. All games are rule-governed. The meaning of a piece (or a chip, or card, or mitt) in the game is derived from its use according to the rules. What is a pawn? A pawn is a piece that moves one square forward, except on its first move, when it may move two squares. It may take the opponent's piece laterally and is converted to a queen if it reaches the opposite side of the board. Similarly with words, phrases, and expressions—they are rule-governed, and their meaning is derived from the use to which they may be put according to the rules of the language game. There are lots of kinds of rules determining language use: grammatical rules, semantic rules, syntactical rules, and what could generally be called rules of context. Some of these rules are very rigid, some are very flexible, and some are negotiable. These variations are true in a comparison of different games (the rules of chess are more rigid than those of ring-around-the-rosy), or even in a comparison within a game (rules governing the pawn's moves are rigid, but those governing the pawn's size

are flexible). But even flexible rules are rules, and they can't be broken without certain consequences. When some of the rules of a given language game are broken in subtle ways, "language goes on holiday" (38), as Wittgenstein said, and one result is a certain kind of *philosophy* (as in the case of metaphysicians), and another result is a certain kind of *madness* (as in the case of *Alice in Wonderland*). The allusion to Alice is not gratuitous. The Alice books were among Wittgenstein's favorites, no doubt because they are compendiums of linguistic jokes showing the lunacy that results when the function of certain features of language are misunderstood. Think of the episode when the White King tells Alice to look down the road and asks her if she sees anyone there. "I see nobody on the road," said Alice. "I only wish *I* had such eyes," responds the king. "To be able to see Nobody! And at that distance too!" What has gone wrong here? The joke is based on what some "ordinary language philosophers" called a "category mistake"—the miscategorization of certain linguistic facts and the drawing of absurd conclusions from the miscategorization. (According to Gilbert Ryle, who coined the term category mistake, this miscategorization was the error made by Descartes that resulted in the mind-body problem. He had placed "minds" in a similar category with bodies, making them "thinking *things*"—ghostly, spiritual *beings* that somehow cohabitated with physical beings, but no one could figure out how.)

Or consider the case of the White Queen, who promises to pay her lady's maid "Twopence a week, and jam every other day" but then refuses to provide the jam on the grounds that it never *is* any other day. Surely this is language gone on holiday.

The Elusiveness of Jam

What about the positivists' search for the simplest constituents of reality on which to base the scientific edifice? Wittgenstein asked,

> But what are the simple constituent parts of which reality is composed?—What are the simple constituent parts of a chair?—The

bits of wood of which it is made? or the molecules, or the atoms?—
"Simple" means: not composite. And here the point is: In what sense
"composite"? It makes no sense at all to speak absolutely of the
"simple parts of a chair." (47)

So much for the search for atomic facts.

In the *Tractatus*, Wittgenstein had written, "Most of the propositions and questions of philosophy arise from our failure to understand the logic of our language" (4.003). He still held more or less
the same view in the *Investigations*, but by then his conception of "the
logic of our language" had changed radically. It was no longer the philosopher's job to reveal the hidden logic *behind* language; rather, it was
to reveal the implicit logic of ordinary language (hence the term "ordinary language
philosophy").
Philosophers were
to show that a failure to grasp
that implicit logic could result in
"a bewitchment of our intelligence
by means of language" (109), and
they were to show that unwarranted
tampering with our ordinary way
of thinking and talking about
the world could produce a
"linguistic holiday," which
generates the jokes
that make up much of
the history of phi-
losophy. Wittgenstein
said, "[My aim in
philosophy is]
to show the
fly the way out of the fly
bottle" (309). Apparently
in Wittgenstein's native

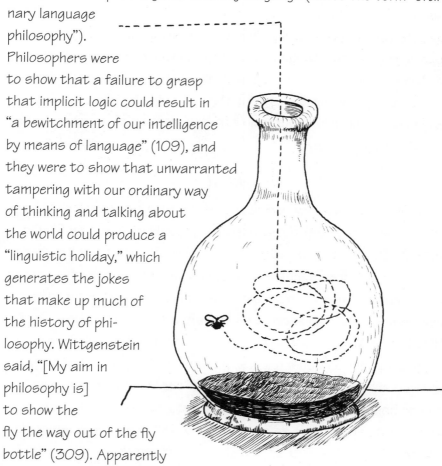

The Fly in the Fly Bottle

Vienna, a common flytrap was made by putting some honey in a vinegar bottle.

The fly, traveling on its merry way, would smell the honey, deviate from its path into the bottle, and either drown in the sticky, sweet stuff or buzz to death. For Wittgenstein, much of philosophy was like that buzzing. To "show the fly the way out of the fly bottle" was not to *solve* philosophical problems but to *dissolve* them by showing that they are the result of deviating from the path of everyday language. This analogy illustrates the conservative side of Wittgenstein's thought. According to him, "Philosophy can in no way interfere with the actual use of language; it can in the end only describe it. For it cannot give it any foundation either. It leaves everything just as it is" (124).

The apparent complacency here is reminiscent of G. E. Moore, but the comparison, though good in some respects, is bad in others. Wittgenstein's mind was in constant turmoil and perplexity. There was a brooding disquietude about the man and his thought that belied the Vermeer-like bourgeois self-satisfaction of passages such as the one I just quoted.

Quine

The most important representative of the analytic tradition in the second half of the twentieth century is probably Willard Van Orman Quine (1908–2000), who was born in Akron, Ohio. He went to Oberlin College for a degree in mathematics, and there he became fascinated with Bertrand Russell's mathematical philosophy. He pursued the topic in his doctoral dissertation at Harvard under the direction of Alfred North Whitehead. After receiving his Ph.D., he visited Vienna, Prague, and Warsaw on a fellowship awarded him by the university and was able to talk with philosophers of the Vienna Circle and with leading Eastern European logicians. He returned to Harvard and took up his career there as a professor of philosophy. Even after his retirement from Harvard at seventy years of age, he continued for the next twenty years to give lectures and otherwise participate in the philosophical profession.

Quine's two most important books are *From a Logical Point of View* (1953) and *Word and Object* (1960). Throughout most of the rest of his work, he has taken the ideas presented in these two books and tinkered with them, elaborating, modifying, and defending them. In *From a Logical Point of View* Quine calls himself a pragmatist, so some have placed him in the tradition of Peirce, James, and Dewey, but it is more generally agreed that he is

W. V. Quine

best understood as responding to the logical positivists with whom he had conversed in Europe and, in his unique way, carrying out their program.

This categorization is in some ways surprising, because by 1960 most philosophers believed that logical positivism had bitten the dust, in no small part due to Quine's pair of silver bullets as represented by his 1951 article titled "Two Dogmas of Empiricism" (included in *From a Logical Point of View*). The dogmas he attacks are two of the positivists' most dangerous weapons. The first dogma Quine challenges is reductionism, the positivists' attempt to reduce each putative synthetic proposition to protocol sentences or confirmation sentences (check the Glossary if you don't recall these terms) and then to correlate these basic propositions with even more basic, incorrigible sense-data experiences. Reductionism is a main feature of the program of empiricism initiated by Locke, refined by Berkeley and Hume, and touted triumphantly by the positivists as the final nails in the coffin of religious, moral, and metaphysical discourse. Instead,

Quine's in Town

this form of reductionism itself seems to have been vanquished, at least in part because of Quine's critique.

The second dogma that Quine targets is the analytic-synthetic distinction (see pp. 184–185 and pp. 207–209 and p. 378). Quine does not claim that there are no such things as analytic sentences ("All bachelors are male" is a clear example of one) or synthetic sentences ("Some dogs are spotted" is one such); rather, he tries to demonstrate that ultimately the boundary between the two supposed types cannot be drawn except arbitrarily. Take this sentence: "Owls hoot." Is it synthetic or analytic? It ought to be synthetic because its negation does not lead to a self-contradiction. Yet our certainty of the sentence "Owls hoot" seems greater than that of the sentence "Owls are members of the order Strigiformes," which proves to be analytic. Similarly, sentences like "Strawberries are red when ripe" or "Heavy objects fall when unsupported" seem to have at least as much certainty as "Tomatoes are fruits, not vegetables" (they are, you know!). Yet the first two examples would normally be classified as synthetic and the third as analytic. Quine is not saying that it is impossible to categorize these kinds of sentences one way or the other, but that ultimately we do so only arbitrarily and that this arbitrariness rules out the analytic-synthetic distinction as one on which we could rest much philosophical weight—certainly not the amount that the logical positivists thought it could bear.

In fact, the real object of Quine's attack is to demonstrate the circularity of a whole cluster of philosophical views sacrosanct to analytical philosophers. Characterizations of *meaning* were made in terms of *analyticity* (that is, the nature of an analytic proposition), analyticity in terms of *synonymy*, and synonymy in terms of *meaning*, and so on forever, without managing to anchor any part of this system outside the vicious circle that had been produced.[31]

One motive for Quine's revision is his dislike of the positivists' claim that mathematics is *necessarily true* but *empty*. He believes that math has content and is not "necessarily" necessary. He does not want to revert to Kant's synthetic a priori to explain this content nor to Mill's view of math as empirical generalization. Instead, Quine develops a type of epistemological **holism** according to which all parts of our system of knowledge are interrelated rather than fragmented into different categories (categories like "the certainty of sense data," "the certainty but emptiness of analytic propositions," "the uncertainty and probabilistic nature of synthetic propositions," "the meaningfulness guaranteed by verifiability," "the nonsense of metaphysics," etc.). Quine defends the power of mathematics in our systems of knowledge by saying that its strength lies simply in "our determination to make revisions elsewhere instead."[32] If something went wrong with an experiment of ours, math would be the last thing we would give up. Yet an extreme discrepancy between our expectations and the data might make us more willing to consider even the abandonment of math. After all, some features of **quantum mechanics,** the most advanced stage of physical theory, have suggested that we might have to abandon the law of the excluded middle in logic.

Much to the horror of the few remaining logical positivists, Quine admits that the dissolution of the synthetic-analytic distinction and the abandonment of reductionism produce "a blurring of the supposed boundary between speculative metaphysics and natural science."[33] You might think that this admission and Quine's attack on the two dogmas of positivism would establish him as an enemy of logical positivism. But, in fact, Quine remained sympathetic to the spirit of the positivist program all his professional life. He believed that responsible philosophy must be a form of empiricism, that it must be scientific, and that it must defend materialism (or "physicalism," as he calls it). From the latter point of view he concluded that a form of behaviorism must be the correct answer to the mind-body problem.

Quine's theory of meaning follows the lead of Frege and Russell in redirecting attention from *words* to *sentences* as the true units of meaning. Hume's empiricism was flawed because it made the mistake of trying to correlate individual words with individual experiences. (Take an idea like "God," "cause," or "self." Hume asked: "From what impression is that idea derived?" If he could find no sense datum corresponding to the idea, then the word naming the idea was meaningless.) On the contrary, by taking the sentence rather than the word as the unit of meaning, Quine avoids Hume's excessive reductionism, and he escapes the opposite extreme, Platonism, as well. For Plato, a word like "green" must name an essence, "greenness," that is more real than individual instantiations of greenness. This move violates Ockham's razor because items like "essences," "meanings," and "Forms" become real things that must be accounted for onto-logically. Meanings become *things* that mediate between words and objects. Quine writes, "The explanatory value of special and irreducible intermediary entities called meanings is surely illusory."[34]

Quine makes great use of a technique that is now generally recognized as a hallmark of analytic philosophy—what he calls *contextual definition.* It is a form of paraphrase in which sentences that seem to provoke philosophical puzzles (for example, "Greenness is a color") are restated in ways that delete the offending terms (for example, "Anything green is colored"). We have already seen this technique used to great effect in Russell's Theory of Descriptions, whose function was to deal with the verb "to be" in ways that relieved us of the need to posit some metaphysical object called "being." This method of contextual definition reveals a suspicion on the part of the philosophers who use it that ordinary language cannot represent ideas in a successful manner and that therefore the philosopher must be constantly alert against language's decep-tive snares. (In this respect Quine is something like Wittgenstein, who wrote in *Philosophical Investigations,* "Philosophy is the battle against the bewitchment of our intelligence by means of language" [109]. The difference is that Wittgenstein did not suspect that ordi-nary language itself is the culprit, rather, that the fault lies with our propensity to saddle ordinary language with monolithic philosophical assumptions.) Unlike Russell or the positivists, however, Quine uses contextual definition pragmatically. He does not claim that it reveals the true, hidden logical structure of thought disguised and burdened by ordinary language. Rather, the convenience of contextual definition is that it provides a way of bypassing certain features of ordinary expression that appear to lead us into an overpopulated metaphysi-cal landscape. It also provides a language that can adequately repre-sent all scientific theorizing.

I should mention as an aside a common objection raised against the method of paraphrasing in terms of contextual definition by op-ponents of the type of analytic philosophy employed by Quine and his tradition. They ask, how do we know that the elimination of the metaphysical problem in the sentence replaced by the paraphrase is not illusory? Perhaps the contextual definition simply disguises a genuine philosophical truth about reality. Generally, philosophers who raise this objection trust ordinary language more than does Quine. Wittgenstein would probably be in this camp.

New Age Analytic Philosophy

Despite Quine's admission that the sometimes stilted language of logical analysis could never replace ordinary discourse, for him only the language of physics is capable of making literally true statements about reality. This belief signals Quine's physicalism—his updated version of the old materialist thesis that there is only matter in motion, a view that we ran into first in Democritus and then later in Hobbes. Ordinary language has *instrumental* value—it helps us muddle our way through life—but it is not equipped to express truths about reality, except sometimes in a metaphorical way. Quine even seems suspicious of the status of the sciences other than physics. Biology and psychology only give us another form of metaphorical truth about what's really there.

You might be surprised to discover that despite Quine's physicalism, he is not a reductionist. He is unconvinced that sciences like chemistry or biology can be reduced to physics or that all mental states can be translated into neurological events. He is satisfied to assert that "there is no mental difference without a physical difference."[35] Apparently the ultimate facts about mental life are the kind of facts that physics talks about, but at least for now—and perhaps forever—there is no way of reducing descriptions of mental events to descriptions of the most basic physical particles. Between these two levels there seems to be a space that only metaphorical language can fill. Yet Quine apparently thinks that this large space is of no interest to philosophy.

It is not surprising that many contemporary analytic philosophers who otherwise respect Quine for his rigor do not agree with him on this topic. Some of them believe that this space to which Quine is philosophically indifferent is the space of greatest interest to thoughtful people, including philosophers, because it is constitutive of human experience. It is in this space, for instance, that we find activities and institutions like art, economics, morality, politics, linguistics, and the experience of selfhood.

Related to Quine's physicalism is a bold theory he produced in 1960 that he calls the "indeterminacy of translation" thesis. This theory has proved to be one of his most controversial themes. Imagine a team of field linguists trying to formulate manuals to allow them to translate into English the unknown language of the subjects among which they find themselves. We are to suppose that these linguists have no access to any knowledge about the culture and institutions that have produced the language in question. The linguists must concentrate on the relation between the verbal and bodily behavior of the speakers and the physical stimuli that provoke these behaviors. Quine believes that if these linguists work independently of each other they will come up with a number of divergent manuals, each of which will be incompatible with the other manuals, but all of which could be compatible with the native speaker's behavior—linguistic and bodily—and the physical stimuli in the environment. Because all these imaginary manuals are compatible with the physical facts (Quine's main concern), there are no physical facts that can determine which of the manuals is the correct manual. A manual that facilitates conversation and cooperation is as correct as all others that do the same thing. This conclusion constitutes a form of radical behaviorism. If the same physical stimuli provoke the same responses, these responses are equivalent to one another.

Quine imagines that the linguists are trying to decipher the expression "gavagai," which the natives utter whenever a rabbit runs by.[36] Furthermore, whenever the linguists point to a rabbit while asking the question, "Gavagai?" the natives always make affirmative gestures and sounds. According to Quine, in this case we can conclude that a correct translation of gavagai would be, "There is a rabbit over there." But he also thinks numerous other translations would be equally correct. In fact, Quine argues that in the situation described, all these sentences are equivalent:

1. There is a rabbit over there.
2. A stage in the development of a rabbit is over there.

3. There are undetached rabbit parts over there.
4. There is rabbit-parts fusion over there.
5. There is an instantiation of rabbithood over there.

Contrary to most theories of meaning, which would say that sentences 1 through 5 are not at all synonymous, Quine concludes that because they are all systematically compatible with the same set of physical stimuli, they *are* synonymous and that therefore an indeterminacy of translation is revealed.

Quine admits that translation 1 is the most likely way of reading *gavagai*, but only for reasons of convenience, not reasons of "truth." His point is that from the perspective of bare physical fact (especially elementary physical particles, etc.), each of these translations is as good as the others. According to Quine, if this indeterminacy thesis rejects not only most philosophical accounts of language and mind but also our ordinary everyday conceptions of them, so be it. Let the chips fall where they may. And certainly Quine's theory *does* wreak havoc with our normal ways of thinking about these topics, so much so that his theory is vulnerable to the charge of being outlandish. For example, a critic has pointed out that if you buy a rabbit as a pet, Quine's indeterminacy thesis turns your perfectly acceptable wish to cuddle such a pet into the perverse desire to fondle undetached rabbit parts.[37] (I would add that the translation of *gavagai* as "rabbit-parts fusion" would make the culinary term "rabbit stew" a tautology.) Another critic suggests:

> Many readers may feel that this consequence of the indeterminacy thesis—apparently, the overthrow of our everyday conception of mind—shows that

something has gone wrong. It may reinforce the feeling that the focus on stimulus meanings was unduly self-denying and was bound to yield a distorted and impoverished picture of meaning and mind.[38]

Quine's theory of the indeterminacy of translation has attracted much critical attention. This attention is not because philosophers feel that the issue of translation itself is necessarily of central importance; rather, they believe that Quine is right to see his thesis as the logical extension of radical physicalism, and by contesting the indeterminacy thesis they may be contesting physicalism itself.

At any rate, even philosophers who are opposed to Quine's overall views find themselves influenced by a variety of arguments in his widely read writings. There are probably few important analytic philosophers on the contemporary scene who have not found themselves incorporating Quinean ideas into their own systems, or at least feeling the need to respond publicly to his views. This list includes names like Donald Davidson, Hilary Putnam, Noam Chomsky, Jerry Fodor, Jerold Katz, Nelson Goodman, Wilfrid Sellars, Ian Hacking, and John Searle, just to name a few. Also, the younger generation of analytic philosophers has felt Quine's continuing influence. Among this group are some outstanding women philosophers, including Lynn Hankinson Nelson and Louise Antony, who have argued that Quine's philosophy should be attractive to feminists.[39]

Farewell to the Twentieth Century

Nussbaum

I will finish the book by turning to Martha Nussbaum, a highly regarded and easily accessible contemporary American feminist philosopher whose interests and writing style contrast greatly with those of the Continental feminists mentioned in chapter 7. Nussbaum, who currently has appointments at the University of Chicago in the

Martha Nussbaum

departments of philosophy, law, and divinity, has published scores of articles in professional journals and written or edited more than thirteen books, including her latest, *Liberty of Conscience,*[40] where we find a manifestation of her commitment to the themes of all three university faculties with which she is associated. The student's main difficulty with Nussbaum will be keeping up with all of her myriad interests. She first trained as a classicist and has written extensively on ancient Greek philosophy and drama. As a result of her study of Greek thought, she has become a supporter of an updated version of Aristotelian ethics—not an obvious choice for a feminist, given Aristotle's **misogynistic** views about women (especially his idea that they are not fully human), his elitist bias against "the working class," and his acceptance of slavery as a social necessity. But Nussbaum is especially good at what is called "winnowing the chaff from the grain" (that is, separating that which is useful from that which is useless)[41] and at applying the best of ancient Greek thinking to the contemporary world. Among other topics, she has written about the roles of luck and of the emotions in ethics, terrorism, animal rights, psychiatric therapy, St. Augustine on love, global justice (including justice for women in India), promoting women's capabilities, a feminist method of hermeneutics (roughly, interpretation), lesbian and gay rights, a defense of universal values (anti-relativism), Kant and cosmopolitanism, family, sex, educational reform, patriotism, the ethics of care, children's rights, Nietzsche, Schopenhauer, Freud, and critiques of postmodernism.

One of Nussbaum's most significant legacies will surely prove to be her concern over the relation between fiction and moral philosophy. We will briefly look at Nussbaum's discussion of this idea, selecting it over her many other interests, because she has been such a pioneer in this area. She has already made a major contribution to it, and her continuing enthusiasm and energy will likely produce even more insights in the future.

We saw in Chapter 2 that Plato had referred to an ancient quarrel between philosophy and poetry (poíêsis, a word that in Greek covered all the linguistic arts, and, by extension, all representative arts) in the search for truth and that Plato weighed in, of course, on the side of philosophy. However, you may recall that Aristotle challenged Plato on this issue, providing a defense of poetry's philosophical value, saying:

> The poet's function is to describe, not the thing that has happened, but a kind of thing that might happen, i.e., what is possible as being probable or necessary . . . Hence poetry is something more philosophical and of graver import than history . . .[42]

In a series of articles, many of which are collected in her book, *Love's Knowledge*,[43] Nussbaum explores this idea in depth and provides specific examples, taken from the works of Homer, Aeschylus, Euripides, Aristophanes, Seneca, Dante Alighieri, William Shakespeare, Jane Austen, Emily Brontë, Charles Dickens, Walt Whitman, Fyodor Dostoyevsky, Leo Tolstoy, James Joyce, Marcel

Proust, W. H. Auden, Virginia Woolf, George Orwell, Samuel Beckett, and Iris Murdoch, among others. In *Love's Knowledge*, the key literary heroes seem to be the ancient Greek dramatists, as well as Dickens, Proust, and, most saliently, the American-English novelist of the late nineteenth and early twentieth centuries, Henry James (brother of the philosopher William James).

In *Love's Knowledge*, Nussbaum states her project clearly:

My aim is to establish that certain literary texts (or texts similar to these in certain relevant ways) are indispensable to a philosophical inquiry in the ethical sphere: not by any means sufficient, but sources of insight without which the inquiry cannot be complete. (23–24)

Nussbaum's theoretical foundation is, as I mentioned, distinctly Aristotelian, and her views presuppose the truth of key features of Aristotle's philosophy. This means that if those features of Aristotle's philosophy are wrong, so is Nussbaum's theory, but she is confident about the correctness of his ethical ideas. Nussbaum has written widely on Aristotle's philosophy,[44] but understanding the argument of *Love's Knowledge* does not require a prior reading of Aristotle; in her book, Nussbaum presents the pertinent features of Aristotle's ethical view in a way that she feels will be convincing to the general reader.

As opposed to Kantianism and utilitarianism, which both stress universal rules (Kant's "categorical imperative" and Bentham and Mill's "principle of utility"), Aristotle stressed what he called "practical wisdom" (see pp. 82–83). This, among other related things, is an ability to recognize the individuality (as opposed to the universality) of situations in which decision and action are required. Nussbaum quotes Aristotle as saying, "It is obvious that practical wisdom is not scientific understanding (*epistêmê*)" (54).[45]

Scientific understanding looks for that which is general—that which is similar to all other cases—but practical wisdom experiments with the particular. It is "the ability to discern, acutely and responsively, the salient features of one's particular situation" and to see that particularity in its relation to the whole complex of temporal, emotional, psychological, and physical features that comprise the situation.

Nussbaum insists on the organic connection between form and content in novels. The very style of a novel such as Henry James's *The Golden Bowl* "makes a statement about what is important and what is not" (7). Form (style) is "expressive of a view of life" (6) and plunges its readers into the very kinds of particular situations in which we come to see just how complicated moral relations are, and we begin to understand what successes and failures of the exercise of practical wisdom are like. According to Nussbaum, a commitment to such *acute perception of the particular* "seems to be built into the very form of the novel as genre" (37). In fact, the insights revealed by James's style in novels such as *The Golden Bowl* and *The Ambassadors* are exactly what a traditional philosophical essay is unable to provide.

One of the things that we come to grasp by reading imaginative literature—and this is something denied by Platonism, Kantianism, and utilitarianism—is the ethical significance of *contingency*, that is, of events that impact the life of an individual but are not in the individual's control. (Nussbaum calls these "uncontrolled happenings" [43]; they force us to realize that

Moral Bad Luck: or, How Godzilla Can Mess Up Your Good Intentions

there is such a thing as "moral luck," as Aristotle insisted.)

Another thing we learn from James's novel and others like it is the legitimate role of emotions in ethical behavior. Some emotional responses are appropriate to situations calling for moral decisions, and these feelings are not opposed to rationality (as Kant and other moralists have held); rather, they are part of rationality. Nussbaum contrasts hunger and thirst with anger and grief, reminding us that the first two are not "belief related" (41), while the second two are. If you discover that certain of your beliefs are false, you do not lose your hunger or thirst, but you may lose or modify your anger or your grief if you discover an error in some of your beliefs. If facts confirm your beliefs, then often your emotional state is justified and, according to Nussbaum, in some cases it becomes part of a correct moral response to the facts.

A Counter Example

Another thing we learn from the novels discussed by Nussbaum is what she calls the "noncommensurability of the valuable things" (36). This is the fact that there is no one value to which all other values can be reduced (as, for example, the case of "utility" for the utilitarians, "duty" for Kant, and "pleasure" for the hedonists). The original Socratic question, "How should one live?" (171) guides both Aristotle's and Nussbaum's moral theories and leads them to claim that there is no one human value or virtue that can conduct a person to a good life. There are, however, many virtues that are qualities that lead to such a life and that can be achieved through the engagement of practical wisdom. Aristotle argues against Plato, saying that imaginative literature can aid in this pursuit, and Nussbaum certainly agrees with Aristotle and his examples. She says of those Greek tragedies that Aristotle admired philosophically—and over which Plato fretted—that they contain the following moral lessons:

> that happenings beyond the agent's control are of real importance not only for his or her feelings of happiness or contentment, but also for whether he or she manages to live a fully good life, a life inclusive of various forms of laudable action. That therefore what happens to people by chance can be of enormous importance to the ethical quality of their lives; that, therefore, good people are right to care deeply about such chance events. That, for these same reasons, an audience's pity and fear at tragic events are valuable responses, responses for which there is an important place in the ethical life, since they embody a recognition of ethical truths. That other emotions as well are appropriate, and based upon correct beliefs about what matters. That, for example, it is right to love certain things and people that lie

Greek Audience

beyond one's own control, and to grieve when these people die, when these things are removed. (17)

However, Nussbaum seems to take a step beyond Aristotle when she argues that the lessons from imaginative literature are not only helpful but *necessary conditions* of any complete and successful theory of ethics. This is an important stance, and it will continue to be developed (and tested) in the future.

Nussbaum's work on the relation between literature and ethics has been well received by important philosophers such as Hilary Putnam and Cora Diamond. There has, of course, been some criticism, as well. For example, the British political scientist John Horton, though generally supportive of Nussbaum's project, has made the observation that every novel of any depth is open to a variety of possible interpretations that contradict other interpretations, and that therefore there is no guarantee that Nussbaum's ethical reading of the novels she selects is superior to other compelling readings of the same novels in which ethical issues are not seen as primary. Why, he asks, do Nussbaum's readings have the authority she seems to claim for them "given the fact that there are invariably many plausible readings of any novel"?[46]

Horton backs up his criticism by offering an alternative reading to Nussbaum's of the character of Josiah Bounderby in Dickens's *Hard Times*, claiming that his interpretation reveals "a rather more complex and morally ambiguous story about the relationship between the ethical and the imaginative than Nussbaum's reading indicates" (90). I suspect that Nussbaum is prepared to

IT'S ABOUT RUSSIA

LEO TOLSTOY WAR

Yet Another Plausible Interpretation. Woody Allen Speed-Reads War and Peace

Quo Vadis, Philosophia?

defend her interpretation against Horton's, or she may be satisfied simply to answer that any reading of a novel that provokes one to lead a better life is a self-justifying moral exercise.

Key Philosophical Ideas in Chapter 8

Pragmatism

Charles Peirce:

- Coined the term "pragmatism" to name a method for clarifying thought, to make ordinary thought more scientific
  - Beliefs are rules for action.
  - The way to distinguish between beliefs is to compare the habits they produce.

William James:

- Theory of meaning: the meaning of an idea determined by tracing its practical consequences.
  - If two apparently differing ideas have the same practical consequences, then there is no difference of meaning between them.

- "There can be no difference anywhere that doesn't make a difference elsewhere."
- <u>Logical consequence</u>: <u>meaning is subjective and relative</u>. (e.g., If a person believes that "God exists" but behaves exactly as she would if she did not believe, then for her, "God exists" and "God does not exist" have the same meaning.)
- <u>Theory of truth</u>: The <u>truth of an idea</u> or belief is <u>its power to "work."</u>
  - A proposition is true if it "gets us into satisfactory relation with other parts of our experience."
  - <u>Logical consequence</u>: <u>truth and falsity are subjective and relative</u> (e.g., if a person's belief in God's existence produces more satisfactory relations with the rest of the world, then the proposition "God exists" is both meaningful and true for her).
  - James's pragmatism attempts to <u>mediate between "tender-minded"</u> philosophers (rationalists) and <u>"tough-minded" philosophers</u> (empiricists).

<u>John Dewey</u>:

- Less interested than James in resolving conflicts between metaphysical beliefs, and more <u>interested in resolving problems in social psychology, politics, education, and morality</u>.
  - <u>Thinking is problem-solving; ideas are plans for action</u>.
  - <u>Universals</u> (Plato) <u>and sense-data</u> (empiricists) <u>are</u> not objects of knowledge, but <u>tools of knowledge</u>.
  - <u>Knowledge</u> does not reflect the world, it <u>changes the world</u> (as in Marx).
- The <u>ultimate goal</u> of action is <u>the full development of individuals as human beings</u>.
  - Therefore, <u>education and democracy have the same goal</u>.
    - Each individual can contribute to the creation of sociality.
    - <u>Social institutions</u> should be <u>judged in terms of whether they contribute to the growth of individuals</u>.

The Analytic Tradition

- So named because it sees the <u>main function of philosophy</u> to be <u>analysis</u>:
  - <u>analysis of meaning and truth conditions</u> of propositions used <u>in ordinary and institutional discourse</u> (scientific, legal, artistic, religious, etc.)

- The analytic tradition, mostly Anglophonic, reacts against the grandiose metaphysical schemes of many traditional philosophers, and especially against those of the "wild years of philosophy" on the European Continent.

Gottlob Frege: analytic pioneer

- Frege looks for the logical structure of meaning and truth.
  - Developed logical analyses of the ideas of "existence" ("There is at least one x") and "generality" ("All x is y").
  - Attempted to demonstrate with logic that arithmetic is internally self-consistent:
    - If true, this shows that arithmetic can be reduced to logic (thereby refuting the mathematical theories of Descartes, Kant, and Mill).
  - Theory of the meaning of "proper names": This meaning cannot be merely "denotation" (naming, pointing at . . .):
    - The difference between "sense" (Sinn) and "reference" (Bedeutung): the example of the "morning Star"/the "evening star"/the "planet Venus."
    - They all denote the same object, but each term has a different meaning: so, besides object, and object named, there is also Sinn—"sense."
  - Deeply influenced all further discussion of meaning and truth by analytic philosophers.

G. E. Moore, and the revolt against British Hegelianism:

- The Hegelians (e.g.,Bradley, MacTaggart, and Royce) made claims that defied common sense (e.g., "Time and space are unreal").

- Moore's reaction: "A Defence of Common Sense": Everything is real that common sense says is real.
  - Moore's list of common sense claims that he knows to be true (e.g., "My body exists; it was smaller when I was first born than it is now; it has always been at various distances from physical objects, which are themselves real," etc.).

- The critique of metaphysics: What do philosophers mean when they deny these well-known truths of common sense?

- Moore's "complacency": "I do not think that the world or the sciences have suggested to me any philosophical problems. . . ."

Bertrand Russell

- Joins Moore in the rebellion against the Hegelian metaphysicians.
  - Attacks their disdain for mathematics rather than their disdain for common sense.
- Co-authors with A. N. Whitehead *Principia Mathematica*, defending and extending Frege's theory of mathematics.
- <u>Philosophy is subordinate to science</u>: <u>philosophy must be primarily analytic</u>.
  - <u>Philosophy's job: conceptual analysis</u> of notions such as "mind, matter, consciousness, knowledge, experience, causality, will, time"
  - Lifelong commitment to <u>Ockham's razor as an analytic tool</u>
- <u>"Theory of Descriptions"</u> as the <u>solution to the problem of propositions involving the concept of "existence," which often dissolve into contradiction</u>:
  - E.g.: The proposition "The golden mountain does not exist" seems to assert, "There is a golden mountain and it doesn't exist."
  - Propositions such as "Scott is the author of *Waverly*" seem to be equivalent to "Scott is Scott" or "The author of *Waverly* is the author of *Waverly*."
  - It seems that one of these propositions is true: "The present king of France is bald," or "The present king of France is not bald." But there is no present king of France.
- Russell's solution: a logical formula into which each of these propositions can be translated and their meaning and truth can be established, eliminating ambiguity and paradox: <u>"There is an entity *c*, such that '*x* is *y*' is true if and only if *x* = *c*."</u>

Logical Positivism: A. J. <u>Ayer</u>, Rudolph <u>Carnap</u>, Otto <u>Neurath</u>, Hans <u>Reichenbach</u>, and Moritz <u>Schlick</u>, among others

- Paradigmatic analytical philosophers.
- Began as <u>"the Vienna Circle"</u> under Professor Schlick whose <u>goal</u> was to <u>make philosophy scientific</u>.
- Exhibited <u>hostility to the history of philosophy</u>, with <u>Hume</u>'s empiricism <u>and Kant</u>'s anti-metaphysical stance <u>as exceptions</u>.
- <u>Key ideas of the logical positivists</u>:
  - Resurrection and updating of <u>"Hume's Fork"</u>:
    - <u>All</u> putative <u>propositions are either analytic, synthetic, or nonsense</u>.
      - Analytic: tautologies whose negation leads to a self-contradiction.

- Synthetic: traceable to empirically verifiable phenomena (theoretically).
    - Nonsense: neither analytic nor synthetic.
  - Result: Metaphysics, ethics, theology all without meaning (as in Hume).
- Theory of meaning and truth:
  - The principle of verifiability: "The meaning of a proposition is its method of verification."
  - A proposition is true if it can be or has been verified.
  - The language of verification:
    - "Protocol sentences," evolving into "confirmation sentences," evolving into acts of indicating sense-data and uttering a sound.
- Theory of moral discourse:
  - Ethical statements are expressions of emotion (which can be true or false: e.g., "I hate this!") combined with "commands in a misleading grammatical form" (which are neither true nor false: e.g., "Don't do that!").

- Standard criticism of logical positivism:
  - Its theory of meaning fails its own criterion: The proposition "All propositions are either analytic, synthetic, or nonsense" is itself neither analytic nor synthetic; therefore it is nonsense on its own terms.
  - Its moral theory is too simplistic, and provides no method for moral criticism of, say, Nazism, from which many positivists fled to Britain and America during World War II.

Ludwig Wittgenstein

- The first phase of Wittgenstein's work: The Tractatus Logico-Philosophicus inspired the positivists because of its logical rigor, but they strongly disapproved of the sudden appearance of mysticism at the very end of the book.

- The Tractatus:
  - "The world" is defined as "the totality of facts, not of things."
  - A "fact" is defined as a "state of affairs."
  - A proposition is meaningful if it asserts a possible fact and true if it asserts an actual fact.
  - The structure of language must reflect the structure of the world.
  - When language does not do so, nonsense is created.
  - Most philosophical theories are neither true nor false, but nonsense.

- The correct method in philosophy is to "say nothing except what can be said—i.e., the propositions of natural science," and correct speakers who fail to give meaning to their philosophical pronouncements. "What we cannot talk about we must consign to silence."
- The positivists were pleased by this program;
- However, Wittgenstein ends the Tractatus saying that his book itself is nonsense, and seems attracted not to what can be said but more to the silence—to "what cannot be said"—which he calls "the mystical."

- The second phase, exemplified by the posthumously published Philosophical Investigations: no more positivism, and no more mysticism.
  - Wittgenstein on meaning: The meaning of a word is its use, its use in accordance with the rules of the "language game" being played in the particular context.
  - Words compared to tools: they get jobs done.
  - Language speaking compared to game playing: both are rule governed.
  - Do the rules of a language game allow only two kinds of proposition (as in logical positivism)? No, there are "countless kinds."
  - When the rules of a specific language game are broken or ignored, "language goes on holiday"—it stops getting work done, producing nonsense ("What time is it on the sun?").
  - Philosophy's job is therapeutic: "To show the fly the way out of the fly bottle"—to dispel philosophical confusion and anxiety.

Willard Van Orman Quine

- The most important analytic philosopher in the second half of the twentieth century.
- Challenges logical positivism, but in some ways carries on with its project.
- The challenge to logical positivism: attacks "two dogmas of empiricism":
  - Attacks the positivists' program of reductionism: reducing the meaning of so-called synthetic propositions to protocol sentences, then to confirmation sentences, then to sense-data, showing that such a program is impossible.
  - Attacks the analytic/synthetic distinction, showing that the boundary between the two can only be drawn arbitrarily.
- In other works, attacks the positivists' compartmentalization of knowledge, replacing it with a holistic model:
  - All features of our systems of knowledge are intertwined.
  - No features guarantee absolute certainty, not even mathematics.

- Quine's sympathy for the positivist program:
  - All responsible <u>philosophy must be</u> a form of <u>empiricism</u>.
  - It must be <u>scientific</u> and <u>defend</u> physicalism (<u>materialism</u>).
  - <u>Behaviorism</u> must be <u>the answer to the mind/body problem</u>.
  - <u>Only the language of physics is capable of making literally true state-ments about the nature of reality</u>.
- The role of <u>logical analysis</u> in Quine's philosophy:
  - "<u>Contextual definition</u>": translation of philosophically perplexing claims into less perplexing components (like Russell's "Theory of Descrip-tions").
  - The controversial theory of "<u>indeterminacy of translation</u>":
    - Meaning is determined behavioristically, but any specific behavior could be described in a number of different ways, all of which would be compatible with one another, so all would be correct and mean the same thing:
      - The variety of possible translations of *gavagai*, running from "There is a rabbit over there" to "There are undetached rabbit parts over there."

<u>Martha Nussbaum</u>: "Farewell to the Twentieth Century"

- <u>The relation between fiction and moral philosophy</u>.
- Nussbaum <u>supports Aristotle's defense of art</u> against Plato's attack upon it.
  - Nussbaum argues that the <u>study of</u> certain <u>literary texts is "indis-pensable to a philosophical enquiry into the ethical sphere</u>."
    - The careful reading of fiction is a necessary condition of ethical study but not a sufficient condition.
  - In ethics, Nussbaum <u>applauds Aristotle's idea of "practical reason,"</u> which <u>recognizes the individuality in each moral case</u> (as opposed the universality sought by all moral systems).
    - E.g., both the style and the content of many of Henry James's novels teach "an acute perception of the particular."
  - <u>Fiction</u> also <u>stresses the ethical significance of contingency</u> (of "un-controlled happenings").
    - There is such a thing as "<u>moral luck</u>," as Aristotle insisted.
    - <u>We learn from</u> some <u>novels the legitimate role of emotions in both rationality and ethics</u>.
    - Emotion is not always opposed to rationality and correct behavior, but is a part of it.

- We also <u>learn from fiction</u> about the "<u>noncommensurability of the valuable things</u>":
  - There is no one thing to which all other values can be reduced, contrary to Kant (duty), Mill (utility), Epicurus and Bentham (pleasure).

Topics for Consideration

1. Analyze the three following assertions, first from the perspective of William James's pragmatic theory of meaning and then from his theory of truth:

   A. The world is flat.

   B. Reality is only a dream.

   C. After your death, your soul will be directed to either heaven or hell, depending on God's judgment of your life.

2. What in general is the pragmatists' idea of useless thought? What kind of thinking is useful?

3. Using examples other than those in the text, explain why Frege believes that the meaning of proper names must involve more than simple denotation (that is, more than reference to the object named).

4. Write an essay in which you imagine G. E. Moore's response to Descartes's claim that, in the absence of a proof of God's existence, Descartes cannot be certain that he has a body (see pages 170–172).

5. In your own words, describe what you take to be the point of Russell's Theory of Descriptions. What philosophical problems does he hope to clear up with that theory?

6. According to the logical positivists, all assertions are either analytic, synthetic, or nonsense. What function does this thesis have for the logical positivists?

7. According to the text, what is the main weakness of the thesis of the logical positivists that all assertions are either analytic, synthetic, or nonsense?

8. What features of Wittgenstein's *Tractatus* did the logical positivists like, and what features did they dislike?

9. Contrast the later Wittgenstein (in *Philosophical Investigations*) with the earlier Wittgenstein (in *Tractatus Logico-Philosophicus*) on the topic of "nonsense."

10. Explain what features of Quine's philosophy would be repugnant to the logical positivists and what features would be attractive to them.

11. Paraphrase Quine's "indeterminacy of translation" thesis as clearly as you can, and then either defend it or attack it.

12. Look back at the material at the end of Chapter 2 on Aristotle's ethics. What feature of it has Nussbaum chosen to support her views about the relation between literary imagination and ethics, and in what ways has she augmented Aristotle's original theory?

Notes

1. Quoted in Morton White, *The Age of Analysis* (New York and Toronto: New American Library, 1955), 158.

2. William James, *Pragmatism and the Meaning of Truth* (Cambridge, Mass.: Harvard University Press, 1979), 28.

3. Ibid., 30.

4. Ibid., 34.

5. Ibid., 32.

6. Ibid., 97.

7. William James, *The Will to Believe* (Cambridge, Mass.: Harvard University Press, 1979), 20.

8. James, *Pragmatism*, 15.

9. John Dewey, *How We Think*, in *John Dewey: The Later Works, 1925–1953*, vol. 8, ed. Jo Ann Boydston (Carbondale and Edwardsville: Southern Illinois University Press, 1986), 199–200.

10. John Dewey, *Experience and Nature* (New York: Dover Publications, 1958), 7.

11. Dewey, *How We Think*, 195.

12. Rüdiger Safranski, *Schopenhauer and the Wild Years of Philosophy* (Cambridge, Mass.: Harvard University Press, 1990).

13. *Begriffschrift* means roughly "conceptual writings." The German title was retained in the section of the book translated by Peter Geach in *Translations from the Philosophical Writings of Gottlob Frege* (Oxford: Oxford University Press, 1952).

14. Bertrand Russell, "My Mental Development," in *The Philosophy of Bertrand Russell*, ed. Paul Arthur Schilpp (Evanston, Ill.: Library of Living Philosophers, 1946), 12.

15. Bertrand Russell, *Philosophy* (New York: W. W. Norton, 1927), 2.

16. G. E. Moore, "A Defence of Common Sense," in *G. E. Moore: Selected Writings*, ed. Thomas Baldwin (London and New York: Routledge, 1993), 111.

17. G. E. Moore, "An Autobiography," in *The Philosophy of G. E. Moore*, ed. Paul Arthur Schilpp (La Salle, Ill.: Open Court, 1968), 14.

18. Christopher Hookway, *Quine: Language, Experience, and Reality* (Stanford, Calif.: Stanford University Press, 1988), 198. Hookway is speaking about W. V. Quine in this passage, but his point applies to Russell as well.

19. Bertrand Russell, "Logical Atomism," in *Logic and Knowledge: Essays 1901–1950*, ed. Robert Charles Marsh (London: George Allen and Unwin, 1956), 341.

20. Ibid., 326.

21. Bertrand Russell, *A History of Western Philosophy* (New York and London: Simon and Schuster, 1972), 831.

22. Rudolf Carnap, *Philosophy and Logical Syntax* (London: Kegan Paul, Trench, Trubner, 1935), 32.

23. Ibid., 31.

24. Moritz Schlick, "Causality in Everyday Life and in Recent Science," in *Knowledge and Value: Introductory Readings in Philosophy*, ed. Elmer Sprague and Paul W. Taylor (New York: Harcourt, Brace, 1959), 195, 206.

25. Carnap, 24.

26. Alfred Jules Ayer, *Language, Truth, and Logic* (New York: Dover, 1952), 113.

27. Jon Wheatley, *Prolegomena to Philosophy* (Belmont, Calif.: Wadsworth, 1970), 103.

28. A recent debate among Wittgenstein scholars pits those who insist that there is an important division between Wittgenstein's two phases (called the "traditional reading") and those who claim that essentially the two stages have the same goal: a "therapeutic one" (called the "new reading"). See *The New Wittgenstein*, eds. Alice Crary and Rupert Reed (London and NY: Routledge, 2001).

29. Ludwig Wittgenstein, *Tractatus Logico-Philosophicus*, trans. D. F. Pears and B. F. McGuinness (London and New York: Routledge, 1994), 5. Subsequent references to this book appear in parentheses in the text, using Wittgenstein's paragraph numbering system rather than page numbers.

30. Ludwig Wittgenstein, *Philosophical Investigations*, trans. G. E. M. Anscombe (New York: Macmillan, 1964), 6–7, par. 43. Subsequent references to this book appear in parentheses in the text, using Wittgenstein's paragraph numbering system rather than page numbers.

31. Not all analytic philosophers agree that Quine has defused the synthetic-analytic distinction. See H. P. Grice and P. F. Strawson, "In Defense of a Dogma," *Philosophical Review* 65 (1956): 141–58.

32. W. V. Quine, "Two Dogmas in Retrospect," *Canadian Journal of Philosophy* 21 (1991): 270.

33. W. V. Quine, "Two Dogmas of Empiricism," in *From a Logical Point of View*, 2d ed., rev. (Cambridge, Mass.: Harvard University Press, 1961), 20.

34. Ibid., 12.

35. W. V. Quine, "Facts of the Matter," in *Essays on the Philosophy of W. V. Quine*, ed. R. W. Shahan and C. V. Swoyer (Hassocks: Harvester, 1979), 163.

36. W. V. Quine, *Word and Object* (New York and London: John Wiley and Sons, 1960), 51 ff.

37. Peter Unger, *Philosophical Relativity* (Oxford: Blackwell, 1984), 18.

38. Christopher Hookway, *Quine: Language, Experience, and Reality* (Stanford, Calif.: Stanford University Press, 1988), 141.

39. Lynn Hankinson Nelson, *Who Knows? From Quine to a Feminist Empiricism* (Philadelphia: Temple University Press, 1990); and Louise M. Antony, "Quine as Feminist: The Radical Import of Naturalized Epistemology," in *A Mind of One's Own: Feminist Essays on Reason and Objectivity*, ed. Louise M. Antony and Charlotte Witt (Boulder, Colo.: Westview Press, 1993).

40. Martha C. Nussbaum, *Liberty of Conscience: In Defense of America's Tradition of Religious Equality* (New York: Basic Books, 2008).

41. Including an essay written with the philosopher Hilary Putnam titled "Changing Aristotle's Mind" in a book edited by Nussbaum and Emélie Ocksenberg Rorty, *Essays on Aristotle's De Anima* (Oxford and New York: Oxford University Press and Clarendon Press, 1992), 27–56.

42. Aristotle, *Poetics*, trans. Benjamin Jowett, in *The Basic Works of Aristotle*, ed. Richard McKeon (New York: Random House, 1941), 1463–64.

43. Martha C. Nussbaum, *Love's Knowledge: Essays on Philosophy and Literature* (New York and Oxford: Oxford University Press, 1990). Subsequent references to this book appear in parentheses in the text.

44. See Nussbaum's book, *The Fragility of Goodness: Luck and Ethics in Greek Tragedy and Philosophy* (Cambridge and New York: Cambridge University Press, 2001), and her articles: "Aristotelian Social Philosophy," in *Necessary Goods: Our Responsibility to Meet Others' Needs*, ed. Gillian Brook (Lanham, MD: Rowman & Littlefield, 1998), 135–56; "Non-Relative Virtues: An Aristotelian Approach," in *The Quality of Life*, eds. Martha Nussbaum and Amartya Sen (Oxford and New York: Oxford University Press, 1999), 247–69; and "Aristotle, Feminism, and Needs for Functioning," in *Feminist Interpretations of Aristotle*, ed. Cynthia Freeland (University Park, PA: Pennsylvania State University Press, 1998), 248–59.

45. Section 1142a24 of Aristotle's *Nicomachian Ethics* in Nussbaum's own translation.

46. John Horton, "Life, Literature and Ethical Theory: Martha Nussbaum on the Role of the Literary Imagination in Ethical Thought," in *Literature and the Political Imagination*, eds. John Horton and Andrea T. Baumeister (London and New York: Routledge, 1996), pp. 70–97; 80. Subsequent references to this article appear in parentheses in the text.

Glossary of
Philosophical Terms

Boldfaced type indicates terms that are cross-referenced within the glossary.

accident In Greek and medieval logic, a characteristic of a **substance** that is not essential to the substance. Rationality is part of the **essence** of human beings, but being bald or hairy is accidental.

aesthetics The philosophy of art. The branch of philosophy that investigates questions such as, What makes something a work of art? Are there absolute values in art, or are aesthetic values always relative? Can there be aesthetic arguments, or are aesthetic judgments based only on preference? What is the status of art among other human intellectual and creative endeavors?

alienation A term usually associated with Hegelian or Marxian philosophy, designating the estrangement of a subject from its own **essence** or the rupture between a subject and its natural object.

analogy A kind of comparison in which there is implied a similarity of sorts between two otherwise differing objects. Analogy was claimed by many **Platonic** medieval philosophers as one of the main sources of our knowledge of God. For example, although we do not know God directly, we know something about his mind based on an analogy between human and divine wisdom.

analytic philosophy The view and practice according to which the main function of philosophy is the analysis of meaning rather than the construction of philosophical theories about the world. Analytical philosophers believe that certain key concepts in ordinary language and in scientific, moral, and religious discourse are philosophically vague

or misleading. Philosophical problems can be solved and pseudophilo-
sophical problems can be dispelled through the clarification of these
concepts. The theories that analytic philosophers do generate tend
to be demonstrations of the logical relationships among these different realms of discourse rather than grandiose **metaphysical** schemes.
Although many of the pioneers of this school at the end of the nineteenth century and beginning of the twentieth century were Continental
Europeans, the movement has become primarily an Anglo-American one.

analytic proposition A **proposition** whose predicate is contained in its
subject (for example, "A triangle has three angles"; here the subject,
"triangle," already entails the notions of "three" and of "angles").
The negation of an analytic proposition always produces a self-
contradiction. Analytic propositions are contrasted with **synthetic
propositions.** The idea of analyticity plays a major role in the philosophies of Leibniz, Hume, Kant, and the **logical positivists.** Quine's
philosophy attempts to demote its significance.

anthropomorphism The projection of human qualities onto the nonhuman
world.

a posteriori A belief, **proposition,** or argument is said to be a posteriori
if its truth can be established only through observation. Classical
empiricism was an attempt to show that all significant knowledge
about the world is based on a posteriori truths.

a priori A belief, **proposition,** or argument is said to be a priori if its truth
can be known independently of observation. Definitions, arithmetic,
and the principles of logic are usually held to be a priori. Classical
rationalism was an attempt to show that all significant knowledge of
the world is based on a priori truths, which most of the rationalists
associated with **innate ideas.**

Arianism A fourth-century heresy named after its leader, Arius, who
denied the **doctrine of the Trinity,** holding that Christ had his own
essence, which was divine, but which was independent of God's essence.

asceticism The religious or moral theory and its practice involving the
requirement that one eschew all luxuries and any material goods other
than the bare essentials.

atheism The claim that there is no God, or that there are no gods.

atomic facts A term of Bertrand Russell's used by him and other
analytic philosophers to designate the most basic, simple facts
out of which all other facts could be constructed. These facts were
"atomic" in the original sense of the word, that is, indivisible. There was

never consensus over what "atomic facts" are exactly. Some analytic philosophers decided that they were facts about *sense data;* others, that they were literally physical facts.

atomism The view of Leucippus and Democritus that the whole of reality is constructed out of invisible, indivisible, ultimate particles of being that they called atoms. The splitting of the "atom" in the twentieth century ended atomism. (The current atomic theory is not really a form of atomism.)

axiology The general term for the theory of values. It incorporates **aesthetics** and **moral philosophy.**

Beatific Vision, the A vision that bestows bliss, or extreme happiness, on the individual who has the vision.

beg the question A fallacious form of reasoning—sometimes intentionally so—in which the thesis that the argument is supposed to prove as its conclusion has been smuggled into the argument's premises (e.g., to "prove" that murder is wrong, when the very word "murder" means "wrongful killing").

canon The documents or books declared to be central to the beliefs of any religious, philosophical, or literary tradition by the authorities of that tradition. For instance, the book of Genesis is canonical to Judaism and to Christianity. The Gospel of Mark is canonical to Christians but rejected by Jews.

Cartesian The adjectival form of René Descartes' name. For example, "Cartesian philosophy" is the philosophy of Descartes.

catharsis The purgation of dangerous emotions. In Aristotle's philosophy this act is accomplished through the engagement with dramatic art; in other theories it is accomplished by a cold shower.

causality The supposed relationship of **necessity** among events such that whenever event X happens, event Y cannot fail to follow. In that case, it is said that X causes Y.

conceptual analysis The logical and semantic analysis carried out by **analytic philosophers** of concepts deemed to be philosophically problematical in order to resolve or dissolve the philosophical problems that these concepts seem to entail.

conceptualism Abelard's theory of **universals,** located somewhere between **nominalism** and **moderate realism,** according to which concepts in the mind are abstractions that the human mind makes from similarities really existing in the natural world. As such, concepts are accurate but not perfect representations of universals.

confirmation sentence A term in the vocabulary of early **logical positivism** designating phrases that express the simplest of all **empirical** experiences, hence are the most likely to be certain; e.g., "Hot here now," or "Painful here now." This category replaced an earlier candidate for certainty, viz., **protocol sentences**.

contingency Used in philosophy to designate the opposite of **necessity.** In the sentence "This square is large," the word "large" stands in a contingent relation to the word "square," whereas the word "angles" in the sentence "This square has four right angles" stands in a necessary relation to the word "square." In other contexts, that part of experience that is unexpected and/or not in one's control: what befalls one, rather than that which is the intended consequence of one's purposeful act.

cosmogony Theories or stories about the origins of the universe.

cosmological argument An **a posteriori** attempt to prove that God exists by showing that his existence can be deduced from certain observable facts in the universe. It was put forth by Maimonides and defended by St. Thomas Aquinas, Descartes, Leibniz, Locke, and Berkeley, among others. It was rejected by Hume, Kant, and Kierkegaard.

cosmology Theories about the nature of the universe.

deconstruction The creation of the late French philosopher Jacques Derrida, based on his eccentric but provocative reading of the linguistic theory of Ferdinand de Saussure. Deconstruction is a theory of texts (philosophical, fictional, legal, scientific), according to which, because of the very nature of thought and language, almost all traditional texts can be shown to "deconstruct" themselves, that is, to undermine and refute their own theses.

deduction A form of argument in which the conclusion follows necessarily from the premises (for example, the **syllogism**).

denotation That feature of meaning that involves naming an object, pointing to it, referring to it. In the phrases, "the brown dog" or "a brown dog," "brown" denotes a color, and "dog" denotes an animal.

determinism The view that every event that occurs, occurs necessarily. Every event follows inevitably from the events that preceded it. There is no **randomness** in reality; rather, all is law-governed. **Freedom** either does not exist (hard determinism) or exists in such a way as to be compatible with **necessity** (soft determinism).

deus ex machina A phony solution. Literally, "god from a machine." Greek dramatists of inferior quality would create complex plots loaded with difficult problems, and then, with the use of a machine, drop a god onto the stage (played by an actor on a cable) who solved the problems supernaturally.

dialectic In the philosophies of Hegel and Marx, the dialectic is a mechanism of change and progress in which every possible situation exists only in relation to its own opposite. This relationship is one of both antagonism and mutual dependency, but the antagonism (a form of violence) eventually undermines the relationship and overthrows it. (However, sometimes the term "dialectical" is used only to emphasize a relationship of reciprocity between two entities or processes.)

differential repetition The **philological** theory that in the cases of many important ancient documents—religious, political, artistic—there are no genuinely original texts to be found; rather, there are fusions of oral and written traditions, including errors, later interventions, and mistranslations of ever-moving textual fragments, and copies of copies of copies of these false "originals."

doctrine of double truth A medieval theory attributed to Averroës and developed by the Latin Averroists, according to which there exist side by side two categories of truth: revealed (religious) truth and philosophical (scientific) truth. These two kinds of truth do not compete with each other even where they appear to contradict each other; they simply offer discrepant perspectives on the same object. Whether a cynical theory, as some believed, or an insight into the nature of truth, as others believed, for a short time it allowed progress in the investigation of topics that otherwise might have been banned by religious authorities.

doctrine of the Trinity An official Christian **dogma** asserting the unity of the Father (God), the Son (Jesus), and the Holy Ghost (or Holy Spirit) in one divine Godhead.

dogma The principal tenets of a religious system as determined and enforced by the authorities. The word has also acquired a pejorative sense, referring to fossilized beliefs held tenaciously and uncritically.

Donatism A fourth-century heresy named after its founder, Donatus, who held that sacraments were invalid if the ministering priest was in a serious state of sin.

dualism The **ontological** view that reality is composed of two distinct kinds of beings, usually (as in Descartes) minds and bodies.

empirical An experience is empirical if it consists in sensorial contact with features of reality: i.e., contact made through any of the five senses.

empiricism The **epistemological** view that true knowledge is derived primarily from sense experience (or, in "purer" strains of empiricism, exclusively from sense experience). For empiricist philosophers, all significant knowledge is **a posteriori**, and **a priori** knowledge is either nonexistent or tautological. The "classical" empiricists were the seventeenth- and eighteenth-century Britons—Locke, Berkeley, and Hume—all of whom denied the existence of **innate ideas** and conceived of the human mind as a "blank slate" at birth.

entropy The hypothetical tendency for systems to achieve a state of maximum equilibrium through reduction of tension.

epiphenomenon "Epi," from the Greek word for "on top of" and "phenomenon" from the Greek word for "appearance." A secondary appearance, implying an appearance that has no causal function in the system in which it appears.

epistemology Theory of knowledge, answering questions such as, What is knowledge? What, if anything, can we know? What is the difference between opinion and knowledge?

eschatology The study of last, or final, things. In theology, the study of death, or of the Last Judgment, or of the end of the world.

essence That feature of an object or concept that establishes the nature and definition of the object or concept. For example, Aristotle said that rationality is the essence of human beings, and even though the ability to laugh or to blush is unique among humans, neither ability is part of the human essence.

ethics Moral philosophy; the branch of philosophy that answers questions such as, Is there such a thing as the Good? What is "the good life"? Is there such a thing as absolute duty? Are valid moral arguments possible? Are moral judgments based only on preference? In this book, used interchangeably with **moral philosophy**. Some writers reserve the term "ethics" exclusively for rules governing the behavior of various professionals: doctors, lawyers, professors, and business people, for example.

etymology The study of the origins and histories of words.

evolution As used here, the transformation over time of one species of natural living being into another species.

existentialism A twentieth-century philosophy associated principally with Jean-Paul Sartre but also thought to encompass the work of Karl Jaspers, Martin Heidegger, Gabriel Marcel, Albert Camus, Simone de Beauvoir, and Miguel de Unamuno, among others. More of a shared attitude than a school of thought, it can nevertheless be roughly defined by saying with Sartre that existentialists are those who believe that, in the case of humans, "existence precedes essence." This is the thesis that there is no human nature that precedes our presence in the world. All humans individually create humanity at every moment through their free acts.

false consciousness A term in Marxian philosophy, originating with Friedrich Engels, designating the psychological state of mind of members of a society dominated by **ideology.**

Forms Usually associated with the philosophies of Plato or Aristotle. For Plato (in whose philosophy the word "Form" is capitalized in this text), everything that exists in the physical or conceptual world is in some way dependent on Forms, which exist independently of the world but are the models (**essences, universals,** archetypes) of all reality. Forms are eternal and unchangeable and the ultimate object of all true philosophizing. For Aristotle, forms are also the essences of things, but they exist *in* things and are not independent of them. The form of an object and its function are ultimately related.

freedom Freedom exists if there are such things as free acts and free agents, that is, if some acts are performed in such a way that the authors of those acts could be held responsible for them. Some philosophers (called libertarians) say that these acts *do* exist, that some acts are freely chosen from among genuine alternatives, and that therefore **determinism** is false. ("I did X, but under exactly the same circumstances, I could have done Y instead. Therefore, X was a free act.") Other philosophers (called soft determinists) also say that free acts exist but define "free acts" not in terms of genuine alternative choices but in terms of voluntary acts. ("I wanted to do X, and I did do X; therefore X was a free act.") Still other philosophers (called hard determinists), while agreeing with the definition of "free act" given by libertarians, deny that any such free acts or agents exist.

functionalism The view in anthropology that socially acceptable behaviors and institutions can be explained by showing that they have survival value for their society, and that dysfunctional individual and group behaviors are deemed morally unacceptable, prohibited by spirits and divine beings.

hedonism Either the view that pleasure and pain *should* be the only motives for correct action (called moral hedonism, defended by Epicurus and Bentham) or the view that pleasure and pain *are* the only motives for voluntary action (called psychological hedonism, or **psychological egoism,** defended by Hobbes).

holism The view that the parts of a system are not independent, discrete units; rather, they are what they are by virtue of their relationship to one another and to the whole system.

idealism The **ontological** view that, ultimately, every existing thing can be shown to be spiritual, mental, or otherwise incorporeal (hence, a version of **monism**); usually associated in Western philosophy with Berkeley and Hegel.

ideology A term in Marxian philosophy designating the status of cultural phenomena (such as art, religion, morality, and philosophy) as systems of propaganda supporting a specific socioeconomic system and its beneficiaries. This propaganda is internalized by the masses, and believed by them to describe natural facts.

immanent Inherent; not external to a system but internal to it, operating from within it.

innate idea An idea or a concept that is present at birth.

incorrigibility An empirical statement has incorrigibility if a person who believes it could not be wrong. An example might be, "I feel pain now," uttered in a case in which one in fact does feel intense pain. Whether such statements actually exist is controversial, but **empiricism** in its classical form (Locke) and modern form (**logical positivism**) put great stock in them.

induction A form of argumentation in which, unlike in **deduction,** the conclusion does not follow necessarily from the premises. Instead, the conclusion makes a claim that is broader than the claim found in any one of the premises or in the totality of the premises. For example, this swan is white; that swan is white; all of those swans are white; therefore all (or most) swans are white. The conclusion of an inductive argument usually stands in a probabilistic relation to the premises.

law of identity See **principle of identity.**

law of noncontradiction See **principle of noncontradiction.**

law of the excluded middle See **principle of the excluded middle.**

logic The branch of philosophy that studies the structure of valid inference; a purely *formal* discipline, interested in the structure of argumentation rather than in its content.

logical entailment A relation of logical **necessity** between two concepts or **propositions.** If concept or proposition X necessarily implies concept or proposition Y, then X logically entails Y. The assertion of X with the simultaneous denial of Y would constitute a self-contradiction; for example, the concept "brother" logically entails both the concept "sibling" and the concept "male." To assert that person P literally is your brother and to deny that he is your sibling or is male is to contradict yourself. See also **deduction**.

logical positivism A development within **analytical philosophy** initiated in Austria and Germany between the two World Wars by scientifically minded philosophers and philosophically minded scientists as a reaction against what they took to be the overblown **metaphysical** grandstanding of European philosophers in the nineteenth century. Their goal was to make philosophy respectable by making it scientific. Philosophy would be restricted to logical analysis whose outcome would be the demonstration that the only truly meaningful **propositions** are those of mathematics, logic, and science. All others would be shown to be merely poetic, emotive, **analogical,** or nonsense.

logocentrism An overvaluation of language, literalness, and reason that fails to recognize limitations of each (according to Jacques Derrida).

Manicheanism A religious system asserting the domination of reality by two opposing irreducible supernatural forces, Good and Evil. Named after Mani or Manes of Persia (ca. 216-ca. 276), who founded the doctrine as a religion, a doctrine that influenced certain later sects of Christianity, such as Gnosticism.

materialism The **ontological** view that, in the final analysis, all phenomena can be demonstrated to be material in nature and that mental and spiritual phenomena are either nonexistent or have no existence independent of matter (e.g., as in Democritus, Hobbes, Marx, and Quine).

mechanism A theory claiming that the whole of reality is like a machine. Reality is made up of material objects in motion or at rest, standing in direct **causal** relationships with one another, requiring no explanation other than the laws of Newtonian physics.

metaphysics The branch of philosophy that attempts to construct a general, speculative worldview; a complete, systematic account of all reality and experience, usually involving an **epistemology,** an **ontology,** an **ethics,** and an **aesthetics.** (The adjective "metaphysical" is often employed to stress the speculative, as opposed to the scientific, or commonsensical, features of the theory or proposition it describes.)

metempsychosis The passage of the soul at the death of the body into the newly born body of another creature, human or animal. The belief in such a transmigration of souls is held in several philosophical and religious systems.

misogyny The hatred of women.

moderate realism An aspect of Thomas Aquinas's theory of mind and language, related to Abelard's **conceptualism,** espousing the Aristotelian view that **essences** are not separate from the physical world—as in Plato and **Platonic realism**—rather, they are embedded in natural objects. The human mind is capable of abstracting these essences from the natural world, along with other general characteristics, thereby forming the **universals,** which are accurate representations of these similarities that exist in the real world.

monad Term from Leibnizian **metaphysics** designating the simplest, most basic **substance,** which Leibniz took to be a unit of psychical energy that is both nonphysical and nonspatial, yet from which all physical and spatial objects are derived—perhaps in the way that neither hydrogen nor oxygen is liquid, yet two parts of hydrogen and one part of oxygen produce liquid.

monism The **ontological** view that only one entity exists (e.g., as in Spinoza) or that only one *kind* of entity exists (e.g., as in Hobbes and Berkeley).

monotheism The belief in one god, as opposed to **polytheism** or **atheism**. Judaism, Christianity, and Islam all purport to be monotheistic religions.

moral philosophy See **ethics.**

mysticism The view that reality reveals its true nature only in a super-rational ecstatic vision.

naive realism The view, attributed both to unsophisticated persons and to certain philosophers who defend a commonsense picture of the world, that reality is pretty much the way it appears to our senses.

naturalism As employed in this text, naturalism is the **epistemological** view that a natural phenomenon can be explained only by references to other natural phenomena; or the **ontological** view that all is nature, that there are no supernatural or unnatural phenomena, and that there is no natural hierarchy of value. For example, humans are no more valuable per se than coyotes.

necessary condition A component, feature, or state of any object or idea X that must be present before the object or idea can correctly be designated as X, and whose absence guarantees that an object or idea is not an X. For example, oxygen is a necessary condition of combustion. Some necessary conditions are also **sufficient conditions.** Life is both a necessary and a sufficient condition of any organic system.

Divisibility by two is a necessary and sufficient condition of an even number. Divisibility by four is a sufficient but not a necessary condition of evenness.

necessity (1) Logical necessity: There is a relation of logical necessity (or logical entailment) between two **propositions** if the assertion of one of them, together with the denial of the other, results in a contradiction. For example, there is a relation of logical necessity between the sentences "Linda is a sister" and "Linda has at least one sibling" because the assertion of the one and the denial of the other would result in a contradiction. (2) Ontological necessity: There is a relation of ontological necessity between two events X and Y if the occurrence of the first event X *must* be followed by the second event Y. (**Determinism** claims that every event is necessary; i.e., every event follows necessarily from the events preceding it. Indeterminism claims that *not all events are* necessary.)

neologism Designates any word in a traditional language, newly coined to name, characterize, or refer to newly emerging conditions or discoveries.

nihilism Either the view that nothing exists or the view that nothing deserves to exist, or the wish for destruction.

nominalism The theory of language and mind claiming that the **universals** do not name independent **Forms, essences,** or general similarities that truly exist in the natural world. Rather, they are mere names designating convenient categorizations of the world for pragmatic human interaction with it. In the medieval world, nominalism (such as that of William of Ockham) was meant as a form of **empiricism.** In the more radical modern versions (such as Nietzsche's and Derrida's), nominalism is a skeptical doctrine, implying that what the human mind knows is not a real, natural world, but rather a world of convention created arbitrarily.

noumenal world Kant's name designating ultimate reality—the forever unknowable but necessarily existent reality behind the phenomenal world, the world of appearance. Phenomena are in fact appearances of noumena.

numerology The study of numbers in order to reveal their supposed esoteric or mystical meanings.

ontological argument An **a priori** attempt to prove that God exists by showing that, from the very concept of God, his existence can be deduced. This argument has been defended by a number of religious philosophers in the **Platonic** tradition. It was first formulated by St. Anselm and appears in one form or another in the work of Descartes, Spinoza, Leibniz, and Hegel. It has some able twentieth-century defenders, for example, Charles Hartshorne and Norman Malcolm. But it has been rejected by some notables too, including St. Thomas, Hume, Kant, and Kierkegaard.

ontology Theory of being; the branch of philosophy pursuing such questions as, What is real? What is the difference between appearance and reality? What is the relation between minds and bodies? Are numbers and concepts real, or are only physical objects real? A question about the ontological status of anything (e.g., about mathematics, God, universals, or frumious bandersnatches) is a question about that thing's status in reality—not only whether the thing in question exists, but *how* it exists. How does it relate to other existing things? (E.g., how do minds relate to bodies? How does God relate to the world?)

pantheism The view that everything is divine, that God's "creation" is in fact identical with God; from the Greek *pan* ("all") and *theos* ("god").

Pelagianism A religious view named after its founder, Pelagius, declared heretical by early medieval Christianity. It denied original sin and, according to Church authorities, overemphasized the role of free will in achieving salvation.

philology The study of ancient written records, usually of "dead" languages.

Platonic realism The medieval **Platonic** theory of language and mind that claimed that the **universals** denote real **essences** and other general characteristics. Indeed, essences (**Forms**) are more real than the physical objects in which they are instantiated.

Platonism A theory basing itself on any of these interrelated ideas in Plato's philosophy: the idea that the intellectual or spiritual world is more real than the physical world, which is a mere copy of that superior world; the idea that **essences** are not merely abstractions but exist eternally as **Forms**; the idea of reality as a hierarchy of dependencies, each less real than that upon which it is dependent.

pluralism The **ontological** view that reality is composed of a plurality of beings rather than just of one kind of being (**monism**) or of two kinds of beings (**dualism**).

polytheism The view that more than one god exists.

postmodernism A loosely applied term (1) designating an intellectual posture skeptical of **epistemologies, ontologies**, and institutions (governmental, academic, military, medical, religious) of the modern

Western tradition; (2) challenging the basic tenets of liberalism, humanism, individualism, and capitalism; (3) designating a fascination with popular culture and the domination of technology over human endeavors; (4) dwelling on contemporary **semiotic** strategies that privilege signs and images over substance and truth, reproduction over production, and representation over originals.

poststructuralism The Continental European cultural and philosophical movement following **structuralism**. It emphasizes the arbitrary nature of the structures studied by structuralists, often leading to a form of radical **relativism** and **skepticism**. Perhaps the key figure in this movement was Jacques Derrida. See also **postmodernism**.

pragmatism An American philosophical movement developing around the turn of the nineteenth century whose goal was to show that both meaning and truth should be defined in terms of a practical relation between thought and language on the one hand and the natural and social worlds on the other. Language and thought were conceived as problem-solving devices, and philosophical theories, like other ideas, were evaluated exclusively in terms of their instrumentality.

principle of identity Claimed to be one of the three basic laws of thought, this principle states that everything is identical to itself: Fido is Fido; $A = A$.

principle of internal harmony An axiom governing reality that Gottfried Leibniz deduces from God's rationality, power, and goodness, according to which God created reality in such a way that it exhibits the greatest amount of perfection possible ("the best of all possible worlds"). Therefore, we must assume that the relationships among all created beings are as harmonious as possible, even in situations in which there appears to be conflict.

principle of non-contradiction Claimed to be one of the three basic laws of thought, this principle states that it is not the case that something both is and is not A at the same time (where A is any identity or characteristic): it is not the case that Fido is brown all over and not brown all over; $\sim(A . \sim A)$.

principle of sufficient reason A foundational idea in the philosophy of Gottfried Leibniz and others asserting the rational structure of both thought and reality and the concordance between them. For any being that exists, there is some reason—known or as yet unknown—explaining why it exists and why it exists as it does. Leibniz claims that anyone who denies the principle of sufficient reason—such as some mystics—is irrational by definition.

principle of the excluded middle Claimed to be one of the three basic laws of thought, this principle states that, given anything in the world, it is either A, or not-A (where A is any identity or characteristic): Either Fido is brown all over or Fido is not brown all over; A v ~A.

Priscillianism A fifth-century heresy attributed to Priscillian, bishop of Avila, Spain, born ca. 340 C.E., executed for practicing magic in 385 C.E. Those who, after his death, saw him as a martyr, followed a version of **Manichean** dualism, believing in a Kingdom of Light and a Kingdom of Darkness. Both Kingdoms were embodied in each human being; the body was associated with Darkness and the soul, the representative of Light was considered to be a portion of divine substance. Christ came to liberate the soul from the body. Attacked by St. Augustine in his book *Ad Orosium, contra Priscillianistas et Origenistas.*

proper name As used in association with Gottlob Frege's theory of meaning, a noun or noun phrase that designates individual people, places, or objects, apparently without regard to any descriptive component, for example, Sacramento, George Washington, the White House, the Capitol. Proper names are contrasted in grammar with general descriptions and with common names, like "horse" and "triangle," which can designate whole classes of objects. Notice, however, that a noun phrase like "the highest mountain in California" can be a proper name if it serves as a synonym for "Mount Whitney," or it can be a description, as in "Which peak in that mountain range would you say is the highest mountain in California?"

proposition As employed in this text, a proposition is whatever is asserted by a sentence. The sentences "It's raining," "Es regnet," and "Llueve" all assert the same proposition.

protocol sentence A term in the vocabulary of early **logical positivism** designating a **proposition** that was intended to serve as the foundation of knowledge by expressing the simplest of all **empirical** experiences, such as, "The person named Donald Palmer (myself) experienced pain at 5:30 PM on the 4th of September, 2008." Later replaced by **confirmation sentences** that purported to express even simpler truths.

psychoanalysis The theory created by Sigmund Freud (1859–1939) concerning the causes of repressed wishes and fantasies in the unconscious mind and the relation of these unconscious motives to the conscious mind and to normal and abnormal behavior in general. Also, the psychotherapy associated with that theory.

psychological atomism The view held by Locke, Berkeley, and Hume (though not named as such by them) that all knowledge is built up from simple, discrete psychological data, such as the primitive sensorial experiences of colors, sounds, and tastes. (See also **sense data**.)

psychological egoism The view that the goal of all motivation is to achieve a benefit for oneself. This doctrine rules out altruism as a possible motivation unless that altruism is conceived by the moral agent as being in his or her own self-interest.

quantum mechanics A theory in advanced physics about the nature of atoms and subatomic particles such as electrons, protons, or neutrons that asserts that the behavior of these entities cannot be explained in terms of nineteenth-century **mechanistic** physics nor in terms of traditional theories of **causality**.

quietism A philosophy of inaction, rejecting agitation, and recommending the least amount of effort. Or, the passivity associated with that philosophy.

randomness If there are events that are totally uncaused and in principle unpredictable, then those events are random events. If there is randomness (i.e., if random events exist), then **determinism** is false.

rationalism The **epistemological** view that true knowledge is derived primarily from "reason" (or exclusively from "reason," in the purer strains of rationalism). Reason is conceived as the working of the mind on material provided by the mind itself. In most versions, this material takes the form of innate ideas. Therefore, for the rationalists, **a priori** knowledge is the most important kind of knowledge. In rationalistic **ontologies**, the mind and the world are seen to be in conformity—the real is the rational. The classical rationalists were the seventeenth- and eighteenth-century Continental philosophers Descartes, Spinoza, and Leibniz, but the concept is broad enough to include such philosophers as Parmenides, Plato, and Hegel.

reductio ad absurdum A form of argumentation in which the philosopher feigns acceptance of the premises of the argument of the philosopher's opponent, then the philosopher demonstrates that absurd consequences can be deduced from those premises, thereby refuting them.

reductionism The project of trying to demonstrate that all apparently complex levels of reality can be shown to be reducible to simpler, more basic levels, for example, the attempt to show that all physical objects can be explained as atomic structures or that all mental events can be explained as neurological events.

reification The result of illegitimately concretizing that which is abstract, that which is general, or that which defies concretization. From the Latin, *res* (thing), hence, to "thingify."

relativism In **ethics** and **aesthetics,** relativism is the view that there are no absolute values; all values are relative to time, place, and culture. In **epistemology,** relativism is the view that there are no absolute truths; all truths are relative to time, place, and culture.

scholasticism The name given to the philosophy practiced in the "schools" of the medieval universities, where all branches of philosophy, **logic,** and linguistics were developed and systematized according to theological schemata.

semiology (sometimes called semiotics) The study of the system of signs. A "sign" is an arbitrary mark or sound that has become imbued with meaning by virtue of its membership in a system of conventionality. Language is the most obvious case of such a system of signs, but behaviors and rituals can also be studied semiologically.

sense data That which is perceived immediately by any one of the senses prior to interpretation by the mind. Sense data include the perceptions of colors, sounds, tastes, odors, tactile sensations, pleasures, and pains. Classical **empiricism** based itself on the supposedly **epistemologically** foundational nature of sense data.

skepticism (or scepticism) A denial of the possibility of knowledge. General skepticism denies the possibility of *any* knowledge; however, one can be skeptical about specific fields of inquiry (e.g., **metaphysics**) or specific faculties (e.g., sense perception) without denying the possibility of knowledge in general.

solipsism The view that the only true knowledge one can possess is knowledge of one's own consciousness. According to solipsism, there is no good reason to believe that anything exists other than oneself.

sophism (1) The doctrines of a group of teachers in fifth-century-B.C.E. Athenian democracy who espoused **relativism** against **epistemological** and **ethical** absolutism and who emphasized rhetoric over reason in argumentation. (2) Sometimes a derogatory term designating a form of deceptive argumentation.

structuralism Based on the philosophical anthropology of the late French theorist Claude Lévi-Strauss (but also finding followers in all the human sciences), structuralism is the view that the human mind is universal in that, everywhere and in every historical epoch, the mind is structured in such a way as to process its data in terms of certain general formulas that give meaning to those mental data. Social relations imitate these mental formulas, adapting them to local and historical conditions. Both the mental and the social structures are best understood by studying them the way the linguist Ferdinand de Saussure studied linguistic structures, stressing not the contents of systems, rather the relations among the different components of systems.

subjectivism The view that there are no objective truths or values; all truths and values are relative to the subjectivity of the individual. (Subjectivism is a version of **relativism.**)

subjectivity The sense of private selfhood that one experiences.

sublimation A term usually associated with Freud, but employed earlier by Schopenhauer, Marx, and Nietzsche, naming the process of refinement or of spiritualization whereby the more base and crass elements are transformed into more subtle or sublime elements; for example, the sexual or aggressive drives are transformed into art.

substance In philosophy, "substance" has traditionally been the term naming whatever is thought to be the most basic, independent reality. Aristotle defined a substance as whatever can exist independently of other things, so that a horse or a man (Aristotle's examples) can exist independently, but the color of the horse or the size of the man cannot. The seventeenth- and eighteenth-century rationalists took the idea of substance as *independent being* so seriously that one of their members, Spinoza, claimed there could be only one substance in the world (i.e., only one *thing*), namely, God, because only God could exist independently. Under Berkeley's criticism of material substance and Hume's criticism of spiritual substance, the concept of substance was very much eroded away. It turned up again in Kant, but only as a category of knowledge, not as a basic reality itself.

sufficient condition A component, feature, or state of any object or idea X that, if present, guarantees that the object is indeed an X. For example, fire is a sufficient condition for heat, but it is not a **necessary condition.** (Heat can be generated without fire.) Sometimes a condition is both necessary and sufficient. Life is both a necessary and a sufficient condition of any organic system. Divisibility by two is a necessary and sufficient condition of an even number. Divisibility by four is a sufficient but not a necessary condition of evenness.

syllogism A logical argument containing two premises from which a **necessary** conclusion can be deduced. The necessity of the conclusion does not guarantee its truth. E.g., if one or both premises of the syllogism are false, the conclusion—though valid—may be false; as in: (1) All pigs fly. (2) Herbert Hoover is a pig. (3) Therefore, Herbert Hoover flies. On the other hand, some syllogisms with false premises have true conclusions: e.g., (1) All pigs are the 31st president of the U. S. A. (2) Herbert Hoover is a pig. (3) Therefore Herbert Hoover is the 31st president of the U. S. A.

synthetic a priori proposition According to Immanuel Kant, such a proposition expresses a truth about the real world (hence is synthetic) but cannot be derived from sense experience (hence is a priori). E.g., all true statements about the physical world presuppose the truth of the proposition, "Objects exist in space and time." This is a synthetic a priori proposition because it is necessarily true but there are no sense data of either space or time.

synthetic proposition A **proposition** that can be either true or false and that asserts factual claims about reality. The negation of synthetic propositions, unlike for **analytic propositions,** does not produce self-contradiction ("The cat is on the mat" and "The cat is *not* on the mat" are both possible factual claims about reality). The **empiricists** hold that synthetic propositions are always **a posteriori;** that is, they can be verified or refuted only through observation. By contrast, Kant held that **synthetic a priori** propositions are possible.

teleology A teleological explanation is an explanation in terms of goals, purposes, or intentions (from the Greek *telos,* meaning "goal"). For example, "John closed the window because he didn't want his budgie to escape" is a teleological explanation because it explains John's behavior in terms of his intentions.

theology The systematic study of God and his properties, from the Greek *theos* ("God") and *logos* ("theory," or "study of").

universals A term in medieval theory of language designating common names like "redness," "quickness," "animality," "mammality," "wealth," and "humanity." The status of the universals was hotly debated throughout the Middle Ages, producing theories such as **Platonic realism, moderate realism, conceptualism,** and **nominalism.**

Selected Bibliography

Includes primary sources (some of the original works of the main philosophers discussed in this book) and secondary sources (some suggestions for further study) as well as a few personal comments concerning some of the books recommended.

Wherever possible, inexpensive paperback editions are cited.

General Histories of Western Philosophy

Copleston, Frederick, S. J. *A History of Philosophy*, in nine vols., now gathered in three books (New York: Doubleday, 1985). The author's biases are evident, but this work is a "must" for serious research.

Jones, W. T. *A History of Western Philosophy*, 2d ed., in five vols. (New York: Harcourt Brace Jovanovich, 1969). Many long passages from the philosophers, clear presentation, and reasoned discussion.

Russell, Bertrand. *A History of Western Philosophy* (New York: Simon and Schuster, 1945). This eminent philosopher's biases balance out those of Copleston. Beautifully written.

The Pre-Socratic Philosophers
Primary Sources

Barnes, Jonathan. *Early Greek Philosophy* (New York: Penguin Books, 1987). Pertinent selections with commentary.

Nahm, Milton, ed. *Selections from Early Greek Philosophy* (New York: Appleton-Century-Crofts, 1962).

Wheelwright, Philip, ed. *The Presocratics* (New York: Odyssey Press, 1966). It's good to have several anthologies of the fragments of the pre-Socratic philosophers in order to compare translations.

Secondary Sources

Ring, Merrill. *Beginning with the Pre-Socratics* (Mountain View, Calif.: Mayfield, 1987). A short, well-written commentary on the fragments.

Taylor, C. C. W., ed. *From the Beginning to Plato.* Vol. 1 of *Routledge History of Philosophy* (London and New York: Routledge, 1977). Composed of chapters on the pre-Socratics, each written by a different expert from the perspective of the most recent scholarship in the field. Not directed primarily to the beginning student, but usually accessible. Get this work and the rest of the *Routledge History of Philosophy* from the library.

The Athenian Period
Primary Sources

Aristotle. *The Basic Work of Aristotle,* edited by Richard McKeon (New York: Random House, 1941). This is the main text for all serious students of Aristotle's philosophy.

Plato. *Great Dialogues of Plato,* translated by W. H. D. Rouse and edited by E. H. Warmington and P. G. Rouse (New York: New American Library, 1956). Contains the *Republic,* "Apology," "Crito," "Meno," and "The Symposium," among others. This is only one of many inexpensive paperback editions now available.

Plato. *The Republic of Plato,* translated by Allan Bloom (New York: Basic Books, 1968). Perhaps the most accurate and literal translation (but therefore not the most readable).

Secondary Sources

Adler, Mortimer J. *Aristotle for Everybody* (New York: Bantam Books, 1985). A readable, enticing defense of Aristotle's views by a real Aristotelian.

Barnes, Jonathan. *Aristotle* (New York: Oxford University Press [Past Masters series], 1982). Almost all the books in this series are good, cheap, short, and readable.

Barrett, Harold. *The Sophists* (Novato, Calif.: Chandler and Sharp, 1987). A short, spirited defense of the views of the Sophists.

Murdoch, Iris. *The Fire and the Sun: Why Plato Banished the Artists* (New York: Oxford University Press, 1978). The author is both a foremost novelist and a top-rate philosopher.

Pirsig, Robert. *Zen and the Art of Motorcycle Maintenance* (New York: Bantam Books, 1982). A (mostly) fascinating contemporary personal investigation of the problem of value that obsessed the Sophists, Socrates, and Plato. Pirsig sides with the Sophists and repairs his Harley.

Stone, I. F. *The Trial of Socrates* (New York: Doubleday [Anchor Books], 1989). Wonderful depiction of Athenian political life at the time of Socrates. Annoyingly simplistic criticism of Socratic and Platonic philosophy.

Vlastos, Gregory, ed. *The Philosophy of Socrates: A Collection of Critical Essays* (Garden City, N.Y.: Doubleday, 1971). A fine sampling of scholarly work about Socrates.

The Hellenistic Period
Primary Sources

Hadas, Moses, ed. *Essential Works of Stoicism* (New York: Bantam Books, 1961). Contains Marcus Aurelius's "To Himself," Epictetus's "The Manual," and Seneca's "On Tranquility."

Oats, Whitney J., ed. *The Stoic and Epicurean Philosophers: Epicurus, Epictetus, Lucretius, Marcus Aurelius* (New York: Modern Library, 1940). A standard source book.

Plotinus. *The Six Enneads,* translated by S. MacKenna and B. S. Page (Chicago: Encyclopedia Britannica, 1952).

Sextus Empiricus. *Sextus Empiricus,* trans. R. G. Bury (London: Loeb Classical Library, 1917–1952), 4 vol.

Medieval Philosophy
Primary Sources

Fremantle, Anne, ed. *The Age of Belief* (New York: New American Library, 1954). This is the first of "The Age of . . ." series. These books are short anthologies of works from the period treated. Each selection is preceded by a brief introductory essay. Very helpful.

Hyman, Arthur, and James T. Walsh, eds. *Philosophy in the Middle Ages: The Christian, Islamic, and Jewish Traditions* (Indianapolis: Hackett, 1974). Excellent samplings of the work of the main medieval philosophers, including selections from Augustine, Eriugena, Anselm, and Thomas Aquinas.

Secondary Sources

Eco, Umberto. *The Name of the Rose,* translated by William Weaver (New York: Warner Books, 1984). A best-selling philosophical novel by a medieval scholar. (You get a mean murder mystery as well.)

Gilson, Etienne. *History of Christian Philosophy in the Middle Ages* (New York: Random House, 1955). By one of the great students of the medieval mind.

Kenny, Anthony. *Aquinas* (New York: Hill and Wang, 1980). This is in the Past Masters series, which are short, usually insightful accounts directed to introductory students.

Luscombe, David. *Medieval Thought* (Oxford and New York: Oxford University Press, 1997). A short, expert, up-to-date discussion of the topic.

Price, Betsy B. *Medieval Thought: An Introduction* (Cambridge, Mass.: Blackwell, 1992). Particularly good in relating philosophy to the rest of culture in the Middle Ages.

Renaissance Philosophy
Primary Sources

Cassirer, Ernst, Paul Oskar Kristeller, and John Herman Randall Jr., eds. *The Renaissance Philosophy of Man* (Chicago: University of Chicago Press, 1948). An excellent selection of works by a number of Renaissance philosophers, with good introductory essays.

Santillana, Giorgio de, ed. *The Age of Adventure: The Renaissance Philosophers* (New York: George Braziller, 1957). The second in the fine "The Age of . . ." series.

Secondary Sources

Parkinson, G. H. R., ed. *The Renaissance and Seventeenth-Century Rationalism.* Vol. 4 of *Routledge History of Philosophy* (London and New York: Routledge, 1993). The first half contains a sampling of contemporary scholarship on the subject.

Schmitt, Charles B., ed. *The Cambridge History of Renaissance Philosophy* (Cambridge and New York: Cambridge University Press, 1988). A large collection of essays by specialists in the field of Renaissance intellectual history. Get this one at the library.

Thomas, Keith, ed. *Renaissance Thinkers* (Oxford and New York: Oxford University Press, 1993). A collection of four short books originally published in the Past Masters series. Includes *Erasmus* by James McConica, *Bacon* by Anthony Quinton, *More* by Anthony Kenny, and *Montaigne* by Peter Burke.

Continental Rationalism and British Empiricism
Primary Sources

Berkeley, George. *Philosophical Works* (London: Dent [Everyman's Library], 1992). See especially *Three Dialogues between Hylas and Philonous.* Very readable.

Berlin, Isaiah, ed. *The Age of Enlightenment: The Eighteenth-Century Philosophers* (New York: George Braziller, 1957).

Descartes, René. *Discourse on Method and Meditations,* translated by L. J. Lafleur (Indianapolis: Bobbs-Merrill [The Library of Liberal Arts], 1960).

Descartes, René. *A Guided Tour of René Descartes' Meditations on First Philosophy*, edited by Christopher Biffle and translated by Ronald Rubin (Mountain View, Calif.: Mayfield, 1989). Annotated with questions in the margins for students.

Descartes, R., B. Spinoza, G. Leibniz. *The Rationalists* (New York: Doubleday [Anchor Books], 1960). An excellent anthology selected from the key works of these philosophers.

Hampshire, Stuart, ed. *The Age of Reason: The Seventeenth-Century Philosophers* (New York: George Braziller, 1957).

Hobbes, Thomas. *Leviathan* (New York: Penguin Books, 1982).

Hume, David. *An Inquiry Concerning Human Understanding* (Indianapolis: Hackett, 1993).

Hume, David. *A Treatise of Human Nature* (New York: Penguin Classics, 1984).

Kant, Immanuel. *Critique of Pure Reason*, translated by J. M. D. Meiklejohn (London: Dent [Everyman's Library], 1991).

Kant, Immanuel. *Foundations of the Metaphysics of Morals*, translated by Lewis White Beck (Indianapolis: Bobbs-Merrill, 1976).

Kant, Immanuel. *Prolegomena to Any Future Metaphysics* (Indianapolis: Bobbs-Merrill [The Library of Liberal Arts], 1950). Difficult but much more accessible than *The Critique of Pure Reason*.

Leibniz, Gottfried W. *Philosophical Writings*, edited by G. H. R. Parkinson (London: Dent [Everyman's Library], 1990). See especially "Discourse on Metaphysics" and "Monadology."

Locke, John. *An Essay Concerning Human Understanding* (London: Dent [Everyman's Library], 1991).

Locke, John. *Two Treatises of Government* (New York: Hafner, 1964).

Locke, J., G. Berkeley, D. Hume. *The Empiricists* (New York: Doubleday [Anchor Books], 1961). The companion to *The Rationalists*.

Spinoza, Benedict de. *On the Improvement of the Understanding, The Ethics, and Correspondence*, translated by R. H. M. Elwes (New York: Dover Books, 1955). See especially *The Ethics*. (Benedict is the latinized version of Baruch, his real name.)

Secondary Sources

Ayer, A. J. *Hume* (New York: Hill and Wang [Past Masters series], 1980).

Hampshire, Stuart. *Spinoza: An Introduction to His Philosophical Thought* (New York: Penguin Books, 1992). Very readable; written by an excellent philosopher.

Martin, C. B., and D. M. Armstrong, eds. *Locke and Berkeley: A Collection of Critical Essays* (Garden City, N.Y.: Doubleday [Anchor Books], 1968). A good selection of scholarly studies.

Scruton, Roger. *Kant* (New York: Oxford University Press [Past Masters series], 1989).

Warnock, G. J. *Berkeley* (Baltimore: Penguin Books, 1953). Still one of my favorites.

Post-Kantian British and Continental Philosophy
Primary Sources

Aiken, Henry D., ed. *The Age of Ideology: The Nineteenth-Century Philosophers* (New York: George Braziller, 1957).

Hegel, G. W. F. *The Phenomenology of Mind*, translated by J. B. Baillie (New York: Harper and Row [Torchbooks], 1967). Will look impressive on your shelf, but not recommended for the casual reader.

Kierkegaard, Søren. *Fear and Trembling*, translated by Alastair Hannay (New York: Penguin Books, 1985). A fascinating little book.

Marx, Karl, and Friedrich Engels. *Marx and Engels: Basic Writings on Politics and Philosophy*, edited by Lewis S. Feuer (Garden City, N.Y.: Doubleday [Anchor Books], 1989).

Mill, J. S. *On Liberty and Utilitarianism* (New York: Bantam Books, 1993).

Nietzsche, Friedrich. *Basic Writings of Nietzsche*, translated and edited by Walter Kaufmann (New York: Modern Library, 1968). See especially *The Birth of Tragedy, Beyond Good and Evil*, and *On the Genealogy of Morals*.

Nietzsche, Friedrich. *Thus Spake Zarathustra*, translated by R. J. Hollingdale (New York: Penguin Books, 1969). The students' favorite.

Schopenhauer, Arthur. *The World as Will and Idea*, translated by R. B. Haldane and J. Kemp (London: Routledge and Kegan Paul, 1964). Big and imposing but surprisingly readable.

Secondary Sources

Barrett, William. *Irrational Man* (New York: Doubleday [Anchor Books], 1990). Classical work on existentialism. See chapters on Kierkegaard and Nietzsche. Also good for twentieth-century figures.

Fromm, Erich. *Marx's Concept of Man* (New York: Frederick Ungar, 1969). Contains philosophical essays by the early Marx and a long essay by Fromm. Both very good.

Kojève, Alexander. *Introduction to the Reading of Hegel: Lectures on "The Phenomenology of Spirit,"* translated by James H. Nichols Jr. (Ithaca, N.Y., and London: Cornell University Press, 1993). A very influential, brilliant, but quirky interpretation of Hegel that makes the connection between him and Marx closer than it is usually thought to be.

Mooney, Edward. *Knights of Faith and Resignation: Reading Kierkegaard's "Fear and Trembling"* (Albany: State University of New York Press, 1991). A fine little book by a friend of mine. Buy it; he can use the money.

Popper, Karl. *The Open Society and Its Enemies.* Vol. 2, *Hegel and Marx* (Princeton, N.J.: Princeton University Press, 1966). Sir Karl was a foremost philosopher of science. This book is a very interesting and very biased account of Hegel and Marx, blaming them for just about everything that has gone wrong since their time (except those things that Popper had already blamed on Plato in Volume 1).

Rius. *Marx for Beginners* (New York: Pantheon, 1979). Cartoons and text by one of Mexico's leading political cartoonists.

Safranski, Rüdiger. *Schopenhauer and the Wild Years of Philosophy* (Cambridge, Mass.: Harvard University Press, 1990). A good way to break into the strange world of nineteenth-century German philosophy.

Singer, Peter. *Marx* (Oxford, England: Oxford University Press [Past Masters series], 1983).

Westphal, Merold. *History and Truth in Hegel's "Phenomenology"* (Atlantic Highlands, N.J.: Humanities Press, 1990). You'll need a guide to Hegel's work. This one's good.

The Phenomenological Tradition and Its Aftermath
Primary Sources

Derrida, Jacques. *Of Grammatology*, translated by Gayatri Chakravorty Spivak (Baltimore: Johns Hopkins University Press, 1976). Not easy!

Heidegger, Martin. *Being and Time*, translated by John Macquarrie and Edward Robinson (New York: Harper and Row, 1962).

Husserl, Edmund. *Ideas: General Introduction to Pure Phenomenology*, translated by W. R. Boyce Gibson (New York: Collier-Macmillan, 1969).

Irigaray, Luce. *Speculum of the Other Woman*, translated by Gillian C. Gill (New York: W. W. Norton, 1977).

Lacan, Jacques. *Écrits: A Selection*, translated by Alan Sheridan (New York: W. W. Norton, 1977). Ouch!

Lévi-Strauss, Claude. *The Savage Mind*, translated by George Wiedenfeld and Nicolson Ltd. (Chicago: University of Chicago Press, 1968).

Lévi-Strauss, Claude. *Triste Tropiques: An Anthropological Study of Primitive Studies in Brazil*, translated by John Russell (New York: Atheneum, 1964).

Sartre, Jean-Paul. *Being and Nothingness*, translated by Hazel Barnes (New York: Washington Square Press, 1992).

Sartre, Jean-Paul. *Existentialism and Human Emotions*, translated by Hazel Barnes and Bernard Frechtman (New York: Citadel Press, 1990). Start here.

Sartre, Jean-Paul. *The Philosophy of Jean-Paul Sartre*, edited by Robert Denoon Cumming (New York: Random House [Vintage Books], 1972).

Saussure, Ferdinand de. *Course in General Linguistics*, translated by Wade Baskin (New York: Philosophical Library, 1959).

Secondary Sources

Archard, David. *Consciousness and the Unconscious* (La Salle, Ill.: Open Court, 1984). This comes as close to an "easy access" to Lacan as I've found.

Danto, Arthur C. *Jean-Paul Sartre* (New York: Viking Press [Modern Masters series], 1975). Great!

Dreyfus, Hubert. *Being-in-the-World: A Commentary on Heidegger's "Being and Time, Division I"* (Cambridge, Mass.: MIT Press, 1991). The best guide to *Being and Time*.

Leach, Edmund. *Claude Lévi-Strauss* (Chicago: University of Chicago Press, 1989).

Moi, Toril. *Sexual/Textual Politics: Feminist Literary Theory* (New York: Methuen, 1986). Good chapters on Cixous, Irigaray, and Kristeva.

Norris, Christopher. *Derrida* (Cambridge, Mass.: Harvard University Press, 1987).

Steiner, George. *Martin Heidegger* (New York: Viking Press, 1979). A sensible introduction to difficult stuff.

Wilcken, Patrick. *Claude Lévi-Strauss: The Poet in the Laboratory*. New York: Penguin, 2010.

Pragmatism and the Analytical Tradition
Primary Sources

Ayer, A. J. *Language, Truth, and Logic* (New York: Dover Publications, n.d.). This short book is the student's best approach to logical positivism. Be careful Sir Alfred doesn't convert you!

Dewey, John. *The Quest for Certainty* (New York: Putnam [Capricorn Books], 1960).

James, William. *Pragmatism* (Cleveland: Meridian Books, 1961).

Moore, George Edward. *G. E. Moore: Selected Writings*, edited by Thomas Baldwin (London and New York: Routledge, 1993). See especially "A Defence of Common Sense."

Nussbaum, Martha C. *Love's Knowledge: Essays on Philosophy and Literature* (New York and Oxford: Oxford University Press, 1990).

Quine, W. V. *From a Logical Point of View*, 2d ed., rev. (Cambridge, Mass.: Harvard University Press, 1961).

Quine, W. V. *Word and Object* (New York and London: John Wiley and Sons, 1960).

Russell, Bertrand. *The Problems of Philosophy* (New York: Oxford University Press, 1967).

Weitz, Morris, ed. *Twentieth-Century Philosophers: The Analytic Tradition* (New York: Free Press, 1966). Representative selections from Moore, Russell, the logical positivists, Wittgenstein, and ordinary language philosophers.

White, Morton, ed. *The Age of Analysis: The Twentieth-Century Philosophers* (New York: George Braziller, 1957).

Wittgenstein, Ludwig. *Philosophical Investigations*, 3d ed., translated by G. E. M. Anscombe (New York: Macmillan, 1968).

Wittgenstein, Ludwig. *Tractatus Logico-Philosophicus*, translated by D. F. Pears and B. F. McGuinness (London and New York: Routledge, 1994).

Secondary Sources

Castaneda, Carlos. *Journey to Ixtlán* (New York: Pocket Book, 1975). An unusual introduction to the idea of phenomenology. Somewhere between anthropology, philosophy, and fantasy.

Duffy, Bruce. *The World as I Found It* (New York: Ticknor and Fields, 1988). A good novel about G. E. Moore, Bertrand Russell, and Ludwig Wittgenstein.

Hookway, Christopher. *Quine: Language, Experience, and Reality* (Stanford, Calif.: Stanford University Press, 1988). Quine is tough, but this book is a big help.

Monk, Ray. *Ludwig Wittgenstein: The Duty of Genius* (New York: Penguin Books, 1990). An excellent biography with philosophical summaries.

Passmore, John. *Recent Philosophers* (La Salle, Ill.: Open Court, 1985). Good, clear account covering philosophical developments up to the early 1980s.

Pears, David. *Wittgenstein* (Cambridge, Mass.: Harvard University Press [Modern Masters series], 1971).

Index

Note: **Boldfaced** type indicates the first significant appearance of a term, and implies that the term's definition can be found in the Glossary.